LIVING JEWISH
LIFE CYCLE

How to
CREATE
MEANINGFUL
JEWISH RITES
of PASSAGE *at*
EVERY STAGE
of LIFE

RABBI GOLDIE MILGRAM

JEWISH LIGHTS Publishing
Woodstock, Vermont

Living Jewish Life Cycle:
How to Create Meaningful Jewish Rites of Passage at Every Stage of Life

2009 Quality Paperback Edition, First Printing
© 2009 by Goldie Milgram

Library of Congress Cataloging-in-Publication Data
Milgram, Goldie, 1955–
Living Jewish life cycle : how to create meaningful Jewish rites of passage at every stage of life / Goldie Milgram.
p. cm.
Includes bibliographical references and index.
ISBN-13: 978-1-58023-335-4 (quality pbk.)
ISBN-10: 1-58023-335-X (quality pbk.)
1. Judaism—Customs and practices. 2. Life cycle, Human—Religious aspects—Judaism. 3. Life change events—Religious aspects—Judaism. 4. Jewish way of life. I. Title.
BM700.M46 2008
296.4'4—dc22
2008026515

10 9 8 7 6 5 4 3 2 1

Manufactured in the United States of America
Cover Design: Melanie Robinson

Published by Jewish Lights Publishing
A Division of LongHill Partners, Inc.
Sunset Farm Offices, Route 4, P.O. Box 237
Woodstock, VT 05091
Tel: (802) 457-4000   Fax: (802) 457-4004
www.jewishlights.com

In loving memory of
Percy Bub,
uncle by marriage, patriarch, and role model.
In the spirit of Jacob he wrestled.

CONTENTS

INTRODUCTION

"Rabbi, our wedding will be at sunset on a small island off the coast of western Canada. The beaches are great; there's even a small mountain. We'll fly you in and put you up for a few days. But please understand, we want the ceremonial mumbo jumbo out of the way as quickly as possible so our guests can have a good time on the party boats before it's too dark."

Ronnie and his fiancée, Debra, are highly detail-oriented, thirty-something architects. They've thought through every bit of site design, catering, color scheme, and music for their wedding. They appear utterly stressed out, and I note that they are not meeting each other's eyes. Engagement can be a time of enchantment and deepening of relationship, but something here is amiss.

It seems that Debra's ninety-three-year-old grandmother won't come to the wedding unless they have a rabbi, rather than the justice of the peace they had planned—which is how I entered the picture. Although he had a bar mitzvah at age thirteen, Ronnie is a confirmed atheist; he's going along with this out of respect for how Debra feels about her grandmother.

What to do, what to say? "Ronnie, do you remember how to say Kiddush, the blessing over the wine?" He reels it off flawlessly at express train speed. "Ronnie, Debra, the blessing recited over wine is part of many Jewish life cycle events—weddings, baby namings, bar mitzvahs, and most holy days, too." They both nod vigorously; they know this already. "But why is wine part of these events? Could we take a few minutes so I can show you?" Too polite to dismiss me outright, they look at each other with minor exasperation and nod their okay.

I take down a silver wine goblet and ask them to imagine they are at the finish line of the detail-driven marathon they have been on en route to the wedding. Their posture changes; they seem to relax a bit—just a bit. I invite them to synchronize their breathing. Their faces soften. I quietly fill the goblet to the brim with sweet kosher wine and hold it cupped, as is traditional, in the palm of my left hand.

"Wine in Judaism symbolizes the life force—vitality, the joy of living. And a blessing is a springboard to happiness. Each symbol, word, and sacred sequence in the wedding has meaning and can help you become closer to each other. Each blessing is meant to expand your ability to perceive and receive the good things in life that can come from marriage. Vitality is definitely one of those good things.

"Any blessing that is going to be effective becomes a whole-body experience; it is not just the rote recitation of words. If your hands shake, your cup will run over. That's totally fine; there's a saucer to catch the drops. Your cup running over is a metaphor for joy from the Torah, the Jewish scriptures.

"Now, focus your intention by casting your gaze on the shimmering liquid and visualize the cup of your marriage full to the brim with joy and energy for living, a strong current that will carry you both for many years to come.

"And now expand your vision; imagine those near and dear to you filled with blessing, their vitality expanding with the joy of witnessing this special moment.

"I'll actually be chanting this blessing for you on your wedding day, but just for now, Ronnie, would you be willing to slowly, with the feelings you are having, chant or say the first verse of the blessing again? Chant it to Debra, your beloved. Let your feelings fill your voice, no matter if your singing isn't perfect, or if each word doesn't have an exact meaning for you yet."

Debra's deep brown eyes fill with tears, the good kind, as Ronnie reveals a side of himself she has rarely seen. His sound is rich and full; his heart seems to pour from his chest as he comes alive. Plenty of drops spill from the cup.

The warm silence of pure togetherness reigns.

Debra's lips have begun to quiver as she speaks: "I want to try, but I don't know the words and I don't know the tune ... but I feel ... awe, and something I'd almost forgotten in all the planning ... I feel so loving and centered."

We decide that Ronnie will chant the words one by one, and Debra will echo him. The reenchantment has begun. On their wedding day they will again gaze upon their cup of life, full to the brim, and pray for vitality for each other, their family, and the guests who happily will now include Debra's grandmother. They will each drink the wine, sweet and fruity on their tongues, the warmth in their chest as it goes down adding a small rush of energy. Each blessing in the wedding ritual sequence carries powerful ways for them to braid themselves together in commitment and love.

When understood and properly performed, the life cycle ceremonies and traditions of the Jewish people are very powerful. Ronnie and Debra discovered that preparing themselves would prove to be as important as attending to the mitzvah, the sacred responsibility, of preparing for their guests. In our study sessions they learned, as you will here, all the components and many dimensions of meaning in this life cycle event, as well as the full sequence of sacred practices needed to prepare for it.

Jewish rites of passage are designed to cultivate the qualities of intimacy, growth, support, and awe that are beneficial to navigating life's transitions. *Living Jewish Life Cycle* provides both education and mentoring so that you will be better able to understand, create, and enter wholeheartedly into Jewish life cycle ceremonies, preparatory practices, and celebrations. Mentoring, in this sense, means that you will be guided in how to make your Jewish rites come alive with meaning, beauty, and impact. *Living Jewish Life Cycle* will take you beyond facts, beyond surviving, and directly into accessing Jewish rites of passage as a force for thriving.

Respectful pluralism prevails in these pages. Diverse approaches drawn from across the spectrum of Jewish practice and perspective are offered with the expectation that readers come from a wide variety of family structures, as well as religious and ethnic backgrounds. Jewish families have always been diverse, comprising virtually every nationality, race, ethnicity, orientation, religion, and language group. Not every Jewish group and family has adopted the concept of respectfully acknowledging each other's differences. Accordingly, *Living Jewish Life Cycle* also offers upfront guidance for finding our way during such challenging situations. A method called *Focusing* is demonstrated, and sample encounters are offered for navigating situations such as intermarriage, divorced parents, finding a sacred name, and responding to differing levels of religious observance in the family that tend to erupt during life cycle event planning.

THE EXPANDING RANGE OF JEWISH RITUAL

While it is not possible to cover all the permutations of events that can happen in a life, the goal here is to empower you by providing the tools you need to appreciate Jewish life cycle traditions, as well as to contribute to the evolution of Judaism by customizing practices to your own life and family situation. You can read this volume straight through or use it as a resource for each major stage of life as it arrives.

Humans are living decades longer than when the traditional Jewish rites of passage were first developed. Our society has undergone major changes in health care, free time, morality, transportation, and communication, all of which impact Jewish practice. Opportunities to advance Jewish culture through the creation of new and expanded rituals are emerging daily. Attention to matters such as organ donation and transplantation, miscarriage, single-parent adoption and foster parenting, same-sex marriage, breakups by couples who live together and have not married, the profound need to upgrade bar/bat mitzvah and Jewish divorce processes, and much more will be addressed in this volume, which also strives to provide firm and respectful grounding in Jewish text and tradition.

Wherever possible, I have drawn upon real-life experiences from my own life and work with congregants, students, family, and clients as a rabbi, seminary professor and *mashpia* (Jewish spiritual guide), ritual designer, wife, and mother. First we cite existing ritual; then we access the sources within Judaism and each individual's life experience that will create a new ritual tailored to the situation and the individual. What you will find here are not cookie-cutter rites that you can paste into your own life, but rather guides to understanding that will allow the symbols, stories, sacred sequences, and metaphors within Judaism to link with the story of your own life so that your rites of passage will become holy and healing, and will promote the healthy growth of your relationships. The goal in this series is to assist you in developing a "practice" for life. Having a continuing "practice" of connecting to the Source, sources, and wisdom of Judaism will serve profoundly in times of joy and in moving through the difficult times when we can feel so very alone and challenged even to choose to survive.

CONSIDER THE JEWISH CALENDAR
BEFORE SETTING YOUR DATE

For those scheduling Jewish life cycle ceremonies, there are hundreds of available dates as well as a number of blackout dates when rites cannot be held. With advance planning, conflict need not occur. Why care about this?

To destroy a culture, deny a people the life of its calendar. The first rule the Greeks, Romans, Babylonians, Nazis, communists, and all oppressors asserted to destroy peoples was to make it illegal for those they conquered to follow their own ethnic calendar. To best save, support, or savor a culture, enter into the culture's calendar with depth of curiosity and treat it with the utmost respect.

At life cycle events, you are transmitting Jewish culture to several generations by way of your example. That's big. Jewish groups—secular and religious—do their best to schedule events in ways that maintain the integrity of the Jewish calendar. It is equally important for individuals to follow the conventions of the Jewish calendar when planning rites of passage.

For the sake of convenience, employers, vendors, and even some family members may urge a fuzzying of the boundaries around dates and times when Jewish rites are meant to be held and not held, but that undermines Jewish identity and respectful pluralism. So it's very important to know the general guidelines for dates and times that are widely observed by Jews worldwide.

JEWISH WEDDINGS, CELEBRATIONS, AND CONVERSIONS. Jewish weddings and conversions can be held six days a week, but not on Shabbat. Why is that? Shabbat is reserved for the celebration of a cosmic wedding between our weary soul and the bride of rest, *Shabbat*; thus weddings for individuals are not held on this day. You might say there's a cosmic conflict of interest. Traditionally, a person is allowed to break Shabbat with labor and travel only for reasons of health. Contracting or solemnizing a marriage is an act of labor, and weddings are certainly not medical emergencies.

Additionally, as a major *simhah*, "celebration," a wedding is supposed to add to the happy days in the calendar, and one that overlaps with a major holiday causes each one to dilute the other. Therefore, weddings and other happy celebrations are not held on any major holiday, such as Rosh HaShannah, Yom Kippur, Sukkot, Pesach (Passover), or Shavuot.

Rosh Hodesh (new moon), Hanukkah, Tu B'Shevat, and Purim, when these do not fall on Shabbat, are days on which Jewish weddings, bar/bat mitzvah rites, and other happy events can be held.

The other exception is Lag B'Omer, the thirty-third day in the Counting of the Omer, the days between Passover and Shavuot. Lag B'Omer is a popular wedding date. Some also include Yom Ha-Atzmaut, Israel Independence Day, as a permitted wedding day. Tuesday is considered a good day to have a wedding because in the account of creation (Genesis, chapter 1), it is written *ki tov* ("it is good") twice on the third day, which correlates with Tuesday since the Jewish week begins on Sunday.

BAR/BAT MITZVAH RITES, BIRTHDAY PARTIES, AND BABY NAMINGS. These celebrations (along with weddings) are not held on days of public mourning because the mood of such days would diminish the joy. These include Tisha B'Av, the fast of Gedaliah, the tenth of Tevet, the fast of Esther, the seventeenth of Tammuz, any of the first thirty-two days between Pesach and Shavuot, and the three weeks from the seventeenth of Tammuz to Tisha B'Av.

Baby namings for girls are typically held within a month of birth on Shabbat morning at services, typically during the Torah reading, or on Mondays and Thursdays, when the Torah is read. A home ritual is also appropriate.

CIRCUMCISION. This rite is held on the eighth day after birth even on Shabbat or a holiday, barring medical contraindications. Why? Our ancestors discovered that the eighth day of life is the healthiest for the covenantal rite of circumcision and required it even on Shabbat. Interestingly, science now shows that the blood clotting factor optimal for an easy and healthy circumcision occurs on the eighth day after birth.

JEWISH NAME CHANGES. Don't like your Hebrew name? Change it. Jewish name changes are typically done on Shabbat morning or afternoon during services as a blessing during the Torah reading.

JEWISH FUNERALS. These are held within twenty-four hours of death for the peace of the soul and to honor the body as the image of God, which must be returned to nourish the earth. Exceptions are made for the Sabbath, major holy days, and to save a life in cases where information from an autopsy could lead to detection of a killer. *Killer* in this sense means either an actual murderer or a previously unidentified genetic disorder, the detection of which could save the lives of other family members over time.

Caution: It's difficult to find an ethical, talented Jewish clergy person on short notice for a major Jewish life cycle event. For a funeral, be sure to arrange for your clergy person before working out a time with the funeral home. Calling a year or more in advance for weddings, bar/bat mitzvah rites, and anniversary rituals is a really good idea if you want a particular rabbi or cantor for a particular date. We do get booked up. Why not plan in advance, so you can savor the time of your engagement or bar/bat mitzvah preparation? A lot of the good gets lost when rites of passage are rushed.

TRANSLITERATION AND FORMATTING DECISIONS IN THIS VOLUME

1. Transliterations are done with a schema created to make it as easy as possible for you to sound out a passage. In Hebrew the letters *haf* and *het* have a similar guttural sound, much like clearing your throat or saying "kh." Often depicted as "ch" and mispronounced accordingly, these letters are both translitered in this series as "ḥ."

2. Since Hebrew has no capital letters, from this point forward transliterated Hebrew words will not be capitalized unless they appear at the beginning of a sentence or refer to the proper name of a prayer. The absence of capitalization is the reality of all Hebrew text.

3. Keeping God as an infinite mystery with many facets that we numerously name, while recognizing that none could ever fully define this category of awareness—this is a core Jewish spiritual practice. Out of respect for this, G*d is the symbolic term used from this point forward in this book.

Tradition and Transition
The Evolution of Jewish Rites of Passage

Overheard on the subways of New York:

"Benjy, you can go ahead and eat that. It's kosher." "Sorry, Grandpa, it's not. The standards have changed a lot since you were in yeshiva."

"Helen, is it true that Rabbi Cohen is marrying your daughter to another woman?!" "Yes, it's true. The one she was engaged to changed her mind."

More than three thousand years ago, the Jewish people began to emerge as a unique people, indigenous to the Middle East. While many peoples disappeared under the crush of the Egyptian, Greek, Roman, Babylonian, and Ottoman empires, we stayed afloat by both adapting to the surrounding society and preserving our own culture and religion.

For most of Jewish history we have divided ourselves up into sub-groups. In biblical times we were tribes. Under the Greek and Roman empires various religious sects developed, such as the Sicarii, the Essenes, the Pharisees, the Zealots, and the Sadducees, as well as non-religious cultural Jews. Later came the Karaites and the Rabbanites, plus some smaller groups. In the past two hundred years or so, larger groupings, typically called movements, have emerged—some religious, some not. Each group continues to refine Jewish rites of passage in accordance with its own ideology and in response to changing times. A sampling of today's many hundreds of Jewish religious groups and organizations (each is briefly defined in the Glossary) includes: Agudath Israel, ALEPH: Alliance for Jewish Renewal, Jewish Reconstructionist Federation, Folkshul, National Havurah Committee, The Orthodox Union, The Society for Humanistic Judaism, Society of Jewish Science, Union for Reform Judaism, United Synagogue of Conservative Judaism, Young Israel, and variants of Hassidism, among the major existing sects being: Belz, Bubov, Karlin, Lubavitch (Chabad), Munkacz, Puppa, Sanz, Satmar, Skver, Spinka, and Vizhnitz.

Gradually some of the new ideas get cross-fertilized from one group to the others—some to be embraced and some rejected. For example, bat mitzvah, an adolescent rite of passage for girls now found in a variety of forms in almost every Jewish group, was at first stridently denounced by Conservative, Orthodox, and Hasidic Jewish leaders. Bat mitzvah was first introduced by the Reform movement in Europe in 1814 as a group ritual for twelve-year-old female classmates. In 1922 it became an individual rite parallel to bar mitzvah in the United States when the founder of Reconstructionism, Rabbi Mordechai Kaplan, arranged for his daughter Judith to be called to the Torah. But it took several decades for bat mitzvah to be appreciated as a valuable addition to the Jewish people's repertoire and customized to the ideology of each group. The process of shaping bar mitzvah and bat mitzvah to serve useful and healthy roles continues.

While differences among Jewish subgroups can sometimes seem quite pronounced, it is important to remember that we are a coherent people, all of whom share the same basic calendar of holy days, most core principles, many practices, and a great deal of liturgy.

We are all grounded in a common legacy, the Torah, and in our dedication to living justly as elaborated in the substantial commentaries and the cultural and religious works that followed the Torah.

Biblical Judaism brought exceptionally original ideas to humanity and also shifted norms by reacting to and adopting components of regional cultures. For example, in Genesis, Sarah suffers from infertility and gives Hagar, her maidservant, to Abraham to produce an heir. This approach to surrogate motherhood is well documented as a legally viable approach under Mesopotamian law, which predates Sarah and Abraham by more than a thousand years. Then and ever since, some of the music, foods, languages, and philosophies of the nations in which we lived have become braided into our daily and holy day religious practices and rites of passage.

Klezmer music, beloved for Jewish wedding and bar/bat mitzvah parties, incorporates elements of Gypsy music. This is because in Ukraine, Poland, Hungary, and Romania, Jewish and Romani musicians often played together. Yiddish, so prominent in Klezmer lyrics, was forged from elements of Hebrew, Jewish-French dialects, Jewish-Italian dialects, and various German dialects. In the late Middle Ages, when Jews settled in eastern Europe, Slavic elements were incorporated as well. At some point between 900 and 1100 CE, Yiddish became a complete, independent language. *Webster's Dictionary* cites more than a hundred Yiddish words—including *bagel*, *chutzpah*, and *kvetch*—as having made their way into the English language.

Speaking of food, gefilte fish and borscht, both common eastern European dishes, have been adopted as part of Jewish culture. In exchange, two Jewish foods have made it around the world. Bagel is the easier of the two to guess. The second is kugel, which is a potato or noodle pudding. Kugel entered Jewish culture from German culture, where it started out as a savory bread and flour pudding. It was not until the seventeenth century that the sweet version with egg noodles was invented. The Yiddish name for this dish is variously pronounced "*koogel*," "*kih-gl*," or "*kuh-gl*," depending on the region from which your family derives. Polish Jewish homes typically add raisins and cinnamon to kugel. Hungarian-style kugel incorporates extra sugar and a nice *shmeck*, or dollop, of sour cream. Jerusalem kugel was born sometime after the founding of the State of Israel in 1948 via the addition of caramelized sugar and black pepper. North American Jews have been known to improvise kugel toppings that range from cornflakes to graham cracker crumbs, and some of us add mushrooms for savory kugel, or fruits such as mango, apple, and pineapple, for sweet kugel.

Today, whenever Middle Eastern Jews emigrate, their cultural traditions are also inevitably transplanted. Hence the arrival of falafel stands, hummus restaurants, and henna (a washable vegetable dye) hand-painting bridal parties in almost every country in which such families take root. Argentine Jews are a recent group to emigrate from their country in large numbers. They have brought with them the custom of a wedding cake with numerous long ribbons hanging out of it, one tied to a thin golden ring hidden inside the cake. Single guests—in some circles only the women—gather around the cake to pull out the ribbons, and, voilà, the one who gets the ring is predicted to be the next to marry.

RITES OR WRONGS?

Traditional rites tend to evolve over the generations as well, so *traditional* turns out to be a relative term. For example, the wedding canopy, or *huppah*, today virtually emblematic of a Jewish wedding, didn't exist in biblical times. Try your hand at the quiz that follows to prime yourself for studying the next section. The answers follow.

	Jewish Life Cycle Not-So-Trivial Pursuit	True	False
1.	The Torah, the Five Books of Moses, describes how Abraham, Isaac, and Jacob read from the Torah when they each became bar mitzvah.		
2.	Moses said *Kaddish*, the mourner's prayer, for his sister Miriam.		
3.	Cremation is not a permitted practice in traditional Judaism.		
4.	The first intentional covenantal gathering solely for naming a Jewish baby girl was in 1970.		
5.	Moses and his wife Tziporah's son, Gershom, was circumcised, given his brit, by a woman.		
6.	In the Torah, when a baby was weaned from its mother, the family would throw a party.		
7.	In the Book of Ruth, Ruth did not immerse herself in a ritual bath, a *mikvah*, as part of her conversion process.		
8.	The first bat mitzvah in Jewish history was that of Judith Kaplan in 1922.		
9.	When King David was married, there was no ritual breaking of a glass at his wedding.		
10.	Gender-inclusive Jewish weddings and divorce rites were first introduced in the twentieth century.		

ANSWERS

1—FALSE. Actually bar mitzvah did not exist during biblical times. The first report of bar mitzvah is in an eighth-century CE text, and there it is only the father who is on center stage, saying a blessing of release from monitoring his thirteen-year-old son's religious education and practice. Today's predominant bar/bat mitzvah norms, whereby a youth or adult chants from the Torah scroll and then gives an interpretation of that section of sacred text, first appeared in the 1700s and took centuries to catch on. Today, many communities are already entertaining ideas for new methods of bar/bat mitzvah preparation, ceremony, and celebration.

2—FALSE. Moses would not have said *Kaddish* because a Jewish prayer liturgy did not exist in his time. The holiness prayer we know as *Kaddish Yatom* didn't become a well-established Jewish practice until the sixteenth century. Additionally, there is no evidence that Moses or his brother Aaron paused at all from the work of full-time leadership to mourn Miriam's death.

3—TRUE. Cremation and the dispersing or burial of ashes, while against Jewish law and custom, was practiced by a minority of Jews in the late twentieth century, and—please excuse the expression—is beginning to die out in the twenty-first century. Why? Because the high temperatures required by crematoria contribute to global warming.

4—TRUE. The first record of an intentional full-fledged covenantal communal gathering for naming a Jewish baby girl appears in 1970, though fathers have traditionally gone to synagogue for a blessing during an *aliyah*, going up to the Torah, that includes the baby's Hebrew name at the first service after her birth.

5—TRUE. The primary covenantal rite for males, circumcision, *bris* in Yiddish and *brit* in Hebrew, was in place by the biblical period, but was not always left in the hands of men. Tziporah, Moses's wife, circumcised their son; this act was not performed by Moses or a *mohel* (typically pronounced in the Yiddish fashion, *moyl*), the ritual expert who would officiate today. Records show circumcision occurring in subsequent generations with the baby situated in the comfort of his mother's lap. By the fifteenth century religious authorities deemed this approach unseemly and the rite became the domain of the father, male relatives, male witnesses, and male professionals. In the twentieth century, a few Reform and Reconstructionist rabbis stopped requiring circumcision to covenant males. In the twenty-first century, in the Reform movement, women as well as men have been trained as professional *mohalim* (pl.), those highly skilled and certified in both the surgical and ritual aspects of circumcision.

6—TRUE. Sometimes rites disappear, only to reappear centuries later. The Torah clearly records that there was a party held to celebrate Sarah's cessation of breastfeeding her son, Isaac: "The child grew up and was weaned, and Abraham held a great feast on the day Isaac was weaned" (Genesis 21:6–8). Weaning as a cause for a celebratory gathering is next documented in the twentieth century when women rabbinical students in several seminaries were touched by this verse and created weaning rituals, blessings, songs, and celebrations. In the twenty-first century, while not yet a firmly established ritual, there have been women in almost every branch of Judaism experimentally creating such practices.

7—TRUE. A moving ritual of the rebirthing of identity, immersion in a ritual bath, river, lake, or ocean, known as *mikvah*, is a part of the conversion process required by almost every rabbi. Scholars have recently noted that the immersion of women who are becoming Jewish was not instituted until Jews lived under the Greek empire. Evidence of this innovation does not appear in the biblical Book of Ruth. When Ruth converts to Judaism, she undergoes no immersion; she simply says: "Where you go, I will go. Where you lodge, I will lodge. Your people will be my people, and your God, my God" (Ruth 1:17). Note the absence of a formal study process and a *beit din*, a court of three rabbis to approve her worthiness, which characterize conversion in our times.

8—FALSE. Please see page 2 for a discussion of the origins of bat mitzvah. In brief, photographs and records have emerged revealing that bat mitzvah was first introduced by the Reform movement in 1814 as a group event for classes of adolescent Jewish girls. The first known *individual* bat mitzvah was Judith Kaplan in 1922, held in the United States.

9—FALSE. King David would not likely have broken a glass at his wedding, as the practice is not described in Judaism until the Talmudic period. Stories from the Talmud reveal glasses being smashed at weddings to call attention to the need to limit raucous rejoicing. Curiously, the wedding minstrel also sang a lament at one of these weddings (Bera<u>h</u>ot 30b–31a). Scholars now interpret these passages as indicative of an intention to avert evil-intentioned demons thought by premoderns to thrive on thwarting happy human circumstances. By the fourteenth century, although communities retained the tradition of breaking a glass at weddings, they have rein-terpreted the action to be in memory of the destroyed Temple of Solomon, the first temple of the Jewish faith tradition built under the reign of Solomon, son of King David. Today, this latter interpretation and many other creative options are used, and the tradition prevails.

10—TRUE. Egalitarian and gender-inclusive Jewish marriage and divorce rites were introduced and became appreciated in the twen-tieth century. With the exception of part of the Conservative movement and all Orthodox communities, inclusiveness in ritual is increasingly well-accepted with every passing year. Jewish rites for dealing with infertility and miscarriage, the onset of menstruation and menopause, the breaking up of a long-term relationship, retire-ment, and many other newly acknowledged Jewish ritual needs originating in the late twentieth century are, by the twenty-first century, already appearing in published ritual guides.

As Rabbi Abraham Isaac Kook, the first chief rabbi of the State of Israel, put it: "What's old becomes new and what's new becomes holy."

DIVERSITY: OPPORTUNITY AND CHALLENGES

> Creation does not have
> only one kind of
> butterfly
> apple
> tree
> rose
> frog
> owl
> …
> How could there
> ever be only
> one kind of Jew?

Is there a right way and a wrong way? This depends on who you ask. For the most part, diversity is how all species on the planet survive. Anything that has only one kind left is on its way to extinction. If you look upon all the varieties of Judaism thriving at present like flowers in a bouquet, diversity becomes quite beautiful. But not only beauty comes from diversity; there are challenges and friction to be aware of as well.

My cell phone goes off. When I answer it I hear weeping on the line.

"Shalom, this is Reb Goldie. How can I help you? Has there been a tragedy?"

"A disaster, Reb Goldie. My sister Ellie, who is a *baalat teshuvah* [newly Orthodox], says she will not attend my wedding for three reasons. One, because her husband can't hear your voice, or any woman's voice, leading a Jewish rite; two, because our hall's kosher caterer is not approved by her local rabbi; and three, because there will be mixed seating and mixed dancing.

"Rabbi, Ellie was going to be my wedding prep buddy, my *shomeret*, the one person helping me for the twenty-four hours before the wedding. We love each other so much, we're more than sisters, we have always been best friends. This is awful. And Reb Goldie, you are our rabbi, you did my bat mitzvah! I'm not about to substitute some strange Orthodox man. Why don't Richard and I have the right to choose our own level of Jewish observance? My sister is free to hold her baby's bris [circumcision] her own way. And my family always has mixed dancing. We aren't Orthodox!"

Kelly breaks into intense weeping. I listen to her sobs and reflect carefully before speaking.

"Kelly, this is painful to you, and it must feel utterly unfair. I want you to know there are things you can do to help your family celebrate this precious time together without changing your plans or compromising your own integrity.

"First, rabbis are not in the business of breaking up families. I'm willing to bet, from experience, that your sister's rabbi can help her find a way to participate, if she calls him and discusses the situation.

"Let me explain further. First, it's likely your sister can still be with you as your *shomeret*, since your wedding is on a Sunday night. She can start right after the Sabbath on Saturday night—there's no real conflict with any Jewish law in her doing that. Next, her husband might not be required to miss the ceremony. He should check with the rabbi. Waivers are given by some Orthodox rabbis for the weddings of first-degree non-Orthodox family members. Rabbis care about families a lot.

"Now, think airplane food. Find out if your caterer can have a special meal brought in for the reception by a caterer approved by your sister's rabbi. If not, her family can bring their own wrapped food to the reception and your caterer can arrange for a spot in the fridge for it. Also, as long as your sister and her husband don't engage in mixed dancing, their rabbi might allow them to attend the reception.

"And finally, family from out of town is often hosted for a Friday night dinner and a Sunday brunch. If all else fails, her family can bring their own food, miss the ceremony, and attend one or both of those events as their way of celebrating with you. Remember that they will need a place to stay within walking distance of any events occurring on the Sabbath, and they'll need lights kept on in public rooms and bathrooms, since they probably won't turn the electricity on or off on the Sabbath.

"Kelly, your sister has dedicated herself to living in a system where she has to first secure permission from her rabbi on such matters. As a *baalat teshuvah*, she is probably using her intellect to extrapolate what she thinks are the right decisions, and as a layperson she hasn't studied all the precedents and principles upon which her rabbi can make decisions. Most Orthodox rabbis try to be compassionate, to look for ways to hold families together. I think you'll be surprised by the outcome that is often possible."

Curious about how the situation turned out? Kelly calmly suggested that her sister call her rabbi for clarification, and she did. The rabbi gave the couple permission to attend everything as long as they brought their own food, didn't travel on the Sabbath, and didn't engage in mixed dancing. He also instructed her husband to be careful not to focus his attention on any scantily clad guests. I've seen rabbis rule more or less stringently, but most will try to find ways that are ethical within their worldview to support family ties.

FINDING BLESSED COMPROMISES

Working things out takes goodwill and a safe method for talking through the issues with one another. It is usually best for each person to first work through his or her emotions. It can be terribly painful to be told that your voice can't be heard in song because of your gender, or that your way isn't appreciated by someone you love. For Kelly's sister, this was as painful and challenging as it was for Kelly. Here's a guide to getting yourself in balance before trying to deal with a religious curveball that's come your way.

- Anticipate that in your extended kinship and friendship system there will be at least one person who comes from a part of the spectrum of religious practice that is different from yours.
- Reach out proactively to those who may have sensitive issues to address, so they feel supported rather than overlooked from the get-go.
- Remember, religious conviction–driven decisions are not about you personally; they are principles being passionately applied to a situation.
- Realize that your love for each other will have opportunities to be expressed whether or not you are, in the end, both able to be present at the rite of passage.
- Become clear about your own values and practices. Know how far you can go to accommodate someone else's need, while still maintaining your own integrity.

THE BOTTOM LINE

When attending or planning a Jewish rite of passage or religious service, be sure to inquire about the customs regarding food, dress, and touch. Also, be careful not to make assumptions about the religious or dietary practices guests and hosts will be observing—be it vegetarianism, kosher, Glatt kosher, eco-kosher, and the like.

While it is disrespectful for guests to expect a host to change his or her customary practices to suit them, it is equally a matter of respect for the host to listen and help the guests creatively discern how to be as present as possible without compromising the host's values or plans.

MAJOR CONTRASTS IN JEWISH PRACTICE

Because change is one of the constants of Jewish life, the variations in customs, laws, and practices at any point in our history are quite fascinating. It's important from the outset for you to be fully aware that individual homes, congregations, and even certain neighborhoods and individual communities within those neighborhoods have their own uniquely nuanced Jewish culture, norms, and guidelines. For example, there are Jewish communities where the norm is:

- for couples to have a two-ring wedding ceremony and others where only one ring is acceptable.
- to have major infant and adolescent rites of passage for both genders, and communities that do so only for males.
- for the rabbi or cantor to wed only two heterosexual Jews, and other Jewish clergy who will also perform wedding rites for two gay men or two lesbian women or two transgendered people.
- for men and women to sit separately for religious services, life cycle ceremonies, and celebrations, and congregations where everyone sits together.
- for women's voices to be raised in prayer or song not to be audible publicly by men, and communities where women singing publicly is fully welcome.

- for food to be prepared by a certified kosher caterer, and others where kosher caterers are not brought in; there are those who serve only vegetarian or dairy foods, and others who accept commercially prepared food offerings as long as their preferred kosher certification symbol is on the package.
- for guests to dress as they please, and communities that require only modest dress.
- for most couples with eastern European (Ashkenazi) roots to wear white clothes at their weddings, and those with roots from the Iberian Peninsula (Sephardi) and Middle East (Mizrahi) to wear multicolored wedding garb, sometimes with precious gold metallic threads running through the fabric.
- for only heterosexual men to serve as ordained spiritual leaders, and both seminaries and Jewish communities where women, gay men, and lesbians are ordained and welcomed as Jewish clergy.

Remember that scene in *Fiddler on the Roof* where Tevye shrugs and belts out "Tradition! Tradition!"? Jewish life is so full of differing traditions that sometimes it seems as if we were as colorfully crazy as … as … as a fiddler on a space shuttle!

Remember that no matter how hard you try to get things right, sometimes it's actually impossible. In that context, I'm reminded of the story of the daughter-in-law who took her new baby daughter to visit Grandma. She dressed her in one of the two sweaters the grandmother had made by hand and given at the *brit bat*, the baby's naming ceremony. What did the grandmother say? "What's the matter, you didn't like the other one?"

ARE THERE NO LIMITS?

When common sense and decency prevail, there are limits. In my opinion, ethical innovation is grounded in tradition. There was a twelve-year-old girl who loved horses. She was preparing to become bat mitzvah and insisted on horseback rides for her friends in the synagogue parking lot as well as centerpieces decorated with famous horses. She also wanted to wear her riding hat when she read Torah. What's a parent or rabbi to say?

∾

REB GOLDIE: Ashley, I'm so impressed by your love of animals, especially horses, that I've brought you some information from Judaism about animals and horses.

ASHLEY: Judaism has something to say about animals and horses?

REB GOLDIE: Oh, yes. According to Jewish tradition, Moses was chosen to lead the Jewish people because he was kind to the sheep he herded for his father-in-law, Yitro (Jethro). And when Rebecca finished giving Abraham's emissary, Eliezer, a drink she said: "I will also draw [water] for your camels, until they have finished drinking" (Genesis 24:19).

ASHLEY: I see you have more papers, Reb Goldie. What are they?

REB GOLDIE: More from Judaism about animals. An important Jewish book called the Talmud teaches that "It is forbidden for a person to even taste food until he has fed his animal, as it says (Deuteronomy 11:15): 'I will put grass in your fields for your animals, and you will eat and be satisfied'—first your animals should eat, and only afterwards may you eat." (Gittin 62a).

And, Ashley, a great rabbi, Judah Ha-Nasi, is described in the Talmud as being in pain for years because he was insensitive to the fear of a calf being led to slaughter.

ASHLEY: So Judaism is very concerned with animals. They are not just for work or play; they matter a lot in these stories.

REB GOLDIE: Here's one more. Would you be willing to read it out loud?

ASHLEY: "On this day [Shabbat, the seventh day, the Sabbath], do no work, you, nor your son, nor your daughter, not a man who serves you, nor your maid, nor your animal, nor the stranger that is visiting."

Rabbi! Animals are not allowed to work on Shabbat? My dad is a doctor and he works on Shabbat, our housekeeper works on Shabbat, so why do I feel so sad to think about animals working on Shabbat? Maybe that's what my uncle means when he says Dad works like a dog and that he needs to slow down. Well, I can't change Shabbat in the family, and I'm not sure if I want to, but I am definitely not going to have horseback rides at my bat mitzvah luncheon! No animal is going to work for me on Shabbat!

What about horses specifically, Reb Goldie? What does Judaism say about horses?

So for homework, I handed her a batch of stories called *midrash*, which I'd culled from Jewish sources on the topic of horses. One was about Shifregaz, the horse in the Purim story, mounted first by King Ahashverosh and then by a Jewish man, Mordecai, who had saved the king's life. Another was about the magnificent horse ridden by Pharaoh in the Exodus story, and a third was about a horse who refused to eat. I asked her to read them at home and come back to me with her thoughts and a story of her own about what a human can learn from a horse.

Ashley came back with her own story about her horse having a foal and how tottery the foal was when she tried to stand up and how the mare used her face to help the foal stay upright. "I'm like a foal," Ashley said. "I needed help to think more clearly about animals. And you helped me see how Torah and the *midrash* stories are like a mare, helping us to stay upright."

Well, Ashley had just composed the essence of her bat mitzvah speech, though I don't think she realized it at that moment. Her centerpieces did have horses on them, and each one had a flap for people to lift up with a different horse *midrash* on each one. "So my guests will learn the Torah of animals!" Ashley declared.

And, yes, Ashley did wear her riding hat when she gave her Torah teaching at her bat mitzvah. Under the circumstances, it was the perfect thing to do.

So notice how, ultimately, Ashley didn't erase the chain of tradition or run irreverently over it. She chose to integrate her love of horses respectfully into her bat mitzvah experience. Sensitive mentoring is crucial for life cycle events.

When another girl's parents acceded to her wishes to ride into her bat mitzvah reception on a white horse, there was no grounding in tradition. The girl, now in college, looks back on that as a crass, irretrievably materialistic, utterly unspiritual, and narcissistic act. "I thought it was all about me, me, me. No one helped me to realize it was about my becoming a capable member of the Jewish people and helping my distant relatives come together as a family, and that the party was a mitzvah, that of welcoming guests, not them receiving me."

Living Jewish Life Cycle will ground you in both tradition and pathways to healthy innovation, no matter what your passion.

2

Helping Holiness Happen
Jewish Weddings of Almost Every Kind

❏ Flowers   ❏ Marriage License
❏ Caterer   ❏ Invitations
❏ Music   ❏ Clothes
❏ Clergy   ❏ Videographer
❏ Parking Attendants ❏ Hairdresser
❏ Cloakroom Attendants ❏ Thank-you notes

"Honey, are we missing something? Honey?!"

Marriage, in and of itself, is technically a mitzvah, a way of stretching yourself in the effort to add something good to the world. *Hiddur mitzvah*, creating a beautiful rite, is indeed a good and holy thing to do, according to the ethics of Judaism. Beyond beauty, however, there is much more to understand and plan if a couple and their guests are to benefit from the wisdom embedded in the Jewish wedding process. By way of introduction, my experience. The ceremony for my first marriage was rather formulaic and by the book. We had no input, the rabbi just did his thing. The second time around was very different. By then I had become a rabbi myself, and I had become part of the creative phenomenon known as Jewish Renewal.

∞

The violinist has been playing "Dodi Li," "My Beloved Is Mine." I haven't seen my beloved Barry in a little more than twenty-four hours, an old tradition we have followed in order to make meeting up under the wedding canopy even more special. It's now time for me to begin walking toward the garden where our guests are assembled. Ah, I can hear my colleague, Rabbi Shefa Gold, inviting guests to join their voices with hers in the heart-opening chant she has composed based on a verse from the Song of Songs: *kol dodi hinei zeh bah*, "The voice of my beloved, here it comes." What a great way to transform a country club into sacred space.

Brrr. It's much cooler out here than we'd imagined it would be in October. The leaves are still beautiful though, glistening with the rain that thankfully has stopped. A few more steps and it will be time for the *bedeken*, veiling. Many brides whose marriages I facilitate have a veil—that's fine. I had a hint of one at my first marriage, but the practice is just not for me. Rabbi Marcia Prager, who will lead the legal part of our ceremony, said she loved being veiled while awaiting her own wedding. She described her experience as a place of tranquility for her soul while others bustled around her with last-minute preparations. There's no way I can connect with the politics or spirit of hiding a woman's face behind a veil.

That said, there are veils between Barry and myself to be lifted. Rabbi Gold asks for silence. My eyes meet Barry's; his are already awash with feeling. The rabbi is explaining that there are many veils between people, including the roles we take on in life. She had asked us to make a list of these roles in advance, to separately contemplate the impact our various roles tend to have on our relationship. This was one of many stages of preparation that made it possible for us to arrive at our wedding open and joyful.

Another chant begins; this one to help us remove the veils of our roles. Those gathered are joining in: *aneini yah elohai, ha-meir eynai,*

"Answer me, oh my G*d, enlighten my eyes." Barry and I also begin chanting softly, gradually dropping our eyes from one another and letting the chant become a prayer. My sight turns inward until Barry whispers the first role on his list—"doctor." I look up into his eyes. Out through the portal of that loaded role word is pouring an ocean of meaning and memories, some shared and many from before we ever met. I move my hands as though removing a veil from over his face, and his roles as a physician and then a psychotherapist are lifted on the wings of the moment. There are many more levels of Barry beneath—some we sense and state; others will take years to discover.

Now it's my turn. I whisper, "rabbi," and the word hovers, so rich in meaning and implications for our life together, its weight always present in our public conduct and its demands upon our time. Internally I gently unhook the feeling of rabbi and quickly feel lighter, facing him as more me than "it." As he lifts the veil of rabbi from my face, the chant continues. We become lighter and lighter, lifting "mother," "father," "author," "gardener," "feminist," "critic," "detail person," "American," "South African," "woman," "man," and so on. Each role is a veil over our core selves.

Soon no veils remain. No words can fully describe our sense of ourselves as beings of pure flickering light.

MULTIDIMENSIONAL PLANNING

When Barry and I were married, we made planning decisions that expanded our wedding experience along several parameters that are important for all successful ritual efforts. These parameters are discussed below. Review them first, and then reread the story above and, with a highlighter or pen in hand, mark the components that matched and made each dimension come to life for my husband and me.

ESSENTIAL DIMENSIONS

1. Grounding in the *physical* world, addressing needs, adding beauty.
2. Arousing and supporting *emotions* and concerns.
3. Reflecting values, *thoughts*, and ideals, raising awareness.
4. Building *spirit* and connection.

These four dimensions synergize to yield wonderful moments of pure, "in the flow" (w)holiness.

As interpretive as our wedding described above may appear, if you had been there, it would have become apparent that the traditional Jewish sequence was being carefully followed throughout. The key difference is how meaning-for-living was being elicited—grounding and beauty in the outdoors, the power of veil as a metaphor, engaging everyone present in the strength and beauty of song, and commencing to more deeply weave the couple together, even before the ritual begins, by having them write down their roles in life. You have probably noted several additional points. The depth and height of what is profound and possible when your thinking and planning embrace the four dimensions—physical, emotional, intellectual, and spiritual—will become increasingly clear as you read through this volume. These dimensions are only planning tools, to be used and then released because the synergies among them result in something beyond planning and expectations. Outcomes will be different for every couple and every wedding or other rite of passage.

ELEMENTS OF A CLASSIC JEWISH WEDDING

The Jewish wedding template for Jews across all denominations is short and simple. It was originally designed to be conducted outdoors, under the stars, in order to invoke the Abrahamic blessing for having descendants as numerous as the stars. In the absence of textual referents, old engravings reveal that elements considered standard practice in contemporary weddings are not authentic Jewish practices. For example, we see no bridesmaids, best man, matron of honor, flower girl, or even the parents and siblings joining the couple under the wedding canopy, the _huppah_. These practices were introduced to emulate host civilizations and are elective. All weddings described in this chapter share the basic elements listed below, which are present in most Jewish weddings:

- **There are weeks, days, and times of the day when a Jewish wedding can and absolutely cannot be held.** The guidelines for setting times and dates for Jewish rites of passage appear in the Introduction.
- **Vort,** a few words of Torah, are taught at a family gathering to announce the couple's intention to wed, a.k.a. an engagement party. Ideally the teaching is done by the groom, the bride, a parent, or a local teacher.
- An **_aufruf_** is held, during which the impending marriage is blessed at the Torah during a Shabbat service in the weeks just prior to the wedding. The husband or the couple is "called up"—_aufruf_ (Yiddish for an _aliyah_), which is Hebrew for the opportunity to witness the Torah reading and then receive a _mi sheberah_, a blessing for their upcoming _simhah_, joyous event. They may then be pelted with soft, wrapped candies, suggesting that the blessing is also for a sweet relationship.
- The day before or the morning of the wedding, a private immersion ritual, called **mikvah,** is performed in a lake, ocean, river, or indoor facility specially designed to include living waters, usually rain, to help the couple separately prepare body, mind, and spirit for their marriage. (For more on this, see "Stress 'n' Lessen" later in this chapter.)

- The **ketubah,** a Jewish wedding contract, is signed by the couple and their witnesses. There are significant differences among the range of *ketubot* (pl.) available today. Couples can make sure that the *ketubah* accurately reflects their sensibilities about marriage. It is important for either the *ketubah* or a prenuptial agreement to address denominational differences on issues that could have an impact on a spouse's (generally a wife's) ability to remarry following a divorce. (For more on *ketubot*, see "The Wedding Contract" later in this chapter.)

- A **tisch** ("table"), also called *kabbalat panim* ("receiving faces"), is conducted for each of the two individuals being wed. Various parts of the Jewish spectrum are increasingly reclaiming the joyful practice of holding a creatively ritualized warm-up reception prior to the formal Jewish wedding ritual. Whoever feels closest to a particular member of the couple attends that particular *tisch*, while those closest to their partner-to-be attend the other *tisch*. A *tisch* is usually set up like a reception for a royal couple, each with their own "throne room." Those assembled have the role of raucous "royal advisors," who may freely interrupt with song, spoof, and jokes while their member of royalty offers a spate of carefully prepared Jewish learning. In classical communities, the bride doesn't teach but rather receives her "subjects," one at a time, as they privately whisper blessings and "advice." These approaches are intended to help break down premarital tensions, emphasize the importance of friendship and shared history, and help guests who don't know many attendees get a sense of the many circles of relationship in the couple's lives before and during their engagement. Can you feel the excitement building? The couple will meet *panim el panim* ("face-to-face") for the first time in a week (or a day, depending on local and personal custom and inclination) when one *tisch* comes over to the other bearing the wedding contract, *ketubah,* for formal witnessing and signing.

- ***Huppah,*** the wedding canopy, is symbolic of the couple's home together. A traditional image is that of the biblical patriarch Isaac taking Rebecca to his deceased mother Sarah's tent; as far as the Torah reveals, this was the biblical rite that made her his wife. The text continues by advising us that "He loved her and was comforted from the death of his mother" (Genesis 24:67). Today, as then, the tent image of the *huppah* reflects the couple's home, one rich in love, the beauty of traditions, and the comforts that only those who dearly care about one another can provide. The contemporary *huppah* takes several forms. It can be freestanding or a flowered bower suspended from the wall, or, most often, four approximately nine-foot poles with a prayer shawl or beautiful fabric stretched between them. Most Jewish clergy and/or synagogues own a nice *huppah* they can bring along at no extra charge. Making or commissioning a custom-made canopy for the *huppah* is also perfectly kosher. These may be done in painted silk or even as a quilt with squares full of messages from, and sometimes photographs of, family and friends.

- The simply lovely, historically brief **Jewish wedding ritual** includes the following steps:

    1. Chanting of short psalm verses of welcome and blessing.
    2. *Eirusin,* a blessing of betrothal said over the wine that is sipped by each member of the couple. (Wine is symbolic of life. In other words, wine starts out just fine as grape juice, fermentation sets in and it becomes sour, and the process goes on to become sweet and joyful.)

3. Vows of holy connection, termed *kiddushin*, coupled with the acceptance of a solid gold ring or object of similar value.

4. Presenting, reading, and, if not already done, signing of the *ketubah*, the "marriage contract." In most states witnesses must also sign the civil marriage forms.

5. *Vort*, a brief word of Torah, a story, or an inspirational talk, usually given by the officiant.

6. Chanting of *Sheva Brahot*, the seven wedding blessings, often with seven friends each giving an interpretive version of one. In these blessings the couple's joy is likened to the happiness of Adam and Eve when they find each other in the Garden of Eden, and they are blessed to have that degree of happiness in their marriage.

7. Breaking a wine glass.

8. Shouting out "Good luck—*mazel tov!*" by guests. (For an explanation of the surprising origins of *mazel tov*, see volume II of this series, *Meaning & Mitzvah: Daily Practices for Reclaiming Judaism through Prayer, God, Torah, Hebrew, Mitzvot and Peoplehood*, page 180.)

• **Yihud.** The couple takes some private time together to integrate the awesomeness of what has just transpired. This takes place after the wedding ritual and before entering the party space. Generally having fasted from dawn until this point in order to maintain a pure inner focus on the impending transition, the couple often will enjoy their first marital meal now, in private. Couples do not fast if their rite is held on Rosh Hodesh (monthly new moon), Hanukkah, Tu B'Shevat, or Purim, or if a health problem would make fasting dangerous. Life always comes first in Judaism.

• The wedding reception, called the ***seudah shel mitzvah***, is itself a mitzvah to attend. This allows friends, family, and loved ones to celebrate joyfully as a way to gladden the hearts of the couple. Here the couple's emphasis is on welcoming guests, connecting with dear ones, and leading the way into dancing and expressions of gratitude.

- At the end of the wedding reception meal, the same goblet of wine from which the couple drank under the *huppah* is covered, saved, and brought out for the **Sheva Brahot at the reception.** The blessing over the wine leads the wedding ceremony *Sheva Brahot* but is chanted last during dining *Sheva Brahot.* Typically friends pass the cup of blessing and take turns giving one of the blessings. A strong message of this tradition is the importance of having and nurturing the inner circle of your life.

- **Tzedakah.** It is customary to channel the gratitude elicited by joy and blessing into charitable efforts. Agreeing upon a serious sum and a good cause is a powerful first act for those who have just gotten married. Encouraging guests to honor your union with a donation to a cause to which you draw their attention is also a very holy thing to do. Compensating for the carbon debt to the environment caused, for example, by cooking and travel is a new option for this practice. (Learn more about reducing the environmental footprint of your life cycle event in Appendix 1.)

- Each night during the week after the wedding reception there are additional **Sheva Brahot,** blessing rituals. Newly married couples needn't cook dinner their first week together, as it is customary for a different friend to invite them over to dinner each night. Just as there are seven blessings chanted at the end of the wedding ceremony, so, too, this is done at the *birkat ha-mazon,* the grace after dinner, each night of the wedding week.

The experience of a full-blown Jewish wedding is best depicted by means of a story, in this case my eyewitness report from a <u>H</u>asidic wedding in Jerusalem.

An orphan since adolescence, a Grateful Dead devotee, and minimally involved in Jewish religious practice, our friend Robin discovered himself, at age twenty-three, to be a descendent of the Karliner-Stollen <u>H</u>asidic dynasty. So Robin uprooted himself from America to the ultra-religious Mea Shearim neighborhood of Jerusalem in search of his roots. Welcomed as family, he stayed and studied there in a yeshiva, a religious day school. Not long into his studies he became engaged to Tanya, another young American who was studying in the women's yeshiva a few blocks away from his. One of the more rigorous approaches to Judaism, <u>H</u>asidism also emphasizes joy and transcendence through observance, marital relationship, spiritual mentoring by a master teacher, known as a rebbe, and his senior students, as well as ecstatic traditional dance and song, and strict gender differentiation.

Two days before the wedding, we walk with Robin and Tanya along the narrow cobbled streets outside his yeshiva. Among <u>H</u>asidim, an unwed couple is not allowed to be alone before the marriage. They are always escorted by two friends. Tanya and Robin courted according to strict protocol: three meetings in a public space with a chaperone present, then a decision—yes, make a wedding plan, or no, keep meeting potential spouses. Their two friends shout out to those whom we pass on our walk: "Behold those who are about to be married, come and wish them well!" Blessings are received in return. What a festive walk! The sense of a caring, connected community is palpable.

The wedding is held in the ruins of the ancient Hurvah Synagogue, which includes an illuminated arch that almost defines Jerusalem's evening skyline. All women are directed to assemble on the top level, a stone balcony of sorts open to the night sky. Below us a river of male escorts for the groom is flowing through the streets toward us, chanting wordless melodies called *niggunim* (pl.) and bearing tall tapers that softly fill Jerusalem's Jewish quarter with an ethereal light that seems perfectly suited to the ancient architecture. Robin is barely visible within the black-coated throng.

Here comes Tanya into the women's section. Two yeshiva friends lead her to a seat of honor festooned with white ribbons and flowers. Her full-length, long-sleeved, high-collared heavy white satin wedding dress is trimmed with pearls, which reflect the candlelight.

In the privacy of our balcony perch, the women are taking turns approaching Tanya with whispered blessings and guidance for fertility and happiness. I simply whisper: "Tanya, my blessing for you is that your love and life with Robin will be sustainable and for you to remember we will be there for you in times of need, not only the good times."

It is time for the *bedeken*, the veiling. Pinned on and hanging down her back, the thick lace cloth is brought forward and settled over Tanya's face, down past her neck and shoulders. In a scared-sounding voice she points out that she can see through it only hazily. The matron tells her not to fear; she will be led slowly to the <u>huppah</u> with escorts on either side until she meets her father downstairs.

The candlelight procession approaches with Robin at its center, like a gem reaching for his setting. The veil is lifted as Robin looks for a second upon his bride's flash of blue eyes, long golden hair, and trembling lips, which burst into a brief splash of a smile at the sight of him. Quickly Robin stammers: "Yes, it is she." The veil is lowered. He and his escorts then depart fairly rapidly, to await her arrival at the <u>huppah</u>.

There is a tradition that a wedding is a time when the prayers of the bride and groom have greater power than any other point in their lives. For this reason both Robin and Tanya each hold an index card listing those who are ill within the family and community. The couple is taught to pray for those listed to be healed. It is also customary, I am advised by a voice on my right, to approach Robin at the reception and request a blessing—typical things to ask for are to find a *beshert*, a life partner, or for fertility, and for *parnassa*, a way to generate an income.

I recall that before the ritual, both Tanya and Robin went separately for immersion in a ritual bath, termed a *mikvah*. In their community, *mikvah* isn't just a formulaic dunk. Mentors remind the bride and groom to contemplate any hurts they have done in their lives to others, and to repent these before immersing so as to achieve the greatest possible purity of body, mind, and spirit.

Robin is wearing a *kittel* over his wedding suit. A *kittel* is a white karate-like robe that will one day serve as his burial shroud. Metaphors of death and rebirth abound in Jewish wedding rites.

Below, Tanya enters the men's section. As she arrives beside Robin at the *ḥuppah*, the soulful soaring of sacred song ceases.

The bride's veil is lifted slightly so she can modestly sip the sacramental wine from a huge, ornate silver kiddush cup. From the balcony we cannot hear the proceedings or, as the scene below shifts, make out much detail until a few minutes later when Robin stomps on a wine glass. Immediately all join in as a robust *niggun* picks up again for the recessional, and the long-awaited rite is finished.

The guests meet and mingle as we all walk down to the neighborhood reception hall. A gardenlike lattice wall has been erected within to continue separation of women and men. The members of the band are on the men's side with their backs to the women's side of the lattice, and they erupt into joyful wedding music as we enter. On our side, Tanya's yeshiva friends bring out masks and noisemakers and begin to entertain the no longer pale, but now wildly vivacious bride with spontaneous skits and circle dancing.

What's this? The lattice is being moved aside. Oh, musicians are coming through, playing a march. Now men arrive, bearing Robin aloft in a chair, and they are also carrying an empty chair to similarly honor Tanya. With a cloth napkin for modesty stretched between them, Robin and Tanya gasp out intermittent shouts of delight and fear, their movements become a dance. You might almost say they dance together. The men dance around them, hands raised above their shoulders, in ecstatic nested circles while we women clap the beat in a circle on the periphery. Now they are each tossed higher and higher into the air as they grasp their chairs in roller coaster–like delight and fear of falling. Now the couple is being lowered, and as quickly as the men arrived, they leave. The lattice wall is restored, and we women are again left to our own celebratory traditions.

After midnight the music changes from frenetic to the most graceful and rich of H̲asidic dance melodies. The few of us remaining on the women's side head up to the lattice. The tables on the men's side have been pushed together into a large U. An older woman advises me that the *Maggid* (or "teller of sacred stories") of Yerushalayim, Jerusalem, will soon arrive. He enters wearing a classic large round fur-rimmed hat called a *streimel* and a *kappoteh*, an elegant black medieval-style coat. He appears to be in his nineties until he starts to dance. Alas, my knowledge of Yiddish is limited. I catch the meaning of only one story; it is about the marriage-counseling prowess of Elijah the prophet.

The remaining men leave en masse; it is time for me to leave as well.

RECIPE #1:
Harvesting
Wedding
Ideas

Many of the practices described in the stories above can be adopted or adapted for almost any Jewish wedding. On reflection, see which might be applicable for you.

❏ A candlelight procession to accompany bride and groom to the *h̲uppah*.
❏ Taking pleasure in walking in the company of friends during the weeks before the wedding.

❏ Choosing wordless melodies, *niggunim*, or single-phrase
chants that friends and family sing in order to become less
an audience and more an empowered community that is
fully part of the process.

❏ Selecting individuals with enough dramatic flair from
among family members, friends, or your Jewish guides and
teachers to be honored by holding the *ḥuppah* poles,
reading the *ketubah*, leading your *bedeken* (veil ceremony),
and being part of other components of the ceremony.

❏ Giving thought as to the intent of ritual garments—allure
versus respect and beauty. Is there a difference? What
kinds of thoughts and attention to your body/mind/spirit
are you intent upon creating among those in attendance?

❏ Does gender separation for prayer and ritual speak to you?
When? How?

❏ Is a veil appropriate or inappropriate, based on your
sense of self, fashion, and politics? What is your partner's
desire? Will you hold a *bedeken* ritual? With or without a
veil?

❏ Do you like the *tisch* model? Will either or both of you
teach? Do you want the humorous interruptions? Who will
be the ceremonial leader for each *tisch*? This is usually
undertaken by a close friend or teacher.

❏ Will you gather some psalms to contemplate while
waiting to be called to the *ḥuppah*? Will you gather names
of those who need healing and dedicate your recital of
the psalms as prayers for them?

❏ Who is single, looking, and coming to your wedding?
How can they best be helped to find one another at your
celebration?

❏ Will you reflect upon your past and set up *teshuvah* meetings
to smooth and heal rifts from life's encounters? (For further

information on *teshuvah*, see volume I, *Reclaiming Judaism as a Spiritual Practice: Holy Days and Shabbat*, pages 15–21.)

❑ Will you elect to immerse in living waters, *mikvah*, and emerge a refreshed, resouled bride or groom?

❑ Where will your kiddush cup come from? A family heirloom? Will you ask someone to gift you with a beautiful one that has caught your eye? Borrow one from the rabbi or synagogue?

❑ Will you break the glass together? If just one of you, which one?

❑ Do you want to be lifted on chairs and danced around? Make a note to inform the musicians and/or dance leader.

❑ Will your party have mixed or gender-separated dancing?

❑ Will you encourage friends and family to create skits, bring masks, and perhaps tell family stories up at the mike?

❑ Will you have a *maggid*, a professional storyteller, regale those present with some new and/or traditional tales?

❑ A *badhan* is the Jewish version of a humorist who often knows comedy, miming, and/or clowning and can lightly "roast" family or society. Might you make room to rotate in one or two such sets between musical moments during the party?

❑ Is the *hora* the only traditional Jewish dance your family remembers, and then only barely? Will you hire an Israeli dance teacher to pop up between sets to teach two or three easy and fun traditional dances at the wedding?

❑ After the wedding ceremony's seven blessing section, will you invite friends to rise and call out spontaneous blessings?

Notice how different this list is from the one at the beginning of the chapter—caterer, invitations, parking attendants—all of which involve logistical decisions.

What if you already have children? How do they feel about all this? Flower girls and boys don't typically handle the pressure of such an assignment with ease. An alternative is to give the children an aisle seat and have them throw petals when the couple walks by. They experience far less performance anxiety this way.

Children give vivid reports of how very loved and respected they feel when they're invited under the wedding canopy before the seven blessings to receive a blessing or a vow of commitment from their mom or dad and their new stepparent. Here's an example of how that can work:

"Patsy and Denny, please come join your mom and stepdad up here under the _huppah_. Elliot and Jason, will you come join your dad and stepmom, please?

"Your parents have something to say to you. So that they can hold you, if you wish, in a hugging huddle, I will read aloud, and they will repeat the words after me." Little Elliot, the youngest at age four, leads the way by clinging to his dad, and soon all the children press into the embrace of their parents. I call out the vow written specially for this family situation, which is then repeated with tenderness and feeling:

> On this holy day of our marriage, let it be known before Heaven, family, friends, and community that these children were conceived in love. Elliot and Jason, Patsy and Denny—we both love you so much. We vow to coordinate and act as parents and stepparents must to secure all possible safety, health, education, and happiness for each of you. We pledge never to speak ill of your birth parents or their loved ones in your presence, for we know that hurts you. We will respectfully negotiate time for their needs,

RECIPE #2:
Do Children Belong Under the _Huppah_?

your needs, and ours to be with you. Our marriage unites more than the two of us; we are now a formal family ready to become a real family, which happens through loving and constructive attention to one another. We commit to this with you not only for as long as we are married, but for as long as we both shall live. *Keyn yehi ratzon*. So may it be!

All assembled: *Keyn yehi ratzon*, so may it be!

Do you or the person you are marrying already have children? What are a few key points you'd want to be sure to incorporate in your vow or blessing for them, whether done privately, at the party, or under the *ḥuppah*?

RING ME LATER

One detail of the Ḥasidic wedding story proved elusive. Was there ever an exchange of rings? The couple did not wear wedding bands at the party. Did someone forget to bring the rings?

In fact, there was no exchange of rings at the Ḥasidic wedding. Remember that Jews are among the most ancient peoples in the world. While egalitarian rites are preferred by most Jewish people today, our rites originated with the "man takes a wife" model. This process is described in the early legal records of the Talmud without any romantic overlay: "A woman is acquired in one of three ways: *kesef*, money; a *shtar*, contract; and *beeyah*, intercourse" (Mishnah Kiddushin 1:1). Notice the absence of a ring in that list. The wife's vow was also absent at the Ḥasidic wedding because historically there was none. That said, the world of classical Judaism is not as monolithic as it appears from the outside. Some classical communities stick to financial sums, documents, and the wedding night, while most now have the man place a solid, unadorned gold ring on the woman's finger as the *kesef*, the money exchange, and none on his own. Still others allow the man to add a ring for himself after the ceremony to wear in secular settings so as not to "put a stumbling block before the blind," in other words, not to lead someone to wrongly think him single. A solid gold ring is traditional because its value can be part of the classical wedding agreement, but some couples now use rings with embedded stones since in our time most rings have negligible nego-tiable value. Some select rings are inscribed with or designed to embody a verse from the Song of Songs that is used in the vows for some egalitarian weddings: "I am my beloved's and my beloved is mine," *ani l'dodi v'dodi li.*

EGALITARIAN CONSIDERATIONS

Most Jews no longer follow the most classical path and elect instead for egalitarian communities and ceremonies. This has required the development of a vow for the woman. Two primary traditions exist: use of the verse from Song of Songs above, or, more commonly, a rather profound verse from Hosea, which is also used in our morning prayers. A combination of the traditional male vow with the Hosea verse makes for a powerful reciprocal vow that can be said identically by each. With this background in mind, it's time to consider whether one or both of these vows, separately or in combination, will work for you.

- Study each of the verses in Table 2–1 with your partner by reading each word out loud and sharing what it means in practical terms for your lives together.
- Take special note of the last phrase in the wedding vow from Hosea. This phrase asserts that the purpose of mar-riage is for spouses to help one another "know G*d."

RECIPE #3:
Vows of
Understanding

What could that possibly mean? What can happen in marriage that doesn't with friends or when we are simply living with someone in a loving, enduring, yet uncommitted relationship?

- Several interpretative versions of these verses are offered in Table 2–1. Find words to create meaning and develop your own interpretive version to complement the Hebrew.

- The traditional vow for a man to a woman is as follows:

    Harei aht m'kudeshet li b'tabaat zo k'dat moshe v'yisrael.

    Behold, by means of this symbol you become holy unto me according to the laws (path) of Moses and the Jewish people.

- *Note:* It is often appropriate to alter one word of the traditional vow formula—saying *minhagei*, "customs," instead of *dat*, "law"—since many Jewish marriages performed today are probably not done within a classical Jewish legal framework.

- Above, the term *aht* is feminine singular for "you" and *m'kudeshet* is also feminine. Should a woman recite this verse to a man, the feminine grammar in the verse above would need to be switched to masculine:

    Harei aht ah m'kudash li b'tabaat zo.

    Behold, by means of this symbol you become holy unto me.

- Things get even more interesting as you start to study the commitment verse from Hosea, who was an eighth-century prophet. This is sometimes uttered unilaterally by the wife to her husband, and can also be combined with the verse above to create egalitarian, reciprocal vows.

Table 2–1 Wedding Vows			
JPS* version	ArtScroll** version	R'Goldie Milgram interpretative version	Transliteration
And I will espouse you forever;	I will betroth you to Me forever,	I commit myself to you on every level.	*V'eirastih li l'olam*
I will espouse you	and I will betroth you to me	I commit to share both challenges and resources.	*v'eirastih li b'tzedek*
with righteousness and justice; and with goodness	with righteousness, justice, kindness	To try my best to be just. I will flow loving-kindness your way.	*u'v'mishpaht* *u'v'hesed*
and mercy,	and mercy,	I want to hear your pain, your joy, to understand you, to find compassion for your actions and feelings.	*u'v'rahamim*
and I will espouse you with faithfulness;	I will betroth you to me with fidelity,	I commit to be faithful to you.	*v'eirastih li b'emunah*
and you shall be devoted to the Lord.	and you shall know HaShem.	so that through relationship, you will know God.	*v'yadaht et adonai.*

* Jewish Publication Society   ** ArtScroll is an imprint of Mesorah Publications, Ltd.

Whether exchanging rings or the groom is placing a ring on the bride's finger, Jewish tradition holds that the index finger of the right hand is energetically connected to the heart. So let's say it's a heterosexual wedding and a "he" is going first:

- Face your beloved.
- Say your vow of commitment, the one in Table 2–1 or whatever one you have chosen.

RECIPE #4:
Jewish
Wedding Ring
Ceremony
Stage
Directions

- Place a solid gold ring on her right index finger.
- Of her own free will, she now moves the ring to the ring (fourth) finger of her left hand.
- For egalitarian ceremonies, just reverse roles and repeat.

HISTORICAL BASIS OF THE JEWISH WEDDING

The three ancient formal components of a Jewish wedding still peek through the rituals of today. *Shidduhim*, the making of a *shidduh*, a "match," today refers to all the various ways of helping someone search for his or her *beshert*, "intended," which can include using the services of a professional matchmaker, a *shadhan*. In times gone by, establishing the *beshert* resulted in a premarital contract of commitment, which, in some regions and periods of history, was arranged from birth. A contract like this would cover specifics, such as withdrawal penalties and the assignment of obligations to the families and partners. While such formal *shidduhim* are prevalent in only a small part of the Jewish spectrum today, help in finding a *beshert* is something everyone can offer to friends and family.

Following the *shidduh* comes *eirusin*, a "betrothal" ritual that traditionally comprises the first half of the wedding ceremony and that takes place up to a year before the wedding itself. Historically, at this point, the woman continued, or in a minority of communties continues, to live in her father's house for three months to a year when the Jewish wedding process is then completed under a *huppah*.

As the centuries have progressed, *eirusin* and *nessuin*, the rituals that formalize the marriage, became one unified wedding ritual. In some communities an intellectually interesting homily or meaningful story from a guest or clergy person is also offered at the time of the *huppah* ritual. Psalm verses, songs, and poetry are added to the ceremony by various Jewish communities and couples, as it is customary to embroider a mitzvah with creative additions.

THE ENCHANTMENT PROCESS

Couples are well-advised to take a full year to enjoy being engaged. During that period, memories of great enchantment are inscribed in the couple's mind and enter the foundation of the marriage. Those who choose to compress ritual planning into a few months sometimes endanger viable relationships with the stress. Also, a solid period of engagement provides time to come to know one another's families and personal styles under enough pressure for each member of the couple to have a good indication of what he or she might be getting into. Even if you've lived together already, you'll see that commitment somehow raises the stakes and changes the dynamics. Give yourself time; this is a process that can put holes or holiness into your relationship, depending upon how it is handled.

KNOWING EACH OTHER

There are two more Jewish practices that help couples cultivate healthy intimacy. First, you may have noticed at some Jewish weddings that the bride or both partners circle one another or the *huppah* three or seven times. By now you may have guessed that there must be some meaning in this practice, and there are, indeed, several meanings.

"Kira and Michael will now face each other, engage each other's gaze, and turn seven times, each around the other. They will be braiding their souls together. Each circle is for a different divine quality which our tradition encourages us to cultivate."

Each quality is called a *sephirah*. Practices for cultivating these qualities in various combinations are widely found in the literature of the ancient and contemporary Kabbalists, Ḥasidim, and other

RECIPE #5:
Sacred
Circlings

Jewish cultural creatives across most of the spectrum of Jewish practice.

Each *sephirah* has a Hebrew name. There are ten *sephirot* (pl.) in total, but only seven a human can work on. The rest—wisdom, knowledge, and understanding—are described as coming to us the way a mother's milk comes, as an act of grace toward her yearning child.

The word *sephirah* shares a root with *sapphire*, and each of the *sephirot* is gem-like, so multifaceted that anything said here is going to be no more than a general explanation. (See Suggestions for Further Reading and Learning for a more in-depth study of *sephirot*.)

Here is an exercise to help you prepare for the circling part of the wedding ritual.

- First, sit with your beloved and ask yourself: What do we know about the practical aspects of the first quality, overflowing loving-kindness, **_hesed,_** in marriage? When does *hesed* help? When can *hesed* hurt?
- Now move on to the other qualities, which are generally understood to be:

    gevurah: maintaining healthy boundaries.

    tiferet: beauty wrought from balancing love and restraint.

    netzah: the drive to sustain and succeed.

    hod: the capacity to submit to further work on something.

    yesod: balancing drive with submission by recognizing when a solid foundation has been created and that it is time to let something manifest.

    malhut: letting effort dissolve into manifestation so that new realities immediately surface.

At your wedding, if you choose to do the seven turns, explain their meanings on a handout sheet or booklet. Have the officiant encourage guests to contemplate each quality with regard to your relationship as you make the turns.

Let's return to Kira and Michael, whose story began this consideration of the circling ritual.

❧

The long train on Kira's dress has been unobtrusively lifted a bit by
her best friend, who follows along behind her as she and Michael
circle each other. They are oblivious to the music, the train, the
guests. The rabbi's soft intoning of loving-kindness, healthy boundaries, is simply a guiding voice. Kira and Michael are enraptured, two
beings once as separate as two Shabbat candles, braiding themselves
together to end as the Jewish week ends, with a braided candle,
signifying how, when we take time for conscious loving, wholeness,
happiness, and holiness happen.

❧

Note: Some say only brides may do the circling and then, only three
circles. A possible source verse for this tradition is found in the biblical Book of Jeremiah: "Set up milestones, three major markers, set
a ladder by your heart, the way you went, turn that way again, oh
daughter of Israel, turn … for G*d has created a new thing on earth,
a woman [to] encompass a man" (Jeremiah 31:21). Another source
for three turns is the verse from Hosea offered in Recipe #3, which
three times says: "*v'eirastih li*—I betroth myself to you."

There's more to say about the number seven. Seven has great significance in Jewish tradition. In addition to the seven qualities to be
cultivated, there are seven days of creation, seven days in a week, and
seven blessings to conclude a wedding. A kabbalistic saying teaches
that the bride who walks seven times around the groom removes the
husks of solitude from his soul through her luminescence.

Judaism teaches that human actions have a ripple effect upon all
of creation, and whether you do three, seven, or no turns, the intent

is for us to realize that as we expand and deepen the scope of our relationships, everything and everyone is somehow affected for the good.

The second intimacy-building practice is called *tenaiim*, composing a list of principles and agreements upon which a marriage "depends." Once a norm of the Jewish wedding process, the list would be drawn up in the form of the legal betrothal, *eirusin*, about a year before the marriage, and it would stipulate dowries and disposition of inheritances, among other property concerns. Today, financially oriented civil prenuptial agreements are widely used throughout the spectrum of Jewish life, and those few who do legalistic *tenaiim* sign them at the wedding proper. But what about the couple's vision for their life together?

RECIPE #6:
Cultivating
Spiritual
Intimacy: A
Guide for
Couples

Unspoken or unfulfilled hopes and expectations can sabotage marriages. A reframed and reclaimed *tenaiim* process can help couples clarify, coordinate, and deepen their vision for life together in the years to come.

Privately jot down a few ideas for how you might initiate action on each of the points listed in the Couples' Jewish Life Assessment on the next page.

Then, taking one topic per meeting with your beloved, share your ideas without either of you interrupting or denying the other's excitement or vision.

Now, select one idea you both are willing to try at least once. Consider this a gift of experimental relationship you give each other. Check in afterward to see how it went; perhaps modify or add to your relationship practices. Move on to another idea and another.

COUPLES' JEWISH LIFE ASSESSMENT

1. Ritual is a way of providing a structure within which intimacy can grow. It is part of the glue that keeps couples and generations connected. Reflect on your family's use of traditional and invented rituals in your home.

2. It is important to be connected with other people who care about you, who can celebrate and mourn with you, who show up to support you as individuals and as a couple, and who hold up a mirror to your lives and give guidance. This is the inner circle of your life. Know to your core that you will show up for them as well. List those people in your life who really form your inner circle of mutual support. Do not include siblings, parents, or pets; we are looking beyond the nuclear family here. Are there enough people on your list to ensure a strong support system for both of you? What steps might you take to expand your inner circle if that seems warranted?

3. On Friday night at the dinner table, it is customary to express and model admiration for your partner's qualities and special actions during the week, to see him or her as a blessing in your life, and to express gratitude. Reflect on this practice together. How might you implement this during your marriage?

4. Judaism recognizes the importance of embracing our imperfections and emphasizes the importance of turning hurtful mistakes into opportunities by working through them with the other person. We call this practice *teshuvah* (see volume I, *Reclaiming Judaism as a Spiritual Practice: Holy Days and Shabbat*, pages 15–21). How do you handle the issue of *teshuvah* with each other?

5. In the Torah we find the concept of time-shifting; that is, moving out of work mode and not letting the news, money issues, or any work-related thoughts or effort intrude upon

the sacred time we call Shabbat. How do you plan to work this out in your life as a couple?

6. Jewish tradition embraces the prayer from Deuteronomy found in the mezuzah—which has as its theme "Listen" (*shema*) so that "you will love" (*v'ahavta*)—as a central spiritual principle. How are your listening skills as individuals affecting your life as a couple? Is listening—or failing to listen attentively—enhancing or undermining the sense of love in your relationship?

7. Judaism regards physical intimacy and lovemaking in marriage as desirable, delectable, and holy. Reflect together about times when you could almost feel G*d sigh in pleasure with you. If you were to write a blessing together to say before making love, what might that be?

8. Together you have the ability to fulfill the mitzvah of *tzedakah*, expanding the amount of justice in the world by helping to make life better for others through charitable giving. Reflect upon your philanthropic efforts and values as a couple.

9. Torah depicts the life of the Jewish people as a journey from slavery to increased awareness of holiness, to dreams of a Promised Land, to rebirth, to a wilderness time of feeling lost and needing to learn new skills to adjust to new circumstances, to arriving in the Promised Land. Like the Jewish people, relationships go through many such cycles. Reflect together on the phases and cycles of your relationship as a spiritual journey. Using the metaphors above, drawn from the Exodus story, where does each of you see the relationship right now?

10. The *Amidah* is a silent prayer during services. Each of the blessings within the *Amidah* is a springboard to find the prayer of your heart. Reflect on what you would most like to have emerge for you as a couple—whether spiritual, emo-

tional, intellectual, or physical. Consider what comes up for each of you, and agree on one item from each of your lists to pray for each night at bedtime. Now you can pray for your partner's wish to come true and your partner can pray for yours. After a month, check in. Has anything changed in your relationship?

11. Remembering to say "I love you" and finding new words for the range of feelings and experiences that fill the concept of love are enduring needs in a healthy marriage. The Song of Songs, *Shir HaShirim*, is intended to be read aloud on Shabbat. It is at once a love poem connecting the Jewish people with the Source of Life and a mirror reflecting the light of love in your relationship. Seek out a beautiful copy of this work for your home and take turns reading verses to one another. Each of you might take a different-colored marker and highlight the verses that shine a light on your love for your partner.

Some couples who complete this inventory have found it valuable to write up a Jewish Marriage Vision Statement.

Tenaiim sessions can be done by the couple alone or with a facilitator such as a counselor or rabbi. Sessions are good times to address other important marital issues as well. One discussion that is almost a litmus test for the future relationship of newly engaged couples is this: If one of your parents needs care as he or she ages, how do you envision being a part of this? It is also surprising how often certain basic issues haven't been fully explored by couples looking forward to a Jewish marriage: Do you both want children? Do you want to live in one place your whole life or somewhere else in the future? Do you agree on the importance of savings or a budget? What about travel?

The answers you come up with in your *tenaiim* sessions comprise your record of important agreements, including such considerations as merged or separate bank accounts or the desire to create a prenuptial agreement. You can use the verses you both have found in the Song of Songs to add the flavor of romance to your *ketubah* and your *tenaiim.*

- Throw a party when your *tenaiim* document is ready. Consider reading your document aloud. (Skip those points that are too private for public airing.)
- Witnesses take a scarf or another object of their own and give it to the guarantors of the agreement, who historically were the parents but are now more often the adult couple themselves. The guarantors hold the scarf aloft. It functions much as a raised flag might to signal an agreement. In some communities a ceramic plate would be broken on such an occasion by the mothers of the bride and groom, releasing all the difficult energy that goes into such serious effort and signifying that a new vision has been created.
- People change. On the night before your first and subsequent anniversaries, reread your *tenaiim,* add codicils, and make changes as needed. You might want friends or family to witness these revisions; after all, it is common to hear people say that throwing a party after five, ten, or more years of sustained marriage makes a good deal more sense than throwing one for the original event.

THE WEDDING CONTRACT

The wedding contract, the *ketubah,* is signed on the wedding day either publicly or privately and then held aloft and read aloud during the wedding ritual. The *ketubah* requires the signatures of two independent Jewish witnesses who are neither facilitating the ritual nor members of the immediate family. A *ketubah* generally comprises

Jewish legal phrases, requires the couple and signators' Hebrew names, and specifies the city and country where the ritual is held. It often contains language stipulating the couple's philosophical orientation and even their duties in creating a home together.

Contemporary *ketubot* (pl.) tend to address feeling as well as function. Different templates for *ketubot* exist within the various denominations and can be found in Jewish bookstores, gift and artist shops, and online. Couples need to review and select among the *ketubah* options in advance to ensure that the one they choose will reflect what they really intend to contract for with each other, or alternatively, to commission a professional *ketubah* artist to create one for them. Some couples typically hang their framed *ketubah* over their bed or in the living room or dining room. Your *ketubah* is a legal document that authorities may ask to see at other points in your life, so don't lose it. A civil wedding certificate, which has tax and estate implications, is not a substitute for a *ketubah*.

Aramaic, once the everyday language of Jewish people in the Mediterranean region, has come to be considered the traditional language for a Jewish marriage contract. Aramaic is a primary language in the Talmud, and two biblical works—Ezra and Daniel—are mostly written in Aramaic. Most *ketubot* today are written in Aramaic and in translation.

For much of human history, women and children had a status like chattel, that is, owned property. The *ketubah* represented an ancient breakthrough for women's rights because it mandated that a minimum sum be exchanged as a dowry and that men provide its value and then some back to the woman in the event of divorce, so that she would not be made destitute. Another upgrade was instituted around the year 1000 CE, when a German rabbinic leader known as Rabbeynu Gershom recognized the importance of protecting women financially in the event of divorce. He shifted the nature of the divorce settlement for those under his domain from terms preset in the *ketubah* to a matter that would be decided in the rabbinic courts, should divorce proceedings ever need to be instituted. This practice has expanded to become a widespread norm. Continued social change now invites further modifications, and egalitarian *ketubot* have become widely available (see Table 2–2).

Caution: The Hebrew, or the more traditional Aramaic text found on preprinted *ketubot*, often does not match the translation that appears on them. If you are preparing for marriage, have a qualified reader review the *ketubah* of your choosing to ensure its accuracy, and be sure to obtain your rabbi's approval of it before making an outright purchase.

Some communities' *ketubot* recognize the shift set into history by Rabbeynu Gershom and his students; others keep the older acquisition approach. Two examples follow in Table 2–2.

It is also important to consider a prenuptial agreement to cover financial, estate, and potential issues concerning Jewish divorce (see chapter 3). You might wonder, "Can anyone even think about such a thing *before* marriage?" As my colleague and technical consultant Rabbi Robert Scheinberg puts it: "Addressing issues of future calamity, divorce, and death are important elements for inclusion in the *ketubah* or a prenuptial agreement. This is part of the spiritual value that I find in the content of the traditional *ketubah*. A marital relationship is such that you want to say, 'I love this person so much that even when I imagine the worst possible scenario I want to do right by him/her.'" It is increasingly common for couples to arrange for a prenuptial agreement addressing issues concerning finances and, if there are children from previous marriages, estate issues. They can further use that document to indicate that they will give each other a *get*, a formal Jewish divorce document, in addition to a civil one should matters so evolve. This is essential, as a civil divorce doesn't undo a Jewish wedding, and most rabbis require a *get* that undoes the Jewish marriage before they will remarry an individual to someone new. A qualified rabbi can help you decide how to incorporate such matters into your wedding process.

Caution: In many countries, civil law requires couples to register with their municipality in advance for a marriage license. Jewish clergy do not marry couples who do not do so where required, for, as the Talmud puts it: "The law of the land is the law."

Table 2–2 *Ketubah Variations*	
Egalitarian *Ketubah* Translated	Classical *Ketubah* Translated
On the "x"th day of the week, the "x"th day of the month of 57_ _ in the town, _____state, _____and country of _____ the bride and groom ___ daughter of ___ and _____ and ____son of _____ and _____ affirmed their love for each other saying, "With these rings, we make our love sacred. Let our hearts be interwoven in a flowing tapestry of hope and trust. Let our lives be united, sharing spirituality and ideas, as equals, and best friends. Let love gently comfort our quiet times and enrich our times of joy. May we create a home that surrounds our family and friends with laughter, warmth, and love.	On the ___ day of the week, the ____ day of the month of _____ in the year five thousand seven hundred and ____ since the creation of the world, according to the way of reckoning customarily used here in the city of ____, state of _____, country of _____, did _____son of ____ [father's name of groom, if no known father, mother's name is inserted] of the family ____ say to _____ daughter of ___ [father's name rule as above] of the family _____, "Be my wife according to the law of Moses and Israel. I will cherish, honor, support, and maintain you in accordance with the custom of Jewish husbands who honestly cherish, honor, support, and maintain their wives. "I have set aside for you the portion of _____ silver *zuzzim*, which accrues to you according to the law of _____ [depends whether widow, virgin, etc.], together with your food, clothing, and necessities, and will commence to live with you as husband and wife according to known custom." And _____ daughter of _____ consented and became his wife. Her belongings that she brought to him in silver, gold, valuables, wearing apparel, house furnishings, and bedclothes, all this _____ son of _____, the bridegroom accepted in the sum of ___ silver pieces, with ___[bridegroom's name] adding from his own property the sum of ____ silver pieces, making ____ silver pieces.

May our love last forever.

I am my beloved's and my beloved is mine.
Set me as a seal upon your heart,
as a seal upon your arm, for love is stronger than death."

This covenant of marriage has been signed and sealed according to the laws of Moses and Israel.
Witnesses:
___son/daughter of _____ and _____
___son of/daughter of _____ and _____

Text from ketubah *designed by Shayna Baecker Magid.*

_____, the bridegroom, declared: "The responsibility of this marriage contract, this wedding dowry, and the additional sum, I take upon myself and my heirs after me, so that they shall be paid from the best of my property and assets that have under the whole of heaven, that which I now possess or may later acquire. All my property, real and personal, even the cloak on my shoulders shall be mortgaged to secure the payment of this marriage contract, the wedding dowry, and the additional amount, during my lifetime, from the present day and forever."
___, the bridegroom, has taken upon himself the responsibility of this marriage contract, of the wedding dowry and the additional sum, according to the restrictive usages of marriage contracts and the additions made for the daughters of Israel in accordance with the institutions of our sages of blessed memory. It is not to be regarded as an indecisive contractual obligation or as a stereotyped form. We have effected the binding legal formality, *kinyan*, between ____son of _____, the bridegroom, and ____ daughter of ____, this ____ by an instrument that is legally appropriate for establishing a transaction and everything is valid and established.
Witness: _____
Witness: _____

STRESS 'N' LESSEN

There is nothing like the feeling of being in the flow. It's crucial to step outside the hubbub and into a different state of consciousness that allows for the release of tight muscles and the soothing of abraded spirit. Recognizing how jarring the day before or the day of a wedding can be, the Jewish people have evolved a wonderful immersion practice called *mikvah* that can be transformational. The next story, which describes Craig's preparation for his marriage to Bill, demonstrates four key points. One is the power of the *mikvah* process, the second is that gender is not a factor in making use of traditional rituals, the third is to help us all remember that lives can be complicated, and the fourth is to teach one way of shaping this practice so that the entire experience is healing, whole, and holy.

∾

Perfect. Sunrise at the Jersey shore and not a soul on the beach save for Craig and his brother Dan. Craig's second marriage will be at one o'clock. I join them on the sand beside a blissfully calm sea. Craig has been doing the traditional practice of recalling, honoring, and releasing anew any mistakes, misgivings, and stresses in his life up to this point. In the weeks and months leading up to this day he has already made and kept appointments to work through and resolve issues with people who have hurt him or whom he has hurt in the past.

"Thank you for coming," Craig says. "I've been doing my homework with family, friends, and life review."

Craig looks at me. He knows I won't push him to share further confidences; besides, his brother is here. I don't know what, if anything, they share about their personal lives. Craig can continue his process internally; it need not be our business.

Craig sighs and continues. "I didn't want to get a divorce ten years ago. Even when Beth said the children were being damaged by our fighting, I still didn't want a broken family." He began to weep, repeating, "I did not want a broken family." Dan takes his brother in his arms.

Craig continues, "I couldn't see into the future then. I couldn't know what would come of those three years of therapy, growing by leaps and bounds in self-awareness, then dating, experimental relationships, twice again a broken heart, and finally finding someone so right, so deeply good, so kind and accepting. I couldn't have known that Bill would come into my life. I feel so blessed. Bill recently met Beth, and they made a pact to hold Passover with all our families together whenever possible. I could not have imagined that; I saw a good in her that had been lost in all our demonizing of one another during the years leading up to the divorce. Not all my divorced friends have a good relationship with their formers; we are so blessed."

"How you suffered; you did not want a divorce. You didn't imagine there would be a healthy, happy life in your future," I assure him. Still he weeps, but more softly. "Is there more?"

There was. Once shared, his posture eases visibly with the release.

"I welcome my new life," Craig says, reflecting positively on what's to come as his _huppah_ approaches. "I welcome the changes that will come with shifting from living together for two years to becoming fully committed to one another. I know marrying will help me feel more secure. Bill wants my full commitment, and I am ready to give it. I know I will welcome his mom and dad as very dear relatives. Just think about it—one ritual and soon I'll have three new sisters and brothers-in-law as well as four nieces and one stepdaughter!"

"Reb Goldie, I especially welcome having learned not to force someone to do things my way—whether it be folding the sheets precisely or using canisters rather than bags for coffee. I'm now in a relationship where we both listen and agree on what's needed for both of us to thrive."

Suddenly Craig jumps up and spins around in circles on the beach, throwing his towel in the air. "Let's do it! I'm ready! I'm goin' in!" I have advised him to wade into the sea up to his waist for modesty and only then to take off his trunks. He will immerse in the most traditional form of _mikvah_, in a natural body of flowing water. _Mikvah_ for marriage is a rite of releasing and rebirthing into the state of being a full _hatan_, a groom aligned with his highest self, one who will emerge physically, emotionally, and spiritually ready to cross the threshold into a new chapter in life.

Dan and I will each midwife Craig's birth as a _hatan_, a groom. Dan wades out with Craig holding a dry towel aloft. When they get to waist-deep, I turn my back and focus all my heart and soul on wishing him well, what people probably mean when they say, "I'll pray for you."

Craig slips off his trunks and hands them to Dan. He pauses, letting the list of things to release quickly run through him, and he dives under a wave, trying to stay under like a baby in a womb. When he pops up, Dan shouts, "Kosher," meaning that every bit of Craig, every strand of hair, toes, all have been immersed. Craig dives again, just a human being, and pops back up. Again Dan shouts, "Kosher!" One more, this time Craig arises a groom, as ready as he ever will be for his beloved. He emerges _hatan_ Craig, really _yonatan_, Jonathan, his chosen Hebrew name, because the Torah says King David and Jonathan, King Saul's son, loved one another. "Kosher!" shouts Dan over the waves. And he was and he is and they are.

"Kosher. Repeat after me," I instruct Craig, leading him in the classic blessing for this moment and translating interpretively. "_Baruh_, here I stand at the pond of life's blessings, _atah adonai elo-heynu meleh ha-olam_, G*d-aware at the threshold of eternity, _asher kidshanu b'mitzvotav v'tzivanu al ha-t'veelah_, through this guidance, the mitzvah of _t'veelah_, immersion, I emerge to know my body, my heart, and my intentions are fully pure and _kodesh_, holy."

Some who have prior experience with _mikvah_ may be surprised by the entry above. After World War II much of the emotional and spiritual component of Jewish practice was ceded to the deep grief of the times and almost lost. Diverse approaches to reclaiming the value of _mikvah_ are under development across the entire spectrum of Jewish life today. (For more on this subject, see volume I of this series, _Reclaiming Judaism as a Spiritual Practice: Holy Days and Shabbat_, page 99; and volume II, _Meaning & Mitzvah: Daily Practices for Reclaiming Judaism through Prayer, God, Torah, Hebrew, Mitzvot and Peoplehood_, pages 156–160.)

GENDER CONSIDERATIONS

Inclusive language for same-sex commitment ceremonies has been drawn from the seven traditional wedding blessings themselves, which declare marriage to be between *rey-im ha-ah-hu-veem*, "beloved companions." Most but not all non-Orthodox denominations have recently configured equality of genders into the wedding liturgy and ritual. But how to get around the language in the Torah stipulating that a man shall not lie with a man as with a woman? The simple response is, well, how could he, since it's biologically impossible? Further, it seems never to have occurred to the sages to comment on lesbianism. But homophobia through thousands of years has left a trail of suffering across the face of almost every world religion, and many contemporary religious people, including Jews, are trying to do some remediation.

As a new phenomenon, there is a lot of variation in the nature of same-sex liturgy and commitment rituals. In 1984 the Reconstructionist Rabbinical College became the first Jewish seminary to accept gay and lesbian students for ordination. Congregations were not so quick to adopt nondiscriminatory hiring and ritual policies, so the movement brought the matter to a vote in 1993. Would congregants, regardless of gender identity, be treated as people with full rights to love within the umbrella of Judaism, or would these souls be bashed yet again? The referendum passed and a report was issued, encouraging congregations to study the issue in depth to increase understanding and increase justice as each congregation would be free to review, discuss, and revise its local policies. In 1990 the Reform movement agreed to ordain gay and lesbian rabbis, and passed a referendum in 2000 allowing Reform rabbis to perform same-sex commitment ceremonies. The Conservative rabbinate, long resistant, determined in 2007 that this decision would be essentially a matter of individual clergy conscience. While same-sex marriages are not condoned within Orthodoxy, homosexual desire is recognized among Orthodox leaders as a painful predicament not to be acted upon.

How did our generation secure the *hutzpah*, the audacity, to challenge the status quo? By studying and applying material from within the tradition: "The wise have the power to uproot a matter from the Torah" (Tosafot, Baba Batra 48b; see also K'tzot Ha-Ḥoshen 34 and also Bavli T'murah 14b). And, "For many things it is permitted to uproot matters of Torah because of the protection [around the law, layers of interpretation, and custom], or in cases of honoring people" (Rashi, Talmud Brahot 20a).

At this point, a couple cannot use a *ketubah* to create a same-sex marriage that will be regarded as valid throughout the entire spectrum of Judaism. Still, the creation of a *ketubah* can be a valuable creative process that nurtures a healthy relationship. Civil marriage or civil union documents must also be filed.

Proxies for health care and financial decisions are essential additions that most states and countries use to ensure that a same-sex partner will have the rights automatically assigned when a woman and man marry. Check with your state authorities to be certain of your legal standing.

Susan Saxe, author of *Points to Consider in Counseling Same-Sex Couples for Marriage/Commitment Ceremonies: A Resource Manual*, emphasizes that except where a civil union is permitted, same-sex couples should assume that unless they take explicit action they will be treated as legal strangers even if they live together for fifty years, share everything, and raise ten kids. Her advice is to contact an attorney about regular and durable powers of attorney, wills, property issues, and child custody or coadoption if that is an issue. Even couples living in states that provide for same-sex commitments need to obtain these additional documents if they ever plan to leave the state, even to travel.

INTERMARRIAGE

Two girls in a public school lobby: "Julie, what are you?" "What do you mean? What am I?"

"Well, I'm American, but really three-quarters Irish-Catholic and one-quarter English-Anglican. What are you?"

"Oh, I'm nothing. My grandparents on one side are from Atlanta and on the other side one's from New York and the other Philadelphia. Their parents were all from Europe somewhere. My dad was born Jewish but doesn't practice, 'cause my mom was raised Lutheran and they don't want to fight about religion. They both love doing yoga though. I am hoping to have a bat mitzvah."

The marriage of Jews and non-Jews has gone on since antiquity. Remember, Moses married the daughter of a Midianite priest. Statistics show that the dominant culture of the host country will win out. We want to be inclusive but the practice is risky for the Jewish people because, at today's high intermarriage rates, it could lead to our disappearance as a culture.

Simply put, Orthodox and Conservative clergy cannot perform intermarriages; it is against Jewish law, which is part of their allegiance. Reform, Reconstructionist, Jewish Renewal, and Humanist Jewish clergy associations make the decision a matter of personal conscience for the clergy professional. Some feel doing intermarriages is a healthy, welcoming approach. Others see it as destructive.

I say welcome! Your presence is precious.
Let us savor your new inheritance from your beloved,
this Jewish connection,
and consider your wedding wishes together,
and also the nature of your future Jewish home together.
If you see the Jewish people as an important part of civilization,
    and learn how and commit to raise your children in a Jewish home,
        a rabbi facilitating your marriage surely makes some sense.

WHAT'S MOST IMPORTANT

Love is blind. A truer thing was never said. Those marrying tend to believe everything is possible and that no matter how difficult the relatives are now, "Things will be better after the wedding," and "Love conquers all." There is also, "No worries. We're smart, we'll make it work," and, "We're going to raise them in both and the children will decide religious orientation for themselves when they grow up."

Before we talk about ceremonial design, there's a more important topic to address: children. Children soak up the culture and cultural assumptions within which they are raised. To raise someone as "nothing" is to neglect a huge aspect of parenting. Family culture matters. You are setting the stage before your families at your ceremony for how you envision the culture of your home—your ritual, your party, how you speak to each other, how you relate to them. This is all a microcosm of your future. It's essential to plan the cultural life of the home you are co-creating even more carefully than your choice of wedding dress and décor for the reception. What kind of plans? The *tenaiim* exercise (pages 42–46) offers many related points of couple and familial spiritual intimacy to consider.

AVERTING CULTURE SHOCK

Marriage is not an emergency, though it may feel urgent. Take time to learn your partner's family(ies) of origin, customs, and background. Also explore what you are deeply attached to from the religious tradition(s) in which you are raised. Consider your ethnic roots. How will your child have an answer that differs from, "I'm nothing. What are you?" or "Your way is wrong, ours is the only way G*d accepts." Careful reflection on your family culture merger, which begins with the choice of culture you elect to manifest at your wedding, sets the stage in front of your family and friends for how you intend the culture of your family and home. While couples without children can find ways to appreciate and celebrate a diversity of traditions, children benefit from clarity about who they are and grounding in a spiritual tradition that connects them to their roots and values.

INTERMARRIAGE RITUALS WITH JEWISH CLERGY OFFICIATING

Now that we've talked about what's really important, let's go on to what may feel more urgent: deciding upon your wedding ceremony.

- Most every Jewish clergy person will need to know that you will be creating a Jewish home together and, no matter how religious or secular your preferred lifestyle may be, that you are committed to raising any children born of your marriage with no other faith being practiced by your family in your home.

- Prior to the wedding ceremony, many Jewish clergy will require a period of study to prepare the non-Jewish partner to understand core practices of the Jewish people, Jewish life, and the ways of a Jewish home. Since love, alas, does not conquer all, this is wise. Consider undertaking such study together, to help form the ground of creative discussion about the family and home life you will be co-creating.

- Some of the sancta—the rites, symbols, and actions in a traditional Jewish wedding—aren't a perfect fit with an intermarriage. Jewish clergy who perform intermarriages will help you modify accordingly and will have their own views and policies about this. Also see the section on vows on page 35 and an inclusive reframing of the *Sheva Brahot*, the seven concluding wedding blessings on page 61.

- If in your partner's soul-sense there is an emerging clarity that she or he will become Jewish, wait for the conversion process's completion before scheduling your wedding, or go ahead with a justice of the peace ceremony now. The tradition is to have a Jewish wedding service within twenty-four hours of a spouse's conversion, making for a very special and beautiful life event sequence.

WHERE IS THE LINE?

We all have to draw the line somewhere. Tom is a serious Buddhist embracing his partner's love of Judaism by studying in my Introduction to Judaism class. He's not sure if he's going to become officially Jewish. He's happy to raise Jewish children and to participate in Shabbat and Jewish holiday practices with Jan, his wife-to-be. Since I also teach Jewish meditation, it was easy for me to see how Tom's spiritual skill set would fit easily into our tradition. He's skillful at meditation. Jewish meditation offers a lovely set of practices that I know they will both delight in learning and incorporating into their ceremony.

From the Torah portion that coincides with their wedding weekend, we found a phrase they both loved: *eheyeh imah*, "I will be with you." This is what G*d said to Moses at the Burning Bush when Moses was concerned about going back to Egypt. Tom explained how a sacred phrase helps elevate consciousness and intimacy and helps a person feel centered. This is also true in Jewish meditation. After the chanting there is silence, as though a precious container in time has been created by the chanting. Jan noted that whether they chanted together or separately in any given day, she became more aware of how the human spirit is not alone, we are connected to All Spirit and that, on another level, she felt she was chanting this to her husband-to-be as a commitment, and he to her. Tom fully agreed. A holy, warm silence comes from this kind of practice. While couples may sleep together, being awake together in healthy and holy ways is wonderful. At the wedding ceremony, they had the rabbi teach this simple chant to those assembled. They entered as the chanting began, turned under the *huppah* to face each other, and a long warm, silence began.

A number of friends and family of the couple suggested ways they'd like to be involved in the ceremony. An uncle from Tom's side wanted to play bagpipes; a niece wanted to read a secular poem about love; and a friend who sings opera offered to sing "Ave Maria." The couple elected to have the uncle play the recessional. That was unique!

The niece read the poem, but we passed on the Christian aria. We all agreed we'd found the line in the sands of intermarriage. Otherwise the ceremony was fairly traditional, except for appropriate liturgical modifications such as the interpretive *Sheva Brahot* (see Table 2–3).

CIVIL CEREMONIES AND INDEPENDENT RITUALS

Depending on how much time the justice of the peace has available, civil ceremonies can be expanded to incorporate some symbols, poetry, and music that emphasize your roots and cultural intentions for your home life.

When your partner is not Jewish, the wedding is official by means of the legal status given a Jewish clergy person by most countries and states. It is not "Jewishly" legal because one of the persons is not a "citizen," so to speak, of the Jewish people. But it is Jewishly *cultural*. The power of ritual to forge the depth of experience is dramatic. You can trust in the process. An alternative to clergy-led ceremonies is asking a friend or colleague who is ritually capable to officiate after having completed a quiet civic marriage with a justice of the peace. There is no requirement for clergy to officiate at a Jewish wedding.

There are also no ritual police who can prevent you from incorporating Jewish elements into your ceremony. For example, while civil marriage documents must also be filed, a customized *ketubah* is a valuable creative process that nurtures healthy relationship. The liturgy will need adjustment, since expressions relating to Jewish law or blessings that cover exclusively Jewish partners make little sense in such a setting. Interpretive vow options can be found on pages 35–38, for example. And the *Sheva Brahot* provided in Table 2–3 offer translation and a more inclusive interpretation that are less emphatic about Jews and things Jewish and more embracing of all. You will find that other authors and several websites offer their own contemporary versions as well.

Table 2–3 *Sheva Bra<u>h</u>ot*—Seven Blessings		
Literal Translation	R'Goldie Milgram Interpretive Option	Transliteration
Blessed are You, Lord our G*d, King of the Universe, Creator of the fruit of the vine.	Blessed be the Source, Creator of the fruit of the vine, symbol of vitality and joy.	*Baru<u>h</u> ata adonai eloheinu mele<u>h</u> ha-olam borei p'ri ha-gafen.*
Blessed are You, Lord our G*d, King of the Universe, for He created everything for His glorification.	Let us bless the glory of creation; its organizing principles are eternal, deep, and profound.	*Baru<u>h</u> ata adonai eloheinu mele<u>h</u> ha-olam, sheh-hakol barah li<u>h</u>vodo.*
Blessed are You, Lord our G*d, King of the Universe, Creator of man.	Blessed be the Source of Life, Creator of humanity.	*Baru<u>h</u> ata adonai eloheinu mele<u>h</u> ha-olam, yotzer ha-adam.*
Blessed are You, Lord our G*d, King of the Universe, who created mankind in His image, in the pattern of His own likeness, and provided for the continuation of His kind. Blessed be the Lord, who created the man.	Let us bless the capacity to evolve, to create, to recreate humankind. May you both be filled with awe as you find your relationship evolving through the years. May your marriage help humanity manifest as a divine blessing.	*Baru<u>h</u> ata adonai eloheinu mele<u>h</u> ha-olam, asher yatzar et ha-adam b'tzalmo, b'tzelem dmut tavnito, ve-hitkin lo mimenu binyan ahdei ahd. baru<u>h</u> atah adonai yotzer ha-adam.*
May the uprooted [Jerusalem] be profoundly joyful at her happy gathering of progeny. Blessed be the Lord, who causes Zion's rejoicing with her children.	May the brokenness of times gone by be replaced with joy and happiness. May you be beloved friends. May you always also sense the love and support of your family, friends, and community whether they are close by or across great distances. Blessed is the Source of loving relationships.	*Sos tasis v'tagel ha-akarah, be-kibbutz bane'ha letoha b'simhah. baru<u>h</u> ata adonai, mesame'a<u>h</u> tzion b'vaneha.*

Let the loving companions be very happy, just as You made Your creation happy in the Garden of Eden, long ago. Blessed be the Lord, who makes the bridegroom and the bride happy.	May your joy in one another overflow into the world which surrounds you. May those in need find good friends in you. May your marriage be as happy as Adam and Eve when they found each other in the Garden of Eden [or choose other appropriate pairs to mention]. Blessed be these loving partners.	*Sameah t'samah re'im ha-ahuvim, k'samehaha yetzirha b'gan eyden mikedem. baruh ata adonai, [m'same'ach hatan v'kalah] [for two men: or reyim ha ahuvim] [for two women: reyot ha-ahuvot].*
Blessed are you, Lord our G*d, King of the Universe, who created joy and celebration, bridegroom and bride, rejoicing, jubilation, pleasure and delight, love and brotherhood, peace and friendship.	May you rejoice and be glad, as the Jewish people rejoice in your wedding today. Blessed be the Source of life, filling the universe, creating joy and celebration, loving partners, gladness and jubilation, pleasure, delight, love, unity, friendship, and peace.	*Baruh ata adonai eloheinu meleh ha-olam, asher barah sasson v'simha, hatan v'kalah, gila, rina, ditza ve'hedva, ahava v'ahava, v'shalom v're'ute.*
May there soon be heard, Lord our G*d, in the cities of Judea and in the streets of Jerusalem, the sound of joy and the sound of celebration, the voice of a bridegroom and the voice of a bride, the happy shouting of bridegrooms from their weddings and of young men from their feasts of song.	Soon may we hear in the streets of the city and on the paths of the fields: the voice of joy and the voice of gladness, the voice of lovers from under their canopy and the voices of their friends and family calling out at feasts of celebration.	*M'heira adonai eloheinu yishama be-arei yehudah u'vhutzot yerushalayim, kol sasson v'kol simha, kol hatan v'kol kalah, kol mitzhalot hatanim meyhupatam, (fem pl. hupatan) u'nearim mimishteh negina[tam].*
Blessed be the Lord, who makes the bridegroom and the bride rejoice together.	Blessed be the Source of happiness for these beloved friends.	*Baruh ata adonai m'same'ah [hatan im: ha-kalah] [for two men: reyim ha-ahuvim reyote ha-ahuvote]. [for two women: reyot ha-ahuvot.]*

A challenging point in weddings can be the absence of loved ones recently deceased, as well as those who are too far off to be able to attend, who are doing military service, or who can't be present for other reasons. What to do?

RECIPE #7:
Healthy
Integration of
the Sad with
the Glad

- You can have the person leading the rite invoke the absent one's memory/honor early on, if you wish; immediately after the opening verses of the psalm and before the wine is generally a good time for this.

- Recently an elderly bride marrying a man who had buried her dear friend, his wife of fifty years, only three years before, stepped forward to say these words: "I wish to invoke the memory of a very wonderful woman who helped make Dave the wonderful man I am about to marry. Anne Elliot, I miss you, dear friend; we miss you. And I thank you for bequeathing me this great gift. When on your deathbed you told me to take care of Dave, we had not yet fallen in love. But I think you sensed this could happen and in your way, you gave us your blessing then. I thank you now."

- It is also customary to visit the grave(s) of parent(s) if one or both have passed on before your wedding. There, suspend your disbelief and speak your heart to them. Whether you intuit a response or not, the catharsis is a healthy process. It's customary to ask for their blessing.

- Some have a parent buried too far away to be able to visit the grave. You might instead write a letter as though it were to be given to that parent and share it aloud on an appropriate occasion prior to the wedding.

- To give your new life the best possible chance, it is customary to work on *teshuvah*, relationship healing, with anyone in your world with whom you feel there is residual or active negativity. If someone has died and the negativity was never resolved, Maimonides recommends visiting that person's grave with witnesses and speaking aloud about what happened and what is needed. The more *teshuvah* done during the engagement period leading up to a wedding, the healthier a self and sphere of influence you bring to a marriage. When clearly unsafe though, opt out of the *teshuvah* process. *Unsafe* might mean that someone would be a physical threat to you or emotionally unable to refrain from trying to gut you with words. Whenever possible, the habit of *teshuvah* is essential in the life of a healthy couple. (For more on this, see volume I, *Reclaiming Judaism as a Spiritual Practice: Holy Days and Shabbat*, pages 15–21.)

JUICY JEWISHING

Now it's time to talk about Judaism, sex, and marriage. Although it's still a traditional ideal, few people are virgins when they get married nowadays. Here are some ideas from Jewish sources that contribute to the quality of a couple's wedding night and sex life.

- It is becoming traditional for couples to abstain from sex for a period of their choice before their wedding. A week is a frequently chosen option.
- There is great diversity of opinion and levels of observance on maintaining the traditional Jewish practice of abstaining from touch and lovemaking when a woman has her period, and bracketing those days with additional days. She traditionally concludes those days with a visit

to the *mikvah* involving physical, emotional, and spiritual renewal. This practice is called *niddah*. The upside is widely reported to be sustained ardor over the years. *Niddah* is a requirement for those who adhere rigorously to Jewish law, *halahah*, and a very personal decision for the rest of us. (To learn more about mikvah, see volume II, *Meaning & Mitzvah*, pages 156–160.)

- *Yihud*, "unification," losing a sense of the boundaries even of flesh, is the term for intimacy with G*d in prayer, and the same term is used for the physical togetherness and lovemaking of the wedding night. Folk stories carry the notion that in times gone by the couple would go straight from the wedding ceremony to "consummation" and get to the party later. Since it's customary to fast the day of one's wedding, few think that was ever what really happened, though it's surely possible. A lovely alternative is to go from the ritual to a room set aside for some quiet time together, to just hold one another, bask in the feelings you have after the ceremony, and share a light, private meal. The *shomrim*, the couples' individual support persons, generally siblings or close friends, can be asked to sit outside the door to keep out catering staff or guests who might accidentally disturb the wedding couple.

Congratulatory shouts from guests herald our exit, as we skip more than decorously from our ceremony to a small private dining room for a half-hour of solitude after the wedding ceremony. This is our time to savor our sacred shift. We touch fingertips, trilling pent-up electricity. Barry runs his finger across my collarbone. I place my hand flat against his heart. We cling to one another and, being more than a foot shorter than he, I listen mistily to his heartbeat. He bends to kiss me and we repeat the kiss we had so memorably given each other during the ceremony, when Reb Marcia placed a large rainbow prayer shawl, a tallit, over us, as we'd requested, for privacy.

Thirty minutes we'd set aside for ourselves—sweet serenity. Outside our door are our *shomrim*, Tzepples and Jeremy, the two dear ones who'd watched over us for the past day, managing or deflecting anything that might have taken us off-center. Now they will prevent any disturbance of our *yihud*, our private time.

Yihud is also the time reserved for us to share our first married meal together. Aromas finally reach us from the international repast the caterer has set out for us on warming trays. Since I have followed the tradition of fasting since dinner the night before, my stomach now growls viciously. I make my move toward the food. "Hang on," says Barry. "Bless, then dive."

Time's up. Our *shomrim* go swiftly ahead to alert the troops, leaving us walking hand in hand to the reception. To our delight and surprise, guests bearing eight-foot-long silk scarves dance us into their flowing circles. They bring chairs and lift us up, spinning glorious hues and shapes of joy in the sound and light. *Mazel tov!*

RECIPE #8:
Under the
Covers

There are a variety of Jewish meditations, *kavannot*, to set the stage for lovemaking. In the privacy of your relationship, doing what pleases your partner as long as it doesn't hurt you is a Jewish principle regarding sexuality. One traditional phrase for lovemaking is:

L'shem yihud kudsheh brih-hu
For the sake of the unification of the Holy One blessed be
[the masculine qualities of life, within you, your partner,
creation, and the aspect of G*d that seems remote,
the meta-level organizing principle]

u'she<u>h</u>intei
and the She<u>h</u>ina
[the feminine qualities of life, within you, your partner, creation, and
the aspects of G*d that seem close, visible, intimate].

- Try whispering these words as a meditation. Imagine your
  lovemaking as a holy time.
- What images arise in your mind? What do you notice?
  How do you feel?
- If something gets in the way of full feeling, there may be a
  need to work it through. Relationships can be compromised
  or unduly limited by earlier experiences. Professional help
  can be valuable under such circumstances.
- To the phrase above you might add "and because I love
  you" to help shape the idiom more to our times.
- The energy of your lovemaking can be dedicated as a
  blessing for someone else, and it can be seen as sending
  ripples of pleasure through creation all the way to the
  Source of Life.

3

Loving and Leaving
Jewish Rituals and Practices for When Relationships End

Souls needing to be unbound from each other experience pain of such an extreme intensity that it is equal only to the joy of their time of courting and marriage. Horrible to contemplate and worse to endure, divorce is cited and sanctioned as a necessary option right in the Bible: Leviticus 21:7, 22:13; Numbers 30:10; Deuteronomy 22:19, 29.

Civil law does not undo a Jewish marriage. A parallel context and process of holiness is needed for the unbinding of two souls that once stood under the _huppah_ together. When a Jewish divorce is conducted in a context infused with spirituality, the ritual of giving and receiving a _get_, a document of release, can become a step in your own healing.

Those who engage in Jewish ritual for the purpose of marriage may be unaware of the powerful Jewish rituals for divorce. While the "civil" process oversees the division of your assets and tax status, it often exacerbates the toxicity between sad, warring souls. That is no way to move forward. Whether individually, for your own peace of mind, or, preferably, together as a way to conclude your marriage as it began, with a sacred rite, a Jewish divorce ritual can help you move on.

THE SPIRITUAL POWER OF A JEWISH DIVORCE PROCESS

Midwifing a couple through a divorce is challenging. Often clergy are doing this for people we know, respect, and have come to care for greatly—both of them. Our task is to help two souls disentwine, to remove the *kiddushin*, the "holiness," that sanctified them for each other alone.

∾

Today is the divorce of two longtime congregants. I am standing between them and ask them to stand back to back and hold open their palms. I place a reciprocal copy of their signed *get*, their document of Jewish divorce, onto their palms. His *get* releases her; her *get* releases him. They are each facing three of their closest friends, who are sitting about eighteen feet away on opposite sides of the room.

"People who love and care for you are here. Look to your friends, members of the inner circle of your life. You can go to them in a moment. For now, please look at the darkest print on the *get* that you are holding. It is for you to take turns reading aloud."

Jenny is weeping softly; she's wanted this divorce for so long but waited until the children had gone off to college. Still, it is hard with so much history between them. Stephan is pale and quiet. His new relationship with a woman in another state has not been going well.

"Now, in accordance with the order agreed upon earlier tonight, please take turns reading this declaration of severance aloud."

Stephan's sad yet strong voice begins: "Your doorway is no longer my doorway. I no longer have the right to comment on your actions. Your well-being is now in your own hands. I do this *lishmi*, *lishma*, *u'lesheim geirushin*, for my sake, for her sake, and with the intent of effecting a divorce."

Jenny repeats the same phrase, only corrected for gender, *lishmo*, for him. Together they were able to design and sign a coparenting agreement in the presence of their three children and read it aloud to them. This document was also included in the civil divorce filing.

Earlier in the ritual, each partner was offered the opportunity to speak about forgiveness. Stephan spoke of forgiving being called terrible names. Jenny surprised everyone by speaking of offering forgiveness for the private detective her soon-to-be-ex-husband had retained to report on her every movement.

The *get* was then read aloud to the witnesses, one man and one woman from the congregation; the details checked and rechecked, and they took turns signing it.

Standing between the partners who are still facing away from each other, my hands hover over their heads. I adapt a phrase from the liturgy for the ending of the Sabbath, for moving from sacred time into the everyday. "*N'vareh et ha-mavdil beyn kodesh l'hol*—Let us bless the One who differentiates between those who have been reserved for each other in holiness and those who are now wholly separate and free. This completes your divorce.

"A copy of your documents will be placed on file at the two rabbinical associations to which I belong in case you or future generations should need proof. While you may have an impulse now to turn to comfort one another, it is no longer your province to do so. Your friends are waiting to receive you; walk toward them and they will take you out through separate doorways."

All parts of the spectrum of Judaism allow for a *shlihut*, a "messenger," to represent one of the two parties if one person chooses not to attend. I can recall several occasions when we prepared the documents with only one party present and then went to the door of his or her partner who waited inside, read the statement of closure, and obtained her or his signature on a receipt for the *get*. This allows for those who need ritual to have it, and for those who prefer not to be present for the whole experience to still have Jewish closure on their Jewish marriage.

GET A RECEIPT

Until the formal receipt and signing of documents takes place, the *get* is not in force. Should either member of the couple decide to remarry, the rabbi will need to see documentation of the Jewish divorce. A *get* needs to be executed no less than three months before either member of the couple remarries. Originally intended to determine paternity in case of pregnancy at the time of divorce, three months, from a psychological point of view, seems to be a reasonable minimum constraint before remarriage.

At present, not all parts of the spectrum of Judaism accept the others' divorce documents. Some rabbis and Jewish courts accept only the signatures of males strictly observant in Jewish law on ritual documents. In such communities a woman can never remarry unless she receives a *get* from her husband. In these communities, if a man collects one hundred signatures of support from other Jewish men, the Jewish court, a *beit din* of three specialists in Jewish law, can rule that he is free to remarry if he has offered his wife a *get* and she has refused to accept it. If a woman from such communities remarries civilly without having received a *get* from her husband, any child born of that marriage will be considered a *mamzer*, literally an illegitimate child. Such children either go through life hiding this fact or are deemed ineligible to marry most rigorously traditional Jews because of a verse in Deuteronomy 23:3 prohibiting communal rights to an illegitimate child's descendants to the tenth generation of a family.

Evidence found in a twelfth- to thirteenth-century repository of Jewish writings and legal documents in Cairo shows that our marriage documents once included clauses that freed a woman to marry should her husband be lost at sea or disappear and remain missing for a significant period. Contractual methods to help prevent a woman from becoming an *agunah*, a "woman chained" to a partner who is missing or unwilling to give a *get*, are now widely available and can be made part of a prenuptial agreement.

Various rabbis and rabbinical associations have designed compassionate yet firm and egalitarian rites of divorce, but so far these have not found their way into the Orthodox communities. The classic approach to ritualizing divorce would closely resemble the following.

OVERVIEW OF THE CLASSIC *GET* PROCESS

First, there must be a trained scribe who is knowledgeable about formatting a *get* and who will write the document in formal Hebrew calligraphy. She or he will use a heavy wooden, unleaded stylus to inscribe the back side of a heavy sheet of paper or parchment with twelve long straight lines. Then, two half-lines will be impressed as well. There are many additional technical customs about such things as margins and use of space on a line. The paper is then turned over and the tops of the letters of each word are penned to hang from the almost invisible lines.

Essential details appear in the document, including the precise location of the writing of the *get* (some use meridian degrees or geographical features, such as rivers, mountains, or oceans, that are unlikely to change in the event of wars), the date, the textual formula for separation, and the signatures of witnesses. To make sure that someone does not attempt to use another's *get*, all of a person's nicknames, Hebrew names, and secular names are written into the document as well.

Witnesses to such a Jewish divorce cannot be relatives. They must be adult males who are considered to be objective parties, observant of Jewish law, and who have no direct interest in the outcome. A court of at least three rabbis, a *beit din*, is convened and a scripted dialogue somewhat like this ensues: "Do you give this *get* of your own free will? Are you under any duress or compulsion to give it?"

The husband replies and the court continues: "Perhaps you have bound yourself by vow or any binding statement that would compel you to give a *get* against your will?" The husband replies and again the court continues.

The process of ensuring the husband's clarity and freedom to give the *get* is further examined until he declares that even if he ever said anything that contravened his current intent, he declares it null and void.

A scribe now presents the writing materials and supplies to the husband, declaring them to now have become the husband's property. The scribe only acts on the husband's behalf. The husband now instructs the scribe to write a *get* of divorce—*lishmi, lishma, u'lesheim geirushin*; for my sake, for her sake, and with the intent of effecting a divorce.

There is more dialogue empowering the scribe, and finally the document is written. When it is finished, the witnesses read it and before signing it indicate to one another that they are signing it *lishmo, lishma, u'lesheim geirushin*. A dialogue ensuring that this is indeed the *get* the husband commissioned begins anew. The earlier dialogue concerning his intent is essentially repeated. Every chance for a last-minute change of heart is offered again and again. Finally, those gathered are given an opportunity to testify against what is about to take place.

The wife is then told to remove all her jewelry and open her hands, palms upward. The scribe folds the *get* and gives it to the rabbi facilitating the ritual, who gives it to the husband, who must hold it in two hands and then drop it into her hands saying, "This is your *get*, and with it you are divorced from me from this time forth so that you may become the wife of any man."

With *get* in hand, the wife turns and walks out of the room (in some places she walks just a short distance away in the room), returns, and hands the *get* to the facilitator, who reads it aloud again, asks the scribe and the witnesses to identify the *get* as the correct one, and then reminds all present that any person who tries to invalidate a *get* after it has been delivered will be put outside the pale of community life and shunned as nonexistent.

The four corners of the document are now cut and the facilitator retains it in the court's files. Husband and wife are each given a copy of a certificate of divorce to certify the dissolution of their marriage under the Jewish law of their community. If one spouse prefers not to attend, prior arrangements are made with a *shaliah*, a messenger, to deliver the *get* and obtain a signature of receipt.

RECIPE #9:
Ritual of
Closure for
Any Serious
Relationship

Now for a ritual that can apply to nonmarital breakups, or serve as preparation for going to a *beit din* for your *get*. The model was developed by Rabbi Brian Nevins-Goldman on the occasion of the breakup of my first serious love relationship after my first marriage. Some say that any unfinished mourning from the first divorce is rekindled when the first serious postdivorce relationship fails. They are right. Some prescribe "retail therapy," a.k.a. lots of shopping and redecorating, as part of the recovery process. While not everyone's style, this often proves to be quite on target as an activity to take a person's mind off the trauma of loss. But there is also an important role for ritual:

- Arrange for a leader, a clergy person, or anyone who is a good listener, who keeps confidences, and who is adept at group process.
- Sit with the facilitator and pour out the circumstances so that she or he can take notes and write a eulogy for your dead relationship.

- If any property of yours remains in the control or abode of your former beloved, arrange for a *shaliah*, a messenger, to retrieve it for you and return to that person anything of his or hers that you might have. Your body and spirit tend to remain somewhat connected to those with whom you have been in an intimate relationship, and thoughts of that person may be easily triggered by any interactions, or even the sight of your former partner, for at least six months. A solid period during which you will not be retraumatized is essential to your healing. Let others help you get there. It is a mitzvah to help someone in relationship recovery.
- Invite ten, a minyan of friends and/or family, to attend a closure ritual. These should be people in front of whom you can speak frankly and who are firmly on your side in life.
- Find an item that can be symbolically destroyed during the ritual.
- Put together an album about the relationship, or a memory box that can hold anything obvious in your home that speaks to the relationship.
- Begin with a chant or play music that evokes the sadness of the occasion.
- The facilitator explains why everyone has gathered and gives the eulogy.
- Then you talk about why this relationship must be buried.
- Seal the album or memory box. Indicate that it will go into a deep chest or onto a high closet shelf to serve as a repository of important memories in years to come.
- Take the item you intend to symbolically destroy and tear, break, or burn it.
- Acknowledge and honor your feelings; your friends will wait and understand.

- The facilitator can now invite your friends to speak about you, your strengths, and why they love you. Meet their eyes and take in the depth of their love and support.
- Allow your friends to gather around you so that anyone who desires can offer a blessing for your future.
- Close with a melody that speaks to you.
- Eat. Comfort foods are good at such times.

This ritual will gradually serve as a marker in time that, like the tiny time-release mechanisms in medicine capsules, will exponentially support your necessary transition. The relationship may be over, but the process of mourning and recovery will take its own time. No matter how long it has been since the parties split, the Jewish practices for transition are powerful. Before beginning to seek new relationships, it is important to give yourself time for the full effects to flow through you and for you to integrate your loss, reestablish a full sense of your independent self, and become fully available to bond anew, should you so desire. We all make relationship mistakes, get hurt, and hurt others. We all can heal and move on to future holiness and happiness, if and when we choose to do so.

May you be blessed with sustainable relationships, rich in happiness and good health. May you also be blessed with at least one of the fruits of the human capacity for love: children, whether foster, adopted, natural, students, grandchildren, great-grandchildren, or the neighbors' children, almost all of which, plus the agony of infertility, are the subject of our next chapter.

4

Babies
Longing, Breathing, Loss, Birth, and/or Adoptions and Options

We will rock you
in the cradle
of Jewish civilization,

where learning becomes
like honey on your tongue.

Before you can talk,
a college fund
will be started.
Before you can read,
you will have books
in your room.
Before you can walk,
you'll likely be taught
how to swim.
Before you earn a cent,
charity will be given
in your name.

And,
before we know it,
you will be grown
and contemplating
a family of your own.

When you're seeking to have and raise a family, there are significant decisions to make at various points along the way. Judaism does not shy away from addressing these. Here you'll find discussion of clinical, practical, intellectual, emotional, and spiritual considerations. You deserve to be fully informed so that you are set on a path that will lead to the joy of welcoming a child into your life.

Fertility is considered a great blessing in Jewish tradition. Stories that teach empathy for the pain of infertility are a major motif in the Torah. While most women get pregnant without too much struggle, many do not. While most children will be born viable and healthy, a substantial number are not. While most pregnancies are wanted, some place the mother's mental or physical survival so much in jeopardy that abortion may be appropriate. Judaism has principles and rituals to address this wide range of possibilities. Let's start at the very beginning.

WHEN DOES LIFE BEGIN?

Most often in Jewish sacred literature, a fetus in the womb is considered a human life "under construction." The soul is usually described as arriving when the first breath of life is taken at birth. The primary Jewish imagery for the beginning of life comes from Genesis 1:2, where breath hovers above the waters of earth before life emerges from that cosmic womb. Then, in Genesis 2:7, after the body of Adam is fashioned from the clay of the earth, G*d is described as breathing life into him. These stories frame the basis for the Jewish view that the fetus gains full human rights and status only once the baby's head has emerged from the birth canal (Mishnah Ohalot 7:6).

There is one talmudic passage in which a Greek philosopher presses a rabbi on this issue until—probably for the sake of peace with the then–Greek empire occupiers of the Land of Israel—the rabbi accedes to the prevailing view in Greek culture that the soul is present from conception. This text has not, however, changed the dominant perspective within Judaism, then and now, that the activation of the fetus's status as a human with full human rights occurs upon birth.

THE DESIGNATED SOUL

The soul a baby will receive is traditionally understood to be predestined. The combining of the particular soul with the particular body it enters results in a human. An often-cited commentary relates that all the souls that will ever exist were "created during the six days of creation, and were in the Garden of Eden, and all were present at the giving of the Torah [at Sinai]" (Tanhuma, Pekudei 3). This perspective is reflected in Jeremiah 1:5, "I knew you, before I formed you in the belly, before you left the womb." Most Jewish authorities read this to mean that the soul is decided upon before conception, and conferred with the first in-breath of life after birth. Or as sometimes friends or family are known to say to small children, "We knew you before you were even a twinkle in your parents' eyes." In the Talmud the distinction between body and soul is particularly clear in this passage: "When the time arrives for a person to depart from this world, G*d takes G*d's portion back and leaves the portions contributed by the parents" (Niddah 31a).

The Torah confounds our senses by offering us an impossible paradox: that humans are created *b'tzelem elohim*, "in the image of G*d" (Genesis 11:7). G*d in Judaism has no image; that's foundational. So what kind of koan, or spiritual brain puzzle, is this? Well-respected spiritual leader and author Rabbi Harold M. Schulweis teaches a helpful *midrash*:

The angels, having heard that God planned to create the human being in His image, grew jealous. What does mere mortal man have to deserve such a gift? The angels plotted to hide the image of God from the human being. One angel suggested that it be hid on the tallest mountain. Another suggested that it be sunk into the deep of the sea. But the shrewdest angel demurred. "Man," he said, "is an adventurer. He will climb the highest mountain. He will plumb the deepest ocean. But if we want to hide it from him, let us hide the image in himself. It is the last place in the world that he will seek it."

Another popular *midrash* also emphasizes this notion of not making it easy to uncover our connection to the Big Picture. This story also accords the fetus cognitive ability while in the womb. It goes like this: While the fetus is gestating, an angel is teaching it Torah—all of Torah. When the child is about to be born, the angel flicks the child just above the lip, causing everything that was learned in the womb to be forgotten (Niddah 30b). Just enough residual memory remains for humans to experience the urge to seek, savor, and believe we can find and connect again to that sweet, deep learning in our lives.

MAJOR JEWISH PRACTICES REGARDING CONCEPTION

PREMARITAL AND PRECONCEPTION GENETIC TESTING. Every human grouping has its own genetic disease risks, as do those with Jewish ancestry. Some genetic diseases cause death with great pain or deformity in infancy or early childhood. After having four of his children die in infancy of Tay-Sachs disease, Rabbi Josef Ekstein founded an organization that prescreens couples before marriage to assess whether their genetic combination could result in a child with a deadly disorder. His organization, Dor Yesharim ("An Upright Generation"), uses the power of the rabbi in Rabbi Ekstein's Orthodox part of the spectrum of Jewish practice to rule that the couple is ineligible to marry. Grounds for such activism might include an interesting use of the mitzvah of *periya u'r'viyah*, to be fruitful and multiply. Because such a couple might not be able to produce a healthy child and thus be unnecessarily deterred from fulfilling the mitzvah of reproduction, their marriage is not considered *beshert*, authorized by heaven or meant to be. The mitzvah to not stand idly by when the life of another is endangered applies here as well. As Maimonides puts it: "It is a mitzvah to remove and watch out for any obstacle that could endanger life, and to be extremely careful doing so" (Hil<u>h</u>ot Rotze'a<u>h</u>, 11:4).

Proactive genetic testing prevents the potential for tragic suffering by child and family, and obviates the need to decide whether a pregnancy will end in abortion. In other parts of the spectrum of Jewish practice, a couple might still choose to marry with the knowledge that adoption would be their path to child rearing; some might risk conception with the potential for therapeutic abortion. Often Jewish campus organizations urge students to go for genetic testing so they can advise potential life partners about their status before a relationship progresses toward marriage. Through knowledge, great suffering can be averted. Jewish Family Service agencies in most major cities maintain relationships with medical centers that offer genetic testing and counseling.

ABORTION. Sanction for abortion in Judaism is rare but possible under very specific circumstances, and is always considered on a case-by-case basis that includes the impact of the pregnancy on maternal mental and/or physical health. Given the high rate of early miscarriage noted by ancient sages, the first forty days of pregnancy are considered "like water" in primary Jewish sources (Yevamot 69b, Niddah 30b, and Keritot 1:3). This leaves room for early abortion in cases of rape, incest, and infidelity and for an unpredicted, severe genetic disorder. Abortion sanctions are also found in the traditional Jewish bioethics literature in cases where the mother clearly could lose her mental health and become unable to care for her family, where the fetus is a threat to the mother's physical survival, and where rape has occurred. In the Torah (Exodus 21:22) a case is given where a woman was struck across the abdomen by a man and she miscarried. The man was not given the death penalty; he had to pay a fine to the woman's husband. This story forms the basis of the Jewish understanding that, until born, the fetus is not considered a complete human life. Many centuries later Maimonides upholds the statute of a financial penalty for assault leading to miscarriage (Mishneh Torah, Hilhot Hovel Umazik 4:1; see also Hoshen Mishpat 423:1).

A fetus that could compromise the mother's survival, even if it is considered ensouled, is termed a *rodef*, a pursuer, and an abortion is considered a required therapeutic option and sometimes an imperative by most Jewish bioethicists, contemporary and in antiquity. In Judaism, a guiding principle is that the life of the mother always comes first until the baby's head has emerged into the world (Mishneh Torah, Hilhot Rotze'ah U-Shmirat Nefesh 1:9). Jewish sacred literature is very graphic about this: "If a woman suffers hard labor in travail, the child must be cut up in her womb and brought out piecemeal, for her life takes precedence over its life. [But] if its greater part has come forth, it must not be touched" (Mishnah Ohalah 7:6).

JEWISH RITUAL AND ABORTION

Here and there we know of Jewish rituals of support in relationship to abortion, so the mother, especially, can experience less isolation and better grieve. These rituals may also comfort the father, when he is known, not involved via a criminal act, and wishes to take part. I don't want to contrive such a ritual for the reader, having never been asked to facilitate a Jewish rite for this purpose. The bibliography includes two sources that detail postabortion rituals that have proven helpful. Before an abortion, I can imagine giving some money to *tzedakah*, charity, with the intention of supporting medical research or children in need, and dedicating this action with a personal prayer asking the soul that was waiting to enter the body of this child to understand that this was not the right body, or not the right situation, and blessing it that another parent(s) will soon give it a good home. For some, this sort of language or behavior will feel odd; for others it can help weather this very difficult decision in a way that feels holy and honorable.

SUPPORTING THE INTENTION TO CONCEIVE

Creating life is one of the holiest moments in Jewish tradition. In the Talmud we read that three are present during conception: the essence of the mother, the father, and the Source of Life itself (Niddah 31a). Accordingly, it is traditional to focus completely on one another, releasing thoughts of any others that might arrive at this time (Nedarim 20b; Commentary of Bahya ben Asher on Genesis 30:39). Additionally, lovemaking in anger while intoxicated is considered a contraindication to attracting a healthy soul (Nedarim 20b).

Among the Jewish customs to help strengthen the intention to become pregnant are the following:

Amulets: Those with one small stone nested within another are especially prized.

Etrog: Biting off the end of a citron, an *etrog*, is an emotional gesture that helps to convey a person's yearning for fertility. (To learn more about *etrog*, see volume I, *Reclaiming Judaism as a Spiritual Practice: Holy Days and Shabbat*, pages 50–54.)

Mikvah: Immersing in the community ritual bath, called a *mikvah*, immediately after a pregnant woman. (To learn more about new and traditional *mikvah* practices, see chapter 2; also volume I, *Reclaiming Judaism as a Spiritual Practice: Holy Days and Shabbat*, pages 41 and 99–100, and volume II, *Meaning & Mitzvah: Daily Practices for Reclaiming Judaism through Prayer, God, Torah, Hebrew, Mitzvot and Peoplehood*, pages 156–160, 186.)

Red thread: Wearing a red thread, coupled with the recitation of specific prayers, is a folk custom, dating back to at least medieval times, that is mentioned in the works of the mystic Ḥayim Vital (Otzarot Yerushalayim, chapter 36). Authentic material would be a thread that has been wrapped seven times around the tomb of the biblical matriarch Rachel, who is often called Mother Rachel. Rachel's story is a source of hope because her two successful pregnancies involved a great deal of longing and patience. Associated prayers are the *Ana b'Koaḥ*, "Respond with the strength of Your right hand—untangle our knotted fate" (Psalm 33), which is rich in praises, and *Asher Yatzar*, the morning blessing for the marvelous construction and capacity for healing that is the human body.

RECIPE #10:
The Intention to Conceive a Child

Whether by mood, careful timing of the woman's reproductive cycle, or some other form of birth control, decisions about when and whether to have a child are being made all the time in Jewish homes. When is the time right? Here is a simple guide based on an adaptation of the technique known as Focusing.

Each partner takes a symbol of his or her choice in hand. A pomegranate or another fruit that is heavily seeded is an option if nothing more personal comes to mind. If you are planning to become a single parent, this can be done on your own or with a friend who knows you well.

Breathe softly, with attention to your own breath, the Breath of Life, *nishmat kol ḥai*. Gently turn your attention inside yourself, listening to your body as though it were a radio that transmits the information it receives by means of sensations.

Give yourself a Focusing invitation: "Is now a good time for me to become pregnant?"

Listen inside. What does your body tell you? You may sense information in the form of a sensation anywhere in your body.

Attend to the sensation. You might ask it: "What do you come to convey?" Perhaps an image will form or an inner knowing will grow.

Verbalize what you sense so that your listening partner can reflect it back without reaction or judgment. For example, "There is a green-bilish swirl in my abdominal area; it is bitter."

Partner: "A bitter green-bilish swirl is in your abdominal area."

Focusing invitation: "Take some time to keep this image of green bile company, and see if it has something it wants to tell you. Sense inside for what its meaning might be." Example of one possible response: "Fear. I'm afraid I'll mess a child up; my inherited parenting skills are not promising."

Partner: "You are afraid that a child would be messed up if parented by you."

The message might amount to no, yes, or yes but …, or it might reveal a further concern or obstacle that needs to be addressed.

You might give the next Focusing invitation: "So there is all that about parenting." [Pause.]

Ask "it," the bilious place inside, or whatever this sense may have shifted into, what is needed for this fear to be overcome, for the time to be right.

Note: This is not the time for a partner to vent frustrations; it is an opportunity to manifest curiosity and cultivate awareness and acceptance of "what is." If the findings are very distressing, the listening partner can take private time to honor, name, and let go of strong feelings that are getting in the way of his or her being able to reflect without passing judgment.

Whatever comes, a response or none, the person posing the Focusing invitations simply reflects accurately what is related, without judgment, labeling, analysis, or reaction. "What is" is now available to both of you as important information.

Now give a blessing. Something like, "As our relationship evolves, so too may our capacity for caring and sharing continue to ripen."

Switch places and repeat the exercise.

If the time to attempt conception or parenthood is not right, you might lay the object you were holding in a "pause and contemplate mode" between your Shabbat candlesticks where they sit on your shelf, to one day be redeemed and reviewed.

If the time is right, meaning not this minute as much as this week or in a month or so, you might open the pomegranate and feed it to one another while wishing each other the blessing of fertility.

May you be blessed to conceive in love when the time is right!

WANTED PREGNANCIES

BLESSING A PREGNANCY

The traditional phrase for blessing an existing pregnancy is *b'shah-ah tovah*—may the child be born "at a good hour." That's right, not *mazel tov*. *Mazel tov* comes *after* a successful birth.

There are numerous talmudic discussions of the most auspicious times to undertake certain treatments and procedures. Choosing the eighth day after birth for Judaism's ritual requirement of male circumcision (barring wellness issues, such as hemophilia) is confirmed by the research of Gerald N. Weiss, MD, published in *Clinical Pediatrics*: "Clotting factors become functional by the seventh neonatal day in the healthy infant."

PRAYER

A discussion in the Talmud recommends that during the first three days after efforts at conception, you pray for the pregnancy to be accepted by the body. Next, you pray that there be no fetal deformity. Then you pray that the pregnancy not result in miscarriage. And from six months onward you pray for a safe delivery (Berahot 60b).

CRAVINGS

Tradition considers cravings to be sent by the fetus, and even if "a pregnant woman wants pork on Yom Kippur" (Babylonian Talmud, Yoma 82a) her craving is to be satisfied. Currently, given the rising prevalence of gestational diabetes, pregnant women are routinely advised by physicians to be careful about excesses of sugar and carbohydrates, so satisfaction within healthy limits is important.

TAKE NOTHING FOR GRANTED

Jews traditionally refrain from setting up the baby's room in advance, a holdover from the days of not wanting to tempt fate or "the evil eye." Many still follow this custom and also keep the baby's name(s) secret until the ritual of circumcision or baby naming.

GIVING BIRTH—THE GREAT NAME

Certain sacred phrases are particularly profound to contemplate, breathe, or even shriek while giving birth. A bit of teaching is necessary to prepare you to benefit from a breathing method that draws on the Great Name.

In dealing with the mystery of the gift called life, Judaism provides what is called the Great Name, *shmei rabba*. This is also termed the *shem havaYah*, "the name of existence [or being]," the *shem ha'etzem*, "the essential Name," and the *shem ha-meyuhad*, "the unique Name," the name that represents the innermost soul and light of all that is possible within us and beyond us. This is the name only the high priest knew how to pronounce and would call out in the Holy of Holies in the Temple in Jerusalem long ago. It begins with the letters *yud hey*, and concludes with *vav hey*, as in Figure 3–1.

Yud

Hey

Vav

Hey

Figure 3–1

As Rabbi Arthur Waskow, author of *Godwrestling—Round 2* (Jewish Lights), has pointed out, if you pronounce this letter sequence quickly without consonants—*yhwh*—it sounds like breath!

In classical Kabbalah, the letters of the Great Name are about a process of a cosmic giving birth to life, a process that will sound quite familiar to scientists, doctors, and mothers as well:

yud—contraction of Infinite Light to a point;
hey—expansion in a concealed realm;
vav—extension from the concealed realm to a revealed realm;
and finally *hey*—expansion in the revealed realm.

The four letters of the Great Name, the sound of breath if you will, reflect the most ancient and sacred name given to that Force/Source that makes for life. *Yud Hey, Yah*, on its own, is described in *Shaarei Orah* by the thirteenth-century Spanish kabbalist Rabbi Joseph Gikatilla as a very high term that reaches realms of cosmic mercy and wisdom.

Birthing is a time to appreciate and contemplate the mystery of life and the gift of breath that is required to sustain human life. Let's explore birth and breath by means of the method midwives have identified to assist with the labor of birthing—conscious breathing.

Carla and Robert are having a baby. In a few hours this baby will take his or her first independent breath. The birthing coach encourages Carla to use the Hebrew word for "breath," *n'sheemah*, as a source of literal inspiration—in-breath. *N'sheemah* has the same root letters as the word for "soul," *n'shamah*. So *n'shamah* becomes the out-breath, the goal, symbolic of the soul about to be entrusted to her and her beloved Robert to raise in this life.

RECIPE #11:
Breathing Life

- Try it—*n'* [breathe in] *sheeeeeeeeeeeeeeeeeeeee-mah!*
- *n'* [breathe out and, where appropriate, push] *sha-mah!*

Like most meditations, you can think these words as you breathe during labor; you don't need to vocalize for the effect to work.

Depending on your theology, you might enjoy one of these variations or alternate them within your birthing breathing:

> *kol ha-n'shamah t'hallel Yah*
> Every soul will praise Yah.
> *kol ha-n'shimah t'hallel Yah*
> Every breath will praise Yah.

1. First take a few *Yah* breaths as deep, gradual inhalations and exhalations—not so many as to hyperventilate, just enough to fully feel and focus on the breath experience.
2. Now try a few patterns of breath like the ones you've learned in childbirth classes, using *Yah* as the syllable

of your breath's expression. Let possible meanings emerge for you.

3. For short breaths, try this: out-breath—*t'hallel*; in-breath—*Yah*.

4. Birthing can require determination and perseverance, plus lots of rallying. For this you might now breathe for pushing: *t'hah-lel Yah! Yah! Yah!*

ADDING HOLINESS TO THE EXPERIENCE OF C-SECTION

While most women hope for natural childbirth, a C-section may be necessary. A spiritual approach to this difficult turn of events is revealed in my own birthing experience. After twenty-six hours in labor with not a centimeter of dilation in sight, the doctor said, "It's probably time for a C-section. We have to do some fetal monitoring to make sure things are okay."

Disappointment and fear rushed in. I'd been patiently waiting for the pains to get closer together, despite looking something like the Goodyear Blimp wearing a parachute. On second thought, whatever it took to get this baby out would be very welcome.

A warm, kind voice asked if I'd like to immerse myself in a memory while the spinal anesthetic was being administered. The face of a male nurse-anesthetist appeared in my field of vision. "Does anything come to mind?" he inquired. "Or shall I create a visualization for you?"

The sacred phrase, *Mikveh Israel*, popped into my head and the Mediterranean Sea appeared on the horizon of my memory. I had been there earlier in the year, joyfully floating in body-temperature waters as the largest setting sun I'd ever seen began bathing me in the intensity of its warmth. Beside me, a very pregnant woman floated in visible delight at being temporarily weightless. On the

Tel Aviv beach filled with young parents, infants, and children, I could hear the wailing of babies alternating with the *ima*, mother, or *abba*, father, tossing the fuzzy little one into the air and calling out, "*Yoffi, tinoki*, lovely my baby!"

As I immersed myself in this scene, I was oblivious to the womblike symbolism of the imagery or that my own waters were breaking. I could barely see the portly surgeon, who, with a strong outstretched hand, himself the image of Spirit in action, moved quickly to rescue our beautiful, healthy, and substantial eight-pound, thirteen-ounce firstborn son from danger. When they called out the baby's Apgar score, it was a nine, not a perfect ten. "That's just because it was a C-section," the nurse murmured. "Perfect," I said. "In Israel a baby isn't a ten until eight days after birth, at his circumcision!"

∾

HOLDING YOUR BABY FOR THE FIRST TIME

Judaism has a great prayer for first times. The same prayer is also said on the first night of all holidays with candlelighting. It celebrates *z'man ha-zeh*, this time, this season, that you have been sustained in life long enough to reach this amazing moment. For the words, transliteration, and more about the *Sheheheyanu*, see volume I, *Reclaiming Judaism as a Spiritual Practice: Holy Days and Shabbat*, pages 53 and 93. In some Jewish communities it is customary to say the *Sheheheyanu* for a girl and *ha-tov v'hameitiv*, "the One who is good and bestows good" for a boy.

GRATITUDE FOR RECOVERY FROM LABOR OR C-SECTION

In the face of a successful birth, whether natural or via C-section, it's all too easy to focus on the baby and overlook the mother and what she's just been through. Giving birth can feel like surviving a difficult and dangerous journey, so many communities have adopted the traditional blessing for recovery from a high-risk life experience to honor and support women's birthing experiences, regardless of outcome. This blessing is on page 201.

INFERTILITY AND MISCARRIAGE

Before we get as far as baby naming and covenantal rituals, what if conception proves elusive? Frustration often intensifies under such circumstances. Relationships can suffer from all the pressure. Couples can be helped greatly by medical fertility specialists, together with sessions with a trained *mashpia*, a Jewish guide who helps your spirit. Some are clergy and some are therapists who are trained in this work. Links to finding a *mashpia* are available at ReclaimingJudaism.org. What follows is a ritual for an infertile couple that came out of one such counseling process.

THE PAIN AND LOSS OF INFERTILITY—THE HOPE OF INSEMINATION OR ADOPTION

On occasion couples come to me for pastoral counseling in the face of many years of infertility. In three separate instances it was eventually discovered that the husband was not producing sperm. Many try, but few men can actually leapfrog over something like this directly into adoption or donor insemination without first taking time to integrate this newly discovered reality. Essentially (and do consult a Jewish bioethics specialist for the fine print), Judaism sanctions AID (artificial insemination by donor); some scholars prefer the donor be Jewish and others prefer the donor be non-Jewish. Very few oppose AID. But for the woman or couple inclined to consider AID, there are also emotional issues. The scenario below, for the sake of confidentiality, is a composite of two different couples, counseling and ritual sessions with me on the matter of male infertility, AID, and the additional possibility of adoption.

She longed for a child and, aware of her biological clock's ticking, was preparing to undertake artificial insemination by donor. Her husband, on the other hand, was still angry and grieving from the discovery of his infertility. And it was uncomfortable for her to consider another man's sperm in her body. They asked, "Isn't it immoral, almost adultery, to have alien [her word] sperm inserted into a wife?"

They wondered whether there were biblical resources to draw on. I remembered that Dr. Tikveh Frymer-Kensky, of blessed memory, teaches about the discovery of tablets from, I think, the Amarna civilization in the Middle East. The tablets were inscribed with laws relating to a woman having her maidservant become a surrogate mother for her. This was the case when Hagar bore a child for Abraham. Could we work a version of this? Instead of a surrogate womb and/or egg, surrogate sperm?

This idea resonated powerfully with the couple. But there was still the matter of mourning the loss of potency for the husband. I'd been given a beautiful kiddush cup by an artist a few days earlier, so the metaphor of the "empty cup" came to mind, and I wondered if he might hold this cup and speak about his own bitter, empty cup. Yes. His face showed that my empathic ritual object offering was right for him.

What more was needed? Generally I encourage a minyan to be present at rituals, a minyan of people who are dear to those doing the ritual, and, equally important, with whom it is safe to share personal information. But this couple didn't know anyone at the retreat center except my hubbatzin, Barry, to whom they felt close. They asked me if he could also participate in the ritual.

So we met in gathering darkness in a yurt, a womblike tent on the retreat center grounds that serves as a classroom on campus. Two candlesticks stood on a table—one lit and one unlit. I explained that the candle is the symbol for the soul in Judaism. In their case the unlit candle represented the soul that hadn't yet come down for them, a soul longed for that has not arrived. Barry asked where he might best sit, and the husband proclaimed strongly, "Right next to me." I sat beside the wife.

We chanted a sacred phrase. I took the empty kiddush cup and looked into it saying, "This is the cup of blessing. Wine is a symbol of the life force in Judaism, in our mystical tradition; some see red wine as symbolizing the female life force, the shedding of the egg and bleeding of the cycle of fertility, and white as symbolizing the male, sperm, life's seed itself. I invite you to retell the story of how you discovered why your 'cup' is empty, of the long journey of hope and disappointment that led to this day."

He did. At first haltingly, then with the fullness of frustration and grief eventually arising and showing in his face and posture.

When he was ready, he passed the kiddush cup to his wife, saying that he commissioned her to fill their "cup" as Abraham would have commissioned Sarah to beget him a son by Hagar. Just as the tablets said was done in times of old, his wife lay across his lap, and he placed his hands upon her, commissioning her to return with a full cup, a cup full with child.

Knowing that she might not conceive, even after all this, I felt and said that a soul was ready to come to this couple, a soul seeking this couple as parents. Together they lit the second candle, the candle of hope for a life to be given them to parent. I asked them to speak as though to G*d and to describe the kind of parents they would be. Oh, their glowing faces as they spoke of their dreams and skills, their willingness to grow and learn how to parent. And, as his face lost its expression of depression and despair, the wife told her husband of her love for him.

A *mi sheberah*, a blessing for the occasion, was bubbling up inside of me. "On the merit of the ancestors who suffered so with infertility and yet conceived, may the soul that is destined for you arrive soon, be it as an infant conceived or one adopted, notice of whom comes by fate to your door, may you be blessed to parent, *bimheyra b'yameynu*, quickly and in our time."

The husband began to sing about Elijah the prophet, *Eliyahu ha-navi*, the herald of one with skills for peace so awesome as to be called messianic. We sang the traditional verse, which ends with hopes for the birth of *ben* David, son of King David, then unconventionally—but why not go there?—added *bat* David, daughter of King David, then *ben* and *bat*, followed by each of the parents' names. Aliveness and hope and love filled our tent as the couple held one another, hugging and singing. Soon Barry and I left them alone to savor their experience.

Perhaps a year later they wrote to tell us of their son, born to them through the combined power of artificial insemination and healthy Jewish ritual.

LOSING A PREGNANCY

Beyond the problem of conception are miscarriage, stillbirth, and the neonatal death of an infant. While rare, these things do happen. It took until 1986 for the medical profession to wake up, even a little, to the emotional and physical pain of miscarriage, stillbirth, and neonatal death. To quote a landmark research paper by I. G. Leon that came to the attention of some physicians:

Medical and mental health professionals have been slow to recognize and treat the often traumatic impact of perinatal death. It has only been within the past ten years that researchers have begun to appreciate that a miscarriage, stillbirth or neonatal death can be a devastating loss to the parent, especially the mother.... Bereaved mothers mourn pregnancy loss through the grieving process, which includes denial, yearning, and despair, usually followed by recovery.

Typical maternal reactions during the first months of grief are shock, disbelief, sleeplessness, irritability, crying, sadness, rage, anxiety, somatic distress, and sometimes hallucinatory experience of the dead baby.

The Jewish people have survived numerous plagues and periods of high infant mortality. Thirty days after birth is our people's minimum criterion for the death of a fully viable life that requires traditional mourning rites. Even so, the sages tell us: "If a day-old infant dies, to his father and mother he is like a full bridegroom" (Mishnah Niddah 5:3). And Maimonides teaches that if a person knows for certain that the child was born after a full nine months, "Should [the child] die on the day it is born, we mourn it" (Aveilut 1:7).

Some mourn every miscarriage; some do not. While not required, mourning is natural and necessary in many cases. As the first generation of American women rabbis began to emerge, so too have rituals for miscarriage and other events that impact women's lives and bodies and the men and women with whom we make and raise life. Experimental versions of such rites are now found across the full spectrum of Jewish practice.

Many models for mourning such a loss can be found online. Options range from prayers and poems of rage, despair, and comfort to rituals that adapt Jewish traditions such as havdalah (learn more in volume I, *Reclaiming Judaism as a Spiritual Practice: Holy Days and Shabbat*, pages 190–192) and *birkat ha-gomel* (see page 202). Some models favor personal prayer and complete privacy; others involve larger or smaller circles of community.

I vividly remember miscarrying during the first week of my rabbinical training. Fearful of being thrown out of the program if I started missing classes, I clenched my teeth, gobbled pain pills, and slipped out to the bathroom as needed. According to my gynecologist, 10 to 15 percent of established pregnancies result in miscarriage, usually in the first trimester. "It's not your fault," he told us. "You don't smoke or drink. This is nature's way, literally, of aborting its mistakes. Most miscarriages are of fetuses that could not have survived in this world. Half of all miscarriages are due to chromosomal abnormalities. Actually, 40 to 50 percent of conceptions don't take and the mother just thinks she got her period. Your next pregnancy should, statistically speaking, be just fine." I found little comfort in hearing his assessment and was too stunned at the time, having birthed two healthy boys already, to be able to formulate a question. Could he not have empathized with our disappointment? Or inquired about what impact this would have on our lives? Or advised me that it would take some time to pass the remaining fetal-support material in my uterus and that I should consider staying home for a day or two?

At school, in a file cabinet labeled CREATIVE LITURGY, I discovered a menopause ritual but nothing for miscarriage. Having started serving as a student rabbi in my first semester of rabbinical school, I had, fortunately, also trained as a social worker. One of my congregants miscarried early in her pregnancy for the fourth time, and later that same week a neighbor's twins, conceived after several miscarriages, were declared stillborn, fetal death at just over twenty weeks. These couples came to talk, cry, and express anguish and devastation, and to rail against the unfairness. One of the women had a sister who had just given birth to a healthy boy. She could not bring herself to visit, to watch the baby, her first nephew, thrive. Who else could she tell, she asked? Who would understand her jealousy and rage?

There needed to be a way to reduce their isolation, to honor their suffering, to do what Judaism usually does so well—facilitate the support, inner strength, and faith it takes to one day transcend the greatest of challenges.

I met with the women and their spouses. One, whom we'll call Sandy, took a pillow off the couch and sat down on the floor like a mourner. Immediately, the other three followed suit.

Sensing that it would be appropriate, I lowered the lights, lit some candles, and spoke briefly. "Anticipating a birth, here are the presents I had bought for each of you. Little board books for babies, now addressed as donations to the local center for abused women and children. You share a common grief; I'm glad you agreed to meet one another."

Without prompting, each told his or her story. Sandy's partner, Bill, chose to go first. He spoke of the call he received at work, his race to the hospital, the look on Sandy's face when she received the news that all her amniotic fluid had disappeared; the rush to sign forms to induce labor for the twins. Sandy told of her labor, the days and weeks afterward when she was in shock, enraged, and grieving. Her inability to focus at work or while driving; the flashbacks.

The other woman, Ellen, pulled a photo from a fetal ultrasound out of her pocketbook and spoke to it about her dreams of creating a family beyond coupledom. Nate, Ellen's husband, could not speak; his hands shook, his broken heart was written across his body, eyes, and mouth.

I read aloud the verse describing how Aaron, Moses's brother and high priest of the Israelites, was silent when his sons died in front of him. "What is his silence?" I asked. The silent father took out his wallet and showed pictures of his parents, grandparents, and himself. He put the picture of himself into the flame. "If I cannot give them grandchildren, what am I?" he whispered. "If I cannot give Ellen a child, what am I?" he bellowed, then wept.

Ellen reached over and, from the remains of the disappearing photograph, rubbed ashes onto her forehead and his and took him into her arms. They rocked and wept together. Slowly, into the silence, the other couple rubbed ashes on their foreheads and held one another. We simply sat in silence for a long while.

I asked, "What is the prayer of your heart?" I also read several more rebellious pieces, full of anger at G*d, one by Rabbi Abraham Joshua Heschel and another by Reb Levi Yitzhak of Berditchev. Then, meeting the eyes of each person present, I asked again, "What is the prayer of your heart?"

Ellen spoke. "My prayer is to become a parent. This has been hard, so very hard. Surely there is a soul meant for us to raise."

Sandy put her hand on her husband's heart. "My prayer is for the courage to adopt a child and for the child we find to thrive and appreciate the love we have to give."

Nate said, "My prayer is to stop replaying the hospital scenes in my head, to see Ellen's smile return and hear her laughter filling our home again so that we can go out, qualify, and find children to raise."

Bill was silent and we waited. "My prayer is to reach full acceptance of what has happened to us. It is good not to feel so alone in this; we were hurting each other in our grief. I thank Ellen and Nate for being so forthcoming. I thought my pain was unique, which was unhealthy really. I can almost imagine a future now."

"May I give you a blessing?" I asked. All four nodded, stood up, and spontaneously joined hands. "May you be blessed to speak of your experience in the community. The shock and trauma you have experienced, the isolation and grief—may no others feel alone while coping with this kind of trauma and crushing disappointment. In Psalms we read that even after the devastation of the Babylonian Exile, they prayed for 'those who sow in tears to reap in joy.' May your harvest come to you, even if it is not the harvest you expected, but still a good and satisfying harvest. May we all move forward into life with compassion for those we see pushing a stroller with a child inside, for we know not the pain that lurks in anyone's life, or what toll may have been taken en route to their moments of joy. May you long enjoy life in each other's arms. *Ameyn!*"

"Wait!" Bill called out. "A cup of wine please."

Stymied, I hesitated; it seemed an over-the-top thought. "A cup of wine please." Easy enough to take down the kiddush cup and a decanter of sacramental wine. Filling it to the brim, Bill held it high and said, "As we who blessed and drank from the cup of blessing at our wedding ceremonies, so may we be blessed to find the healthiest way to create the families for which we yearn."

Everyone agreed. "*Ameyn*."

The above is a good example of spontaneous ritual. Feel free to create one yourself or invite professional assistance. Planning new rituals in advance is more customary, as in the previous situation. A guide to new ritual creation can be found in chapter 8.

RECIPE #12:
The Individual without Progeny
(*co-written with Sarah Harwin*)

Some decide not to raise a family. There are many good reasons for this decision. There are many ways to participate in the chain of Jewish continuity. There is a great deal to contribute and pass on to future generations besides your genes or parenting skills. This recipe is written with intent to recognize how hurtful it can be for those who make this choice to feel community pressure regarding the progeny.

- Think about the myriad ways in which you have contributed, or hope to contribute, to Jewish continuity.
- How do you envision your talents affecting the Jewish future? Perhaps through the arts, music, scholarship, books and articles you write, activism, philanthropic generosity, communal work, and/or … ?

ADOPTION

Michal, the wife of King David, never had children (2 Samuel 6:23), yet she is also considered to have been the mother of five sons (2 Samuel 21:8). Tradition resolves these verses by noting that Michal was called on to raise her sister's children. Another good example of foster-parenting or adoption is in the Purim story, when Mordecai raises and advises his orphaned cousin Esther to the point where she becomes queen and is in a position to save the Jewish people from persecution and slaughter.

Judaism doesn't have a formal adoption process; that is a matter of civil law. Taking care of a child who needs a family is full of opportunities to make mitzvot, to do numerous good and holy things. An initial set of mitzvot would include making sure that the child has had the proper Jewish covenantal rituals—and, if not born Jewish, also *mikvah*, immersion in living waters and a certificate of approval from a rabbinic court, a *beit din*.

The Talmud teaches that for those who bring up an orphan in their home, it is as though the child had been born to them.

- Unlike civil law in many countries, in Judaism caring for a child needing a home does not erase the spiritual existence of the birth parents or the child's duties to honor them as much as possible in life and mourn them when the time comes.
- If the child does not come from Jewish parents and was too young to make religious decisions when a formal conversion took place, the child has the option to decline remaining Jewish on his or her thirteenth birthday.
- There is no contraindication to raising a child of any ethnic background. Judaism is not a race; our members are found in every color of the rainbow, and all are welcome.

Adoption adds special considerations to rituals for welcoming a new baby or child. Here is one recent example.

∾

Cherie just called to say the civil adoption approvals and medical clearances have all arrived and she will leave next week for Central America to collect her baby, a girl just over one month old. She wants help with planning a Jewish rite of passage ritual for bringing her daughter home. She is vibrant with excitement until her voice drops and she says, "Reb Goldie, I don't expect the day of the ritual to be easy."

"Why is that?"

"We're very concerned about whether my parents will accept her. Mom keeps asking if we're sure about going through with this. She's upset because our daughter won't look like anyone in our family. We wanted that whole genetic legacy thing too, but we couldn't keep trying. It's taken too much of a toll on our relationship. And this baby, she's so beautiful and she needs us. Mom just has to start to understand she's about to become a grandmother for the first time. Why does she have to be so impossible now?"

"Cherie, you are suffering because your mom isn't accepting your and Matthew's decision to adopt."

"Reb Goldie, what can we do? She has to accept that Carmen is never going to have Grandma Rayzl's eyes or my artistic talent. This girl is going to be her own unique self."

"Cherie, did you pick a sacred name for Carmen yet? Remember, we'll need one for her conversion documents and blessing."

"No, we have time yet to decide that. Why?"

"What was your Grandma Rayzl like?"

"Well, she loved to read novels, to do crewel embroidery, and she loved trees and flowers. Everyone says she was a passionate dancer when she was young. Family legend has it that she once ran for city council because she was angry about crime during Prohibition. She called herself Rosa Raymond for the election and she served one term. She had friends who were beatniks, Mom said. Also, her sister Lena told me Rosa ran off to elope with a boyfriend during the war but actually didn't end up marrying him. Instead, she joined the Army and trained as a nurse. She was sort of a renaissance woman."

"Cherie, might Rosa be a nice name for a soon-to-be Jewish girl from Guatemala? And Rayzl is an honorable, good Yiddish name to have as a sacred name."

"So you're thinking we might name her for my mom's mother? That would be bold. No one's named for Matthew's Grandpa Joseph yet. But it's really a strong idea. If we name her for Grandma Rose, it will give her a real family connection, someone to learn about when she's older. Oh, if Grandma Rose were here she'd be helping Mom understand. Grandma Rose traveled to many countries during the war. Her friends were from every nationality, especially as the neighborhood where she lived changed in her later years. I'm going to talk to Matthew about this."

Notice how wise Cherie is to take this step—to register and embrace the possible feelings of her parents, as well as to speak honestly and honorably about her and her husband's sense of loss in the midst of their joy at Carmen's imminent arrival.

Her inner wisdom is already working well; naming the new baby after her grandmother Rose, who was a real old-fashioned family matriarch, the kind who would have taken charge and wrapped that baby in acceptance and life, could prove to be a great option.

I see that Cherie is looking inward, knowing something important. "Rabbi, remember Wendy Li's Rosh HaShannah talk last year?"

I did remember. It was a heart-stopping talk. Wendy Li had been adopted in 1980 from a Chinese orphanage, where she was suffering from deliberate neglect. As a child, Wendy Li seemed well-adjusted. She did very well in school, had lots of friends, delighted in Jewish summer camp, and became chair of the synagogue's junior youth group. Then, as a teen she became angry about always feeling different, being different; she raged about having been unfairly uprooted. After college, she taught English as a second language for two years in China, and also took time to tour the province of her birth.

On her return to America, Wendy Li met with me regarding her request to speak at High Holy Day services, to reach as many people as possible at one time. She had come to understand just how huge her good fortune had been. She's now doing a doctorate with the intent to work on issues of population balance and control. As part of her talk, she apologized publicly for her accusations of unfairness to her adoptive parents and described her goal as turning challenges into miracles that can help others.

Cherie called a few days after our first discussion to say Matthew had agreed to naming the baby after Grandma Rose. Cherie also had some new ritual ideas. "Reb Goldie, here's my vision. I sense there is a need to have us stand with our baby as a family; for everyone in attendance to tighten a circle around us. We can all be holding hands in a way that each can feel the pulse of the other, until we are one loop of life. Then, let's ask my mom to touch Carmen, to feel for her tiny heartbeat. After a while, into the silence, I can whisper the word *shema*, 'listen,' and you can whisper back *ehad*, 'one.' Then you can amplify the *shema* and encourage everyone to reply with *ehad*, 'one!'"

I was knocked out by the beautiful idea and imagery, great for starters. "But what about the traditional rituals?"

"Oh, we'll do them for sure, too. We could use Grandma Rose's big embroidered babushka, a huge scarf she kept from her own mother, that I have held onto as a family heirloom. We could hold it over Carmen like a _huppah_ while you say the traditional blessing and we welcome her into the Jewish people with her new sacred name.

"We'll have been through most of the formal conversion process earlier in the week, so would it be alright for you to explain about _mikvah_, her ritual immersion, and the formal _beit din_, the court, of three rabbis that signed her certificate? Then everyone can call out spontaneous blessings, respond, '_Ameyn_,' and then we can eat!"

Just right. Cherie had created a beautiful ritual model, customized to address the needs of her particular family. As we move to the next chapter, you will learn the traditional rites for welcoming, naming, and covenanting boys and girls as well as gender-balancing options and perspectives on creating a healthy Jewish family.

5

Belonging and Becoming
Ceremonies of Welcome, Naming, Covenant, and Blessing

Jewish tradition includes many rituals, symbols, prayers, and practices for every stage of life from infancy through bar/bat mitzvah. These rites emphasize appreciation for the gift of life and the covenantal responsibility to raise each child to live an ethical, mitzvah-centered life.

CEREMONIES OF NAMING AND COVENANT

In Judaism the naming process is meant to involve far more spiritual significance and searching. A child's given name is viewed as shaping the evolution of his or her character and lot in life (Berahot 7b and Midrash Tanhuma, Parshat Ha'azinu 7). While parents wouldn't select a name that might prove to be a handicap in popular culture, names chosen would link children to their Jewish lineage and were intended to provoke curiosity, insight, optimism, and growth.

In biblical times, as far as the Torah reveals, children were named at birth. Scholars have found that naming a child at an independent ritual, such as at the Torah or during circumcision, emerged in the twelfth century and became a norm by the sixteenth century (Shulhan

Ar*uh*). Over time, entry of a child into the covenant gradually became ceremonial rather than assumed. So what is meant by *covenant*?

- That as Jews we will be dedicated to aligning with and evolving the ethics articulated in Torah as delivered at Sinai as best we can.
- That we will work within our people, the Jewish people, to model the ways in which a group's internal culture and relationships can shine light on how to realize humanity's highest hopes.
- That *mipnei dar*h*ei shalom*, for the sake of creating universal pathways to peace, we will work for the good of all.
- That we bless our offspring and community members to enter into and make holy their intimate relationships, to raise children, and to have the resources to do so available to them.
- To treasure immediate and extended family, and to gather in celebration and welcome each new member.

With all this in mind, our ancestors managed to keep rituals involving infants fairly brief.

Traditionally, boys have a ritual called a *bris* (Yiddish and Ashkenazi Hebrew) or *brit* (Sephardi and modern Hebrew), meaning "covenant." For girls, the father announces her name by means of a blessing given by the service leader in synagogue. In the twentieth century, as gender equality became more expectation than hope in many Jewish communities, numerous unique rituals were invented for girls. These involve symbolic gestures, often with wine or water, and there is even a record of some discussions about symbolically breaking the hymen to parallel circumcision. Upon study, review, and reflection, it is possible to simply expand the language of the traditional brit ceremony so that it is applicable to both boys and girls.

ENTERING THE COVENANT OF JEWISH PEOPLEHOOD

What does this covenant require of a parent and participants? What is received in return? The rituals of covenanting are beautiful, visceral, and powerful. Essentially, at the covenantal rituals you are committing to raising a child dedicated to living a mitzvah-centered life. To understand the terms of the covenant, let's look at the five biblical points of covenant in their order of appearance in the Torah. Each one shows a maturing process, reflected through the characters of G*d and Israel in the Torah. Whether you view these as foundational myths or historical events, they offer valuable life lessons.

RAINBOW COVENANT

Upon realizing humanity's horrific behavior results from a design flaw, G*d is depicted as realizing that G*d, too, lashed out in inappropriate, consummately destructive anger. The Rainbow Covenant arises here, G*d's commitment to cultivate self-control.

> Then G*d said to Noah and to his sons with him, "I now establish my covenant with you and with your descendants after you and with every living creature…. Never again will all life be cut off by the waters of a flood. Never again will there be a flood to destroy the earth." And G*d said, "This will be the sign of the covenant I am making between Me and you and every living creature with you, a covenant for all generations to come. I have set my rainbow in the clouds and it will be the sign of the covenant between Me and the earth." (Genesis 9:8–13)

COVENANT OF ABRAHAM

PART 1. *New York Times* columnist David Brooks has recently pointed out that childhood, adolescence, adulthood, and old age are no longer sufficient to accurately reflect the human life cycle. He documents a now fully emergent new stage of life we know intuitively to deserve recognition and attention; he dubs this the "odyssey years." These are the years when, after finishing high school or college, instead of heading directly into marriage and/or career, a person visits Israel, India, and beyond on a journey of personal growth and spiritual awakening. This model is not news to the Jewish people; it is one of the first spiritual instructions Abraham receives:

> Go to yourself, out from the land where you were born, from the house of your father, go to a land I will show you. I will make of you a great nation and bless you, your name will become great, and you will be a blessing and I will bless those who bless you, and the one who curses you I will curse, and in you all the families of the earth will be blessed. (Genesis 12:1–3)

PART 2. After the odyssey years of our youth, a yearning for children and a place to nest with them comes naturally to most of us. This is also reflected in the virtually archetypal story of G*d, Abraham, and Sarah. Genesis 15:1–21 records the actual making of the Abrahamic covenant. G*d comes to Abraham in a vision; some call it a dream. In this experience Abraham receives a promise from G*d of great rewards—descendants more numerous than the stars, and a land for his descendants to dwell in.

PART 3. Holding a family together, much less having it remain connected enough to become a people, an enduring nation, benefits from a symbolic sign. In a rather lengthy passage, Genesis 17:1–14, we find the sign of the covenant that Avram, at biblical age ninety-nine, his son Ishmael at age thirteen, and all his household and descendants are to receive. Instructions are given to undertake removal of the foreskin of all males in the household and of all generations of males to come. Since the blessing is one of fertility, perhaps permanently uncovering the portal of male fertility was a substantial way to show it. In this passage, G*d also repeats the covenant with Avram, and as an additional symbol of covenants adds a letter *hey* from the Great Name to Avram's name so that it becomes Avraham, known in English as Abraham.

PART 4. Mothers are a logical and vital part of any fertility blessing. Here we read that a sacred name is also provided to Abraham's wife.

> G*d said to Avraham, "Regarding Sarai your wife, no longer call her Sarai, her name is Sarah; I will bless her, and give you a son by her: Yes, I will bless her, and she shall be [a mother] of nations; kings of people shall be from her." (Genesis 17:15–16)

PART 5. Is there sufficient meaning to maintaining a separate people? What is this all about? Here the answer comes: This is all for the greater good. Childhood selfishness abates with maturity. G*d, in the role of cosmic parent, has seen what cruelty can emerge from those made in G*d's image. It is important to note that this section goes on to the story of Sodom and Gemorrah, which makes it clear that additional official principles for living need to be set into motion. The covenant the Jewish people follow will become increasingly rigorous with time so that as they become able to, they will live just lives. Will G*d give these reasons for the covenant to Abraham or Sarah? If G*d does, what will be their reaction? The text lets us hear G*d as meta-parent thinking out loud and Abraham, like a true son, reacting and debating, pushing the parent's perspective:

> G*d said: "Shall I hide from Abraham what I am about to do since Abraham will surely become a great and mighty nation and in him all the nations of the earth will be blessed? I have chosen him so that he will teach his children and his household after him to follow in the ways of G*d by doing righteousness and justice, so that I can fulfill my vision for him." Then G*d said: "The outcry from Sodom and Gomorrah is so great, and their misdeeds so grave. I will go down to see whether what they have done matches the outcry, so if not, I will know … Abraham came forward and said, "Will You sweep away the innocent along with the guilty? What if there are fifty innocent

within the city; will You wipe out the place and not forgive it for the sake of the innocent who are in it? Far be it from You to do such a thing, to bring death upon the innocent as well as the guilty, so that innocent and guilty are alike. Far be it from You! Shall not the Judge of all the earth deal justly? (Genesis 18:17–19)

SHABBAT COVENANT

So the idea of a healthier form of peoplehood is hatched, but what will it take to implement? A good start is ending abusive work conditions, workaholism, the slavery mentality among the Israelites. This is priority number one and still quite useful today.

> You must observe my Sabbaths. This will be a sign between Me and you for the generations to come, so you may know that I am the Lord who makes you holy…. The Israelites are to observe the Sabbath, celebrating it for the generations to come as a lasting covenant. (Exodus 31:12–16)

COVENANT AT SINAI

Shabbat was among the few important concepts taught to the Israelites in the infancy of the new peoplehood project, what might be called the *Kodesh* Project, the Holiness Project. But the first set of concepts didn't prove sufficient for building a civil society. A system for ethical living proved necessary. Let's take the deuteronomic version of the giving of the Torah at Sinai as our example. Here Moses looks back on his experience at Sinai as his life is drawing to a close. Notice how he expresses himself with the wisdom of an elder who is looking ahead to future generations.

> You stand this day, all of you, before the Lord your G*d, your tribal heads, your elders and your officials, all the men of Israel, your children, your wives, even the stranger within your camp, from woodchopper to water drawer—to enter into the covenant of the Lord your G*d, which the Lord your G*d is concluding with you this day

and into G*d's oath. To the end that [G*d] may establish you this day as [G*d's] People and be your G*d, as [G*d] promised you and as sworn to your fathers, Abraham, Isaac, and Jacob. And it is not with you alone that I make this covenant with its oath, but with those who are standing here with us this day before the Lord our G*d and those who are not with us this day. (Deuteronomy 29:9–15)

EZEKIEL'S COVENANT

The theme of covenant and ritual, expressed in the feminine in the Hebrew original of this passage, which is refreshing, is found in the writing of the prophet Ezekiel, who at the time was mightily focused on getting the Israelites back on an ethical track.

I said to you: "Live in your blood and grow like a plant in the field.... I swore an oath to you and entered into a covenant with you; you became mine," says the Lord G*d. "Then I bathed you with water, washed away your blood, and anointed you with oil." (Ezekiel 17:8–9)

For a people to survive and contribute to the human future
for thousands of years, reproduction is a vital matter.
Equally so is that the children
are taught to perpetuate and cultivate
The pathways of their people.

So is the covenant in which a Jewish child,
or one undertaking conversion, enrolled.
The *Kodesh* Project, the Holiness Project
is to live a mitzvah-centered life,
to manifest the image we've had, and would like to have, of G*d
through learning and living, core Jewish wisdom texts and practices.

The promise continues to unfold.

THE PARENTS' ROLE IN FINDING A SACRED NAME

Abraham's original name was Avram, and Sarah, Abraham's wife's name was Sarai. Their journey includes receiving the Hebrew letter *hey* into their names to reflect their divine experience. So, too, it became traditional for parents to intuit and ritually bestow a sacred name upon each of their children. Tradition holds that the name of a soul exists before birth, and what that name is can actually be perceived by the parents. Parents don't always get this right, so it is possible for you to change your sacred name later in life.

Because your sacred name is made from the *lashon kodesh*, the letters of the holy language of the Jewish people, this name is part of ritually establishing the child's place within the Jewish people and our covenant of ethical living and shared culture. Your sacred name ideally gives inspiration for living by creating connection to personal, biblical, literary, or historical Jewish ancestors, or to important ideals or texts.

- A Jewish sacred name is a first name, not a surname (last name), and can also double as a person's everyday name. Last names didn't come into human society until Roman times; before that a person was known as, for example, *Miryam bat Shmuel*, Miriam the daughter of Shmuel (Samuel). Due to acts of war like rape, scholars typically say that Jewish identity was changed sometime between 200 BCE and 500 CE to be determined by whether the mother was Jewish, so that formulation would read: *Miryam bat Hannah*, Miriam the daughter of Hannah. Increasingly, both parents are listed in naming formats for life cycle rites: *Miryam bat Shmuel v'Hannah*, Miriam the daughter of Samuel and Hannah. A local rabbi will be able to advise you on which format is appreciated in your community.

- The Jewish sacred name will be required on documents for conversion, naming, and circumcision, bar/bat mitzvah, marriage, and, heaven forefend, divorce, in healing prayers when needed, and in the end, on your grave marker.
- If you are a Jewish parent who will be raising a child, and you do not have a Jewish sacred name, this is an appropriate time to take one for yourself or to amend yours, if that is necessary.

In some traditions a master designates a sacred name for an acolyte. In traditional Korean families, for example, the father-in-law names the baby. In the Torah, the mother usually does the naming. In modernity, the parents usually find a name on which they can agree.

Reb Goldie: "Mom, why did you name me Gail?"

"Well, dear, when the doctor's office called to say the test showed I was pregnant, I was watching the *Gail Storm Show* on television. I turned to your father and said, 'If we have a girl let's name her Gail.' He agreed."

"So what would you have called me if you had been watching the evening news? Walter Cronkite?!"

So, some time after a painful divorce, I had a vision to take a new and untarnished name, a sacred name, Goldie. Right away I realized it had belonged to my legendarily amazing great-grandmother, who successfully faced down the Cossacks with a bottle of vodka and a few empty glasses and so survived the war.

- Begin by creating some mental and emotional space for yourself. Register with one sentence each thing waiting for you to do, and promise each item that you will get back to it with focused attention as soon as you are able to. First, you have something essential to attend to—finding the sacred name.

- Now release any prior intentions to name the child (or yourself) after some person, place, or event. Set aside consideration of the pressures various family members may be exerting on you to choose their preferred name. Let your spirit leap beyond all that.

- When you feel empty, centered, and ready, sit comfortably and ask, "What is my [child's] Jewish sacred name meant to be?"

- A quality of being may come to you, something from nature, an ancestor—many things are possible. Collect whatever images or words come to you as valuable information that contains the name or that points you toward it. You may want help with translating what comes to mind into Hebrew or Yiddish.

- Explore the contexts in which the names being considered may appear. Check out Torah stories and popular culture in Israel. Some words take on colloquial meanings within a particular culture that may not be pleasant and are to be avoided. Care is required.

- Inside, where it counts, when you have found it, you will know the name is right.

RECIPE #13: Finding Your Own or Your Child's Jewish Sacred Name

BASIC GUIDELINES FOR SACRED JEWISH NAMES

Upon the establishment of the State of Israel it became popular to take Hebrew rather than regional Yiddish or Ladino names. Recently, some are again taking Yiddish and Ladino sacred names for their children or themselves in order to preserve Jewish culture and honor family connections.

A Jewish person can have a secular name, too (Gittin 11b), but this is not necessary and can inhibit transmission of identity. Names that work equally well in the larger culture in which one lives, for example, Miriam or Dan, may be ideal.

It is recommended to use the selected name in some way for thirty days and then be called to the Torah to affix it ritually (Shulḥan Aruḥ, Even HaEzer 129, and also in Igrot Moshe).

If grandparents-to-be pressure their children to choose a particular name, the code of Jewish law says that the child's parents do not have to choose that name if it does not resonate with them (Yoreh Deah 240:25).

One convention to keep in mind is that while Sephardi Jews can name children after living relatives, Ashkenazi Jews, after the talmudic period, primarily do not. In Ḥasidic communities, when a rebbe has had a positive impact on the parents regarding the pregnancy, some will name their child in his honor.

There are approximately 2,800 original first names in the Bible, which makes for lots of interesting characters and stories to help a child relate to the name a parent chooses. See Suggestions for Further Reading and Learning at the back of this book for recommendations on books of Jewish names.

Sacred names are often related to:

> **The natural world.** Tamar, for example, means "date palm," and Tziporah, or the affectionate diminutive Tzippi, means "bird."

Emotion words. Nahum, meaning "comfort," and Simhah, "happiness," for example.

The twelve tribes, such as Dan and Ruben or Ruvein.

Prophets' or angels' names with the letter *hey* or the term *el* or *yah* for G*d in them, like Nataniel, "Gift of G*d"; Uriel, "Light of G*d"; or Talya, "Dew of G*d."

Descriptive names like Benjamin, or in Hebrew Binyamin, "right-hand son," or Binni or Bibi in affectionate forms.

Hebrew nouns that relate to things or times of the year, such as Vered, "rose," or Tammuz, a month of the year. Israelis often favor this approach.

The season or characters in a major Jewish holiday or the Torah portion near the time of the birth. A child born near Shavuot might be called Rute, Ruth, or Naomi, for example.

The first letter of the child's secular name. The name may also mean something similar to the secular name. This strategy isn't terribly meaningful, but was quite popular in the late nineteenth and the twentieth centuries.

Keep in mind that it is not a advisable to name a child after an evil person, unless that name already exists in the family lineage with good associations. Still, consider the impact on a child of a name associated with evil.

For adopted children, some seek words with an affinity between the child's language of origin and Hebrew. For example, an American dad thinking to name his adoptive son Leonard after his father Leibel, decided to call him LiYam, "the ocean is mine." The cultural resonance of the name's sound connects the child to his original homeland in Asia and his family of origin, the Hebrew meaning to his new people, and the image to the journey from his mother's womb, across this watery world, into the *mikvah*, the ritual immersion, and his new life as an American Jew.

Some follow the tradition of not announcing a baby's name until her or his covenantal ceremony. Sources for this are in Torah because Abraham's name is changed in conjunction with his circumcision—at biblical age ninety-nine! (Genesis 17:15)

RECIPE #14:
Sustaining a
Sacred Name

- If you name a child after someone from your family who has died—an elective Ashkenazi practice—or someone still alive—an elective Sephardi practice—you might create a list of adjectives describing the fine qualities of that person and collect stories about her personality and accomplishments.
- If you name a child after a character from the Torah, or another Jewish sacred source, collect stories about that character from Torah and commentaries to read and discuss regularly.
- On Friday night, when it is traditional after lighting the candles to bless our children, also bless the child with the qualities of the character for whom he is named.
- From time to time give a gift that echoes the sacred name in some clever way. If you name a child Ari ("My Lion"), for example, a toy lion called Ari can be used at bedtime to animate the name as you tell lion stories. Much later, the life and teachings of the great kabbalist Rabbi Yitzhak Luria, known as the Ari, might be introduced to strengthen the name and the person's Jewish connection.
- If you name a child after a quality, start a bedroom wall of verse or prayer in which that quality appears and add to it over the years.

COVENANTAL RITUALS

It's no secret that many traditional societies prized and privileged males over females. In some societies even today, women are the property, first, of their father and then of their husband. The spectrum of Jewish practice today with regard to welcoming children into the Jewish people reflects the reality of our people's own emergence from patriarchal societies. Continuing the tradition of respectful pluralism in the *Reclaiming Judaism* trilogy, *Living Jewish Life Cycle* will provide options within the context of explaining traditional practices and some of the meanings of the texts, metaphors, symbols, and blessings involved.

TRADITIONS FOR THE WEEK BEFORE THE COVENANTAL RITES

Many of these are little-known in some communities and beloved in others. Consider importing a few of them into your own life and evolving circle of personal and Jewish community.

SHEVUAT HA-BEN OR -BAT. Feasting, dancing, celebration, and filling the house with candlelight are among the many traditional expressions of joy practiced in a reemerging ritual called *shevuat ha-bat*, "week of the daughter," and *shevuat ha-ben*, "week of the son," that is held during the first week of a child's life.

VAHT NAHT. We know from rabbinic records that the last night of the birth week, from medieval times until the Holocaust (and within small regional pockets to this day), involved an all-night vigil called in Yiddish *vaht naht*, and known in Salonika as *Veula*, "watch night." Family and friends would visit, celebrate, and stay up beside the baby and mother. Incense would be burned and new *midrashim*—stories based on imagined biblical scenarios—would be composed in the child's honor. For this reason, the Sephardim called the vigil night simply *Midrash*. A possible way to celebrate these rituals follows.

RECIPE #15:
Covenantal
Celebrations

You help build the cradle of civilization within which the life of every child is rocked by cultivating a spiritual community. This recipe draws upon the traditional models described above to create community- and culture-building practices during the week or month after a child's arrival.

- Invite those who know of the pregnancy to compose a *midrash*, a vision of an untold story that lurks between the verses and voices of Torah and to offer this as a gift upon the birth of your child. A *midrash* can be composed as writing, dance, painting, sculpture, or song.
- Welcome visitors during the *shevuat ha-ben* or *ha-bat* week to deliver and/or perform their *midrashim* in person.
- You might have the "watch night" become a salon during which the offerings are performed in your home before a gathering of friends and family.

For those inclined to weekend or Shabbat gatherings, there is a Friday night tradition, similar to the one described above, called *Shalom Zahar Brit Olam.*

- Time was when the first Shabbat of a boy's life was an occasion for creating a booklet called *Brit Olam*, "An Eternal Covenant," that was filled with selected sacred stories and told in honor of the prophet Elijah, who is known as the herald of the messiah. This event was called *Shalom Zahar*, "the peace/welcome of the male."
- We might reclaim this practice by gathering on the first Shabbat of any Jewish child's life and, through a pun on the sound of the term *zah-hahr* [male], grasping instead for

the message of Shabbat, *zayher yetziat mitzrayim*, to remember the miracle that we do leave the narrow times of stress and constricted living for the wider places filled with life, such as welcoming a new baby. A baby represents infinite potential, a being that could help change this world for the better. This is the *Brit Olam*, part of why it is a mitzvah to multiply—to multiply the promise of a better future that comes with each new life.

- Jewish communities might create a Monthly Midrash Salon in the synagogue or Jewish community center. Here all the children born and adults newly covenanted in a given month might be feted by friends, teachers, and community with new works done in the honor of all our beautiful new Jews.

FORMAL COVENANTAL RITUALS

NAMING: FOR GIRLS

Traditionally, a girl from a family of Ashkenazi origin is blessed and her sacred name formalized when her father, or both her parents in many communities, attend synagogue for the first time after her birth. This is done on a Torah reading day, usually a Monday, Thursday, or Shabbat, historically within the first two months of birth, more recently within the first week or two of birth.

Sephardi Jews hold their ritual for a girl in the home, calling it *zeved bat*, meaning "precious daughter." In this ceremony the daughter is likened to the image of the awesome beauty that is expressed in the Songs of Songs: "O, my dove, in the cranny of the rock hidden by the cliff, let me see your face, let me hear your voice, for your voice is sweet, your face is lovely."

After the parental *aliyah* to the Torah, a *mi sheberah*, a blessing using the child's sacred name, is chanted aloud by whomever is leading the Torah service.

Usually the family will sponsor a reception after services with a nice spread for the community in celebration of the naming and birth. Family gathering rituals also celebrate these "new arrivals."

NAMING: FOR BOYS

For boys the naming in most communities takes place at the same time as the *brit milah*, the covenant of circumcision. There is a celebratory meal, a *seudah shel mitzvah*, followed by the traditional blessing after the meal, *birkat ha-mazon*, with additional special blessings included relating to the occasion.

Most Jewish communities—religious or cultural—will be happy to host your baby's naming; usually no membership is required. Some might even extend a full- or half-year free membership to make you feel welcome. Shop around when you are ready to join a community. What you grew up with might not be the right fit at this stage of your life, so explore!

FOR BOTH BOYS AND GIRLS

1. The baby's father, mother, or both, depending on the community, attend synagogue the first Torah reading day that they are able to do so, as close to the birth as is healthy and reasonable for them.

2. By advising an usher that they wish to be called up to the Torah, the parent(s) can participate in a blessing of welcome for the new baby that includes the child's Jewish sacred name.

3. If you own a tallit, a prayer shawl, bring it with you and wear it during the service. If not, you'll find extras in the lobby. In some communities women wear one; in others they don't. If it is not your customary practice, consider what is appropriate for you or ask the usher what is appropriate in this setting.

4. Depending on what other occasions are being celebrated in the synagogue that day, you may also be offered a full *aliyah*, the opportunity to witness and bless before and after the

Torah reading. Should you wish to do so, the steps are simple to follow.

- Touch the Torah with the fringe of your tallit at the site the reader will indicate with the *yad*, the Torah pointer.
- If you know the opening blessing and wish to chant it, by all means do so. Or, you can recite it by using the Hebrew and/or the transliteration that will typically be available on a card set in large type.
- The reader will then chant part of the weekly Torah reading.
- Now, again, touch the tallit fringe at the spot the pointer indicates.
- Now chant the closing blessing from the card. (Learn more about the Torah service in chapter 3 in volume II, *Meaning & Mitzvah: Daily Practice for Reclaiming Judaism through Prayer, God, Torah, Hebrew, Mitzvot and Peoplehood*.)

5. Don't sit down. A version of the *mi shehberah*, "May the One who blessed our ancestors bless ..." will be given; it includes the public announcement of your baby's Jewish sacred name.

6. Parents often contact the congregation in advance and offer to pay for a dessert or brunch buffet for the community after the service. Alternatively or additionally, a donation of appreciation to the youth education fund at the congregation is also appropriate.

CREATING A FULL COVENANTAL SERVICE (AT HOME OR IN THE SYNAGOGUE)

This section is a guide to creating a *brit bat* for girls (also termed *zeved bat*, precious daughter) and a *brit milah* for boys that both follows the traditional liturgy and sequence and also shows you how to use much of this framework to welcome and covenant daughters. But first, here is some basic terminology.

RITUAL ROLES

MOHEL/MOHELET. In recent years some parts of the Jewish spectrum are training and certifying women as well as men to circumcise and lead the rites; other communities will only accept men. Circumcision, or for those already medically circumcised, *hatafat dam brit*, drawing a minuscule drop of blood, is a covenantal rite performed only on males, and then only when there are no health contraindications, such as hemophilia. Secular physicians increasingly seem to be referring parents to these circumcision professionals, as the traditional Jewish methods take far less time, cause the infant little or no pain, reduce the risk of hospital-acquired infections, and can be properly done in the comfort of your home on the eighth day rather than before it is physically ideal, due to rapid hospital discharge policies. A medical circumcision not done by a *mohel(et)* does not qualify as a covenantal ritual, so a *mohel(et)* will still need to be engaged and a *hatafat dam brit* will be required.

PARENT(S). The obligation to conduct, or, if unable, to organize covenantal rites traditionally falls upon the father. If he cannot carry out this obligation, then the community must do so. In many communities the mother's role has become ritual partnership equal with the father's.

BAAL/BAALAT TEFILLAH, LEADER OF PRAYER. In the absence of circumcision, a knowledgeable friend or Jewish clergy person can assist in ritual design and lead the proceedings on the day of the naming and covenantal rite for girls or boys.

BAALAT HA-BRIT. In some communities there is a woman who receives the baby from the mother and conveys the child to the room of the ritual. *Baalat* is feminine for "master of," and *brit* means "covenant."

BAAL HA-BRIT. The designated *baal ha-brit*, master of the covenant, receives the child at the door of the ritual and places him in the lap of the godparent. At some points in history this is the same person as the *sandek*, described below. Where customary, and if the baby is amenable to being handed around, this is a nice opportunity to honor yet another friend or family member.

KVATTER/SANDEK (M) AND/OR *KVATERIN/SANDEKET* (F). Often translated as "godparent," this/these person(s) in communities where women's involvement has been renewed are honored to sit in the chair of Elijah the prophet while holding the child, since Elijah was a powerful advocate of traditional covenantal rites.

THE ROLE OF GODPARENTS

RECIPE #16:
Choosing
Godparents

The term *godparent* sounds a bit odd in a Jewish context. Jews don't use the "G" word lightly. Godparents, if they are to be the guardians of your child(ren) in the event of your untimely death, must be stipulated in your will, or else the government will step in to make that determination, and in some cases can pick a total stranger. So while Jewish tradition does not require the role of godparent to include that of legal guardian, this is a good time to take the ritual in that direction.

- Make a list of your criteria for someone to raise your children if one day you cannot.
- Now, consider the word G*d in *godparent*. What does that add to the idea of legal guardianship?
- Who, in addition to yourself, do you know who can help your child walk in awe in this world and seek to live successfully while also seeking harmony with nature and humanity?

- Who will be able to listen, to hear the prayer of your child's heart? Who will support that prayer to become a vision for a better life that can be worked for, attained?
- Who else will see what your child is capable of, and do everything possible to give nourishment to such seeds of possibility?
- Who would not flinch to dip into her own fiscal and emotional resources to help your child if you cannot?
- Who would be willing to reshape their own home and schedule if your child needs to move in with them?
- Match those you know with the qualities you have listed and then screen the list for those in your life who might agree to take on such a role.
- Meet with your first choice and explore the possibility. Let them know they will appear in your will as the child(ren)'s designated guardians.
- Invite the godparents to write a letter describing how they feel about this godparenting relationship—their hopes, desires, fears, and blessings. Save the letter to be opened at the child's bar/bat mitzvah or in the unfortunate event that they actually need to step into this role and raise the child(ren).
- Grandparents may feel either relieved or threatened by the idea of godparents drawn from your peer group. Be sure they know of your choice, and your reasons, to prevent them from contesting the matter at a time when you can't intervene.
- There is a ceremonial role for godparents in the covenanting rituals to celebrate a birth in a Jewish family. If grandparents are not the designates, they can still be honored appropriately. Have the godparent(s) publicly

acknowledge their role by receiving the infant during the covenanting rituals either before or after the grandparent(s).

- If you are to be a *sandek* for a baby boy, don't pass out yet. You will hold the child only ceremonially. To reduce the chance of medical complications, no longer does either the mother or the *sandek* hold the baby during circumcision. The professional *mohel* takes on this responsibility these days in almost every setting. Some lay the baby on a beautifully embroidered pillow, swaddled in a wrap called a whimple; others use a nicely padded board with Velcro closures. It all amounts to careful restraint lest the cold of the small surgical tools make the child move, risking injury.

Why bear this, or ask it of a baby boy? Important questions; let's go there now.

UNDERSTANDING THE *WHY* OF MALE CIRCUMCISION

Judaism is very serious about life. Our rituals for new babies and new Jews emphasize the gritty details of making and sustaining life. For males, ours is a covenant of blood, an intense practice that delivers a homeopathic dose of reality—how vulnerable we are, how precious this life is.

Tziporah, "Song Bird," Moses's Midianite wife, circumcises their son, whom Moses names Gershom, "a stranger there," while they are on the run. This is a decisive moment for her, whether to raise her child as a follower of the Midianite religion, for which her own father served as a priest, or to choose for her son and family to be Israelites. This mirrors the motif of modernity—that every Jew is a Jew by choice, even the son of Moses.

Exodus tells the story of the marking of our
doorposts with the blood of sacrificial animals.
The message: May death pass over this house.

Onto the doorpost of how males give life
we Jews make a different life-centered sacrifice:
circumcision.

The literal engraving of a body-memory
on the portal through which males
contribute to the creation of life
through a mitzvah that teaches
vulnerability and values,

Circumcision is the first formal lesson
in the education of a Jewish male.

All those who are born Jewish are automatically part of the covenant
originally made with Abraham and Sarah that included circumcision for him and the assignment of a sacred name to each of them.
Circumcision is a sign of how much value parent(s) place on their
son's being Jewish. It is also part of how a male convert affirms his
own "member"ship.

Circumcision is a mitzvah symbolizing our people's sense of
covenant as found in Genesis 17:2: "Throughout the generations,
every male among you shall be circumcised at the age of eight days."
A boy born of a Jewish mother is still Jewish even if his parents
don't arrange for him to be circumcised. The mitzvah falls to
the boy to arrange for this himself when he is old enough to understand. Bar mitzvah, for example, is conditional in most congregations upon this rite.

SYMBOLS USED IN COVENANTAL RITUALS

KIDDUSH CUP FILLED WITH SWEET KOSHER WINE

As has already been explained, wine symbolizes the blood of life. The baby is given a taste of wine immediately after the circumcision and blessed in the words of Ezekiel, "in your blood live." Looking into the rabbinic sources we see that the bleeding of women is equally understood as the blood of life and spoken of in terms of wine metaphors:

> Young women are like vines. There is a vine whose wine is red. A vine whose wine is abundant and a vine whose wine is sparse. Rabbi Judah said: "Every vine has its wine." Reb Hiyya taught: "As leaven is wholesome for the dough so is blood wholesome for a woman." One taught in the name of Rabbi Meir: "Of a woman with an abundance of blood many children may come." (Talmud, Niddah: 64b)

BLOOD

The only time blood is present in a Jewish ritual is at the opening of the male doorway to fertility during removal of the foreskin in the rite of circumcision. For those with the rare condition of having been born circumcised, or for those adults who've already had the procedure done for medical reasons, eliciting enough blood to turn the point of a napkin pink, called *hatafat dam brit*, is done instead, literally drawing of the "blood of covenant." Though wine is a nice touch, it comes afterwards, so a topical anesthetic that takes care of any potential pain is used in both rites by most professionals. Be sure to inquire about methods when booking a *mohel(et)*; there are variations that are important (see the article on circumcision at www.ReclaimingJudaism.org for details). In families where alcohol poses problems, kosher grape juice is always a fine substitute.

WATER

Since the late 1980s, water is often added as a ritual building block when covenanting daughters because in the Ezekiel Covenant (see p. 112), the Jewish people are addressed in the feminine when entered into the covenant and bathed by G*d in water. *Mikvah*, the monthly immersion after menstruation has fully ended, is part of Jewish fertility practice. It is also symbolic of the living waters from which life comes and of the potential for transition, growth, change, and healing.

ELIJAH'S CHAIR

An ornate seat (or seats if there is more than one godparent) is set at the front of the room where the rites will be held. The *sandek(et)* sits here. Some use a female, *sandeket*, for a girl and a male for a boy; others have two. The seat is named *Kisei Eliyahu*, the Elijah chair, because Elijah is called the "angel of the covenant" in the Book of Kings. *Midrashim* about Elijah are delightful tales to tell at bedtime and on Friday nights. Many of these show him to be closely associated with helping family relationships to thrive, and his spirit is viewed as a guardian for children at these rites.

CANDLES

The candle flame is the symbol for the soul. Two candles have many meanings within Judaism—the masculine and feminine qualities in each person; the individual in connection with G*d; the individual covenant of Abraham and the collective covenant of the Jewish people at Sinai. It is customary to have two candles alight during these rites. (Learn more about candles in Jewish ritual in volume I, *Reclaiming Judaism as a Spiritual Practice: Holy Days and Shabbat*, pages 39, 70–71, 148, 168–170, 186–188, 191, and volume II, *Meaning & Mitzvah: Daily Practice for Reclaiming Judaism through Prayer, God, Torah, Hebrew, Mitzvot and Peoplehood*, pages 26–29.)

KOS MIRIAM, MIRIAM'S CUP

Starting in the late 1980s a cup of spring water began to serve as a symbol of the equal importance of women in Jewish life. Miriam the prophetess not only placed her brother in the Nile and was there when the pharaoh's daughter drew him out to safety, she also led the community in song after the crossing of the Sea of Reeds and became known for her ability to locate water in the wilderness. A *midrash* called Miriam's Well (see Suggestions for Further Reading and Learning in the back of this book) inspired the start of this symbol. Some conclude the rituals of *brit bat* and *brit milah* by offering the baby a sip or anointing or spritzing him or her playfully with spring water from such a designated cup.

RITUAL GARB

CIRCUMCISION DRESS

Those who frequent art galleries will recognize that after togas, little boys continued to wear dress-like garments for a good bit of history. There still exist circumcision dresses that have been passed down from generation to generation, although most were destroyed during World War II. It is customary for the infant/child to wear white, the symbol of transformations of the soul, during these rituals. All others dress as for a festive religious occasion in accordance with local customs.

WHIMPLE. These lengthy cloths used to swaddle the baby during the ritual become family or congregational heirlooms, as they are meant to be beautifully embroidered, hand-painted, or quilted and to include the baby's sacred name and date of covenanting. In Ashkenazi communities, when they are donated to a congregation, whimples serve as wraps for the Torah under its dress. Many examples are on view at Jewish museums.

TALLIT. Some also wrap the baby in a tallit, a prayer shawl, during these covenantal rituals, or hold a tallit aloft during some part of the ritual as a symbol of connection to the covenant, per this verse in Torah: "The Lord said to Moses: 'Speak to the Israelites and instruct them to make for themselves fringes on the corners of their garments throughout the ages; let them attach a cord of blue to the fringe at each corner. That shall be your fringe; look at it and recall all the commandments of the Lord and observe them, so that you do not follow your heart and eyes in your lustful urge. Thus you shall be reminded to observe all My commandments and to be holy to your G*d. I, the Lord, am your G*d, who brought you out of the land of Egypt to be your G*d: I, the Lord your G*d'" (Numbers 15:37–41).

DRESS FOR PARENTS AND GUESTS. Dressing in a way that attracts attention to oneself has no place during a religious ritual. Modest dress clothes are always appropriate. All eyes are meant to be on the baby.

KIPPAH. The traditional skullcap signifies the wearer's intent to live a mitzvah-centered life. It is customary to provide these for guests. In some communities they are only worn by males. (To learn more, see volume II, *Meaning & Mitzvah: Daily Practices for Reclaiming Judaism through Prayer, God, Torah, Hebrew, Mitzvot and Peoplehood*, pages 192–194.) Often the *mohel(et)* will place a cute little mini-*kippah* on the baby's head, attached with an elastic band.

BLESSINGS AND TEXTS. The ritual that follows includes traditional as well as clearly identified adapted blessings that may prove to be helpful additions for those preferring a gender-inclusive ceremony. Please consult a local rabbi for the full content of the traditional texts, as there will be some variation across the spectrum of Jewish practice.

Here is a gender-balanced script, based upon the traditional sequence. Anticipate variations for local norms. The presence of a rabbi or cantor is not required. A skillful ritual facilitator is sufficient with the exception being that a *mohel(et)* must officiate for a boy. A full range of Hebrew text and translations are available online at ReclaimingJudaism.org. I recommend your handing out a small program sheet so guests are aware of the basic outline of the service and have access to translations/transliterations of communally chanted prayers. [O] indicates options for community-building and inclusiveness. It is customary for both male and female infants to wear a white dress because white is the Jewish color for spiritual transformation. Some families hand down such outfits from generation to generation.

RECIPE #17:
Brit Milah/Brit Bat: A Covenantal Ritual for Boys and Girls

❧

[O] **LEADER:** Welcome family and guests, my name is _____ and I will be guiding the sequence of *brit*, covenant and sacred naming. Today reflects the joy of this family and the parent's commitment to raise their child as a covenantal member of one the longest continually existing peoples in the world, the Jewish people.

LEADER (pointing to a chair in front of room): *Zeh kisei shel eliyahu ha-navi zahor la-tov*, which means this chair is endowed with the good name earned by the prophet Elijah. [O] *Eliyahu ha-Navi* is the traditional herald of our people's hope for a messianic time of peaceful coexistence for all. Elijah advocated for such rituals of inclusion. May this child be blessed to live in times of enduring peace.

[O] **ALL PRESENT:** So may it be!

LEADER: Please join in as I chant the traditional verse of blessing and the baby is escorted into our midst. It is customary to rise if you are able.

Baruh ha-ba (m)/*Bruhah ha-ba-ah* (f)
May the one who has arrived be blessed!

Note: Links to ritual melody options are available at ReclaimingJudaism.org.

Baalat[ei] ha-brit and parent(s) enter with baby. Depending on community norms they will hold the baby or honor the kvatter(in) *or prominent teachers present with doing so.*

[O] **LEADER:** Please be seated while the parent[s] continue with a message for the baby.

[O] **PARENT(S):** Little one, as Abraham chose for his household, as Tziporah chose for Gershom, so too are we prepared and ready to raise you as a member of the Jewish people, to teach you how to live a Jewish life. It is not for us alone to raise you. Over the years many of those here today will be a support to you, physically, emotionally, intellectually, and spiritually. We invite all those present to say their name and their connection to you through friendship and family.

Family and friends now take turns introducing themselves. If it is not Shabbat, you may want to preserve this on video.

[O] **LEADER:** The candle flame is the symbol of a Jewish soul, as we kindle the lights of covenant at this time, one for the soul of the child, the other for his/her connection to the Source of life. Let us chant a verse from Psalms in honor of this soul's place of welcome among our people.

> Or *hadash al tzion ta-ir, v'neezkeh kulanu bimheyrah l'orot.*
> A new light will illuminate Zion, may we merit to
> enjoy his/her light.

Note: Pachelbel's Canon in D *fits this verse and adds a nice element for families with non-Jewish friends or relatives present.*

[O] **LEADER** (speaking as though to the baby): Your grandparents _____ and _____ [or other relatives] will now give a brief history of your family.

Continue with the video/audio recording and definitely the writing of notes for the child's photo/memory album. (The act of circumcision for a boy is not to be photographed, lest the child one day be embarrassed by the public nudity.) If one side of the family is not Jewish, you can honor their presence by including their family history telling as well, if they so desire. Theirs is also an important part of the child's extended family story. Families take time to get to know each other and create shared lives. Ritual gatherings, which go beyond the formulaic aspects, present a powerful opportunity to do so.

Speakers on family history can be followed by another chorus of Or Hadash *or other appropriate psalm or song.* [O] *A selection of texts that might be read aloud by invited guests with good public speaking skills, include:*

I will establish my covenant between Me and you and your descendants after you for all generations, an eternal covenant, to be your G*d and that of your descendants after you. (Genesis 17:7)

Though the mountains may depart and the hills be shaken, My over-flowing love will never go away, my covenant of peace will not be shaken. (Isaiah 54:10)

Live in your blood and grow like a plant in the field.... I swore an oath to you and entered a covenant with you; you became mine, say the Lord G*d. Then I bathed you with water, washed away your blood and anointed you with oil. [*Note:* "you" is in the feminine in this sacred text.] (Ezekiel 17:8–9)

LEADER: All rise please as I declare the sacred phrase said by G*d to Abraham: *Hithaleh*, make your path, *l'fanai*, as G*d is your witness, *v'heh-yei tamim*, meaning, "be whole, have integrity, try always to manifest your best self."

LEADER OR PARENT:

Hineini
muhan [m] *muhana* [f]
u'm'zuman [m] *u'm'zumenet* [f]
l'kayem et mitzvat aseh

she-tzivanu ha-borei yitbarah
l'mol [b'ni].

l'hikaneis et bati ba-brit.

sibarti li-y'shuathah adonai
u'mitzvoteha ahsiti.
eliyahu mal-ah ha-brit,
hinei shel-ah l'faneha
amode al y'mini v'samheini.
sibarti li-y'shuathah adonai

sahse anohi al amarteha
k'motzei shlal rav.
Shalom rav l'ohavei torateha
v'eyn l'amo mihshole.
Ashrei tivhar u't'karev
yishkone hatzeireha.

Here I am
[the person performing the circumcision or rite of covenant]
ready and invited
to fulfill the positive mitzvah
as required by my Blessed Creator,

For a boy:
of circumcision ["of my son" is added if the parent happens to be
the professional doing the procedure].

For a girl:
to enter my/this daughter into the covenant.

I await Your deliverance, G*d,
I strive to live a mitzvah-centered life.
Elijah, angel of the covenant,
behold, before you, one who is for you.
Stand at my right side as my support.
I await Your deliverance, G*d,
I rejoice in your Torah as one who discovers undeserved riches.
Inner peace comes to those who love Torah, there's no obstacle for them.
Happy is one who chooses and approaches, such a one dwells
in Your courtyard.

All present attest joyfully from Psalms:

Nishb'ah b'toov bei<u>te</u>ha k'dosh hey<u>ha</u>le<u>ha</u>.
Your home (creation) is so good, such a holy palace!

The leader holds the baby and sets him or her in the Elijah chair as if teaching the child about it by again saying and invoking the legendarily sheltering presence of the prophet:

Zeh kisei shel eliyahu ha-navi za<u>h</u>or la-tov.
This chair is endowed with the good name earned
by the prophet Elijah.

[O] **LEADER** (passing the child to the grandparents): Young one, behold your grandparents and as you grow up, do them honor. May they be blessed with long life and may you be blessed to bring them *na<u>h</u>as*, satisfaction.

[O] **GRANDPARENT** (giving the child to the *sandek*/godparent(s) /sage to hold): You hold this child in your role as legal godparent, incorporated into the parents' will as such. May this never come to pass, may you never need to take him/her permanently into your home and even so may you be known and beloved to him/her as an honored and trustworthy mentor of life and tradition.

[O] I pass this child to be held by _____, honored teacher/scholar of our people.

For a boy, the leader returns the baby to the lap of the sandek(et), *who carefully holds the child so he won't move during the circumcision, or a cushion with soft Velcro straps or swaddling is used to briefly immobilize the child for his own safety.*

LEADER (*mohel[et]*):
> *Baruh atah adonai eloheynu meleh ha-olam, asher kidshanu*
> *b'mitzvotav v'tzivanu al ha-milah.*
> Blessed is the Source of life for the healthy holiness
> that comes through living a mitzvah-centered life,
> connecting us through the mitzvah of circumcision.

Ritual circumcision is now done.

FATHER (or if there is no father, the godfather/parent):
> *Baruh atah adonai eloheynu meleh ha-olam, asher kidshanu*
> *b'mitzvotav l'hahniso b'vreeto shel avraham avinu.*
> Blessed is the Source of life for the healthy holiness
> that comes through living a mitzvah-centered life, which includes
> entering this boy into the covenant of Abraham our father.

For a girl (also can be included for a boy), the leader lifts the cup of Miriam, Kos Miriam.

LEADER: This is the cup of the Miriam the prophetess, filled with spring water in honor of she who rescued her brother Moses by setting him afloat in the Nile and then bringing her mother to the Pharoah's daughter as his nurse. After the Israelites crossed the sea from slavery to freedom, Miriam led us in songs of celebration and tradition teaches, she found water for us in the wilderness. Water is the Jewish symbol for the divine blessing of abundance and loving-kindness. May this little one be so blessed.

For a girl only:
> *N'vareh et eym ha-olam, eyn mayyim hayyim asher kidshanu*
> *ba-brit ha-bat.*

Let us bless the mother of the world, wellspring of living waters, for
the healthy holiness conveyed through the covenant
of the daughter.

*Note: As there is no set format yet for this part of Jewish ritual for girls.
Your own innovations are vital and may well enter the stream of tradition.*

*The leader lightly spritzes the baby girl or touches her lips with gauze
dipped in spring water and chants:*

For girl:

MOTHER (or if no living mother, godmother):
N'vareh et eyn ha-hayyim, m'kor mitzvah l'hahnisah b'vreetah shel
sarah imeynu.
Let us bless the wellspring of life, source of the mitzvah to enter
her into the covenant of Sarah our mother.

ALL (for boy or girl):
K'shem nihn'sah (f) sheh-nihnas (m) la-brit, keyn tikaneys (f),
yikaneys (m) l'torah u'l'huppah u'l'maasim tovim.
Just as s/he has been entered into the covenant, so may s/he be
entered into a life of Torah, marriage, and good deeds.

*Note: Some prefer to substitute healthy relationships for the term mar-
riage, given today's multiplicity of lifestyles.*

LEADER: Please join me in chanting the blessing of vitality over this
kiddush cup filled to the brim with kosher red wine.
Baruh atah adonai eloheynu meleh ha-olam borei p'ri ha-gafen.
Blessed is the Source of life, Creator of the fruit of the vine.

*The baby is given a napkin corner dipped in the wine to suck, and in some
communities the mother, father, and siblings take a sacramental sip as well.*

For a boy, the leader continues with a lengthy Hebrew blessing regarding covenant and circumcision that concludes with blessing the Source, the One who koreit ha-brit, *cut the covenant.*

For a girl:

[O] **LEADER:** May the One who remembered Sarah, Rebecca, Rachel, Leah, and Hannah (with the gift of progeny) remember the covenant with Sarah and all mothers of Israel.

For a boy or girl:

LEADER: When Abraham and Sarah entered the covenant they were given Hebrew names to mark this great occasion. Your parents will now talk about your sacred name, why they have chosen it, and some of what they hope you will find in it.

Parents speak about the name[s] they have chosen for the child.

[O] **LEADER:** Will _____ and _____ please come forward to create the canopy of blessing over the baby.

A tallit *or the parents' wedding* huppah *or another symbolic familial fabric is used.*

LEADER:
> *Eloheynu velohei horeinu,*
> *kayeim et ha-yeled ha-zeh* (m)
> *ha-yalda ha-zot* (f)
> *l'horo* (m) *l'hor-ah* (f)
> *v'yikarei sh'mo* (m) *shem-ah* (f)

_____ben/bar _____.

Yismaḥu ha-horim!

Or for single parents:

Yismaḥ ha-av (or ha-eym)!

G*d of our ancestors, sustain this child for his/her parents
and let his/her name be known to the Jewish people as
_____ [Jewish name] son/daughter of
_____ [parent(s)].

Let the parents rejoice!
Let the father/mother rejoice!

LEADER: As it is written in the Torah, let us all recite Ezekiel's
blessing for life.

B'damḥa ḥayee (m) *B'dameyḥ ḥayee* (f)!
In your blood, live!

Some communities give the baby another suckle of wine at this point.

LEADER:

B'damḥa ḥayee (m)! *B'dameyḥ ḥayee* (f)!
In your blood, live!

*For a girl, the leader now requests that the Creator of the Universe accept
the rite of covenant.*

LEADER: Accept this rite of covenant, as if I had brought the child
before Your throne. This little child, may she become great. As she
has been entered into the covenant, so may her parent(s) be blessed
with long life to escort her into the study of Torah, to marriage, and
a life rich in good deeds.

For a boy, the leader continues:

LEADER: May the Source of blessing for Abraham and Sarah bless this child with complete healing of the circumcision site and the parents with long life to raise the child up in Torah, to see the child under the marriage canopy, and a life rich in good deeds.

[O] **ALL PRESENT:** May _____ [sacred name] be blessed with life. Bless _____ [sacred name] with the ability to live life, to give life, to live life, to always choose life. For our sons we pray, may this be the last drop of blood ever shed in your name. May you remember to use your power wisely. To our daughters we recall the talmudic metaphor of women as vines and the bleeding of a woman in her proper time as the wine of fertility. May you remember to use your power wisely. Little ones, male and female alike, are the precious fruit of the vine of the wandering Jews. We welcome you with this sip of wine symbolizing our prayer that you will have a strong, healthy, joyful life. May the covenant and its blessings travel through all our sons and daughters. May this little one be able to be fruitful and multiply and may your mother's recovery from her labor be swift and full. For our daughters and sons, let Ezekiel's blessing be fulfilled: "in your blood live, in your blood live."

[O] **LEADER:** I invite a sharing of blessings from those present.

Such blessings include those for long life, seeing the world, good friends, wonderful teachers, enduring health, and quality time with family. Be sure at least three guests know about this in advance so they can start the blessings rolling.

Now everyone sings:

> *Siman tov und mazel tov, und mazel tov und siman tov*
> May this be a good sign and good fortune
> *y'hay lanu, y'hay lanu, u'l'hol yisrael.*
> for us, for us and for all Israel.

As an alternative, Rabbi Robert Freedman teaches that the Sheheheyanu fits to the tune of Brahms's Lullaby. This would not be done in communities where parents said it already upon holding their baby for the first time.

It is traditional for all present to now share a celebratory meal, a seudah shel mitzvah.

PIDYON HA-BEN/BAT

A ritual for the firstborn child on the thirty-first day after the day of birth, this is traditionally done for a male child when all the following conditions are met. Other options will also be presented here because building family strength and recognizing the psychodynamic that comes with being a firstborn are certainly worthy reasons to gather in discussion and ritual.

- The child must be from a natural birth, not a C-section, and the mother must not have previously miscarried a fetus after forty days, the minimum Jewish criterion for viable fetal life.
- The child must not be a descendent of those who served in the sacrificial system, meaning a *Kohen* or a *Levite*, but from the majority, Israelite.

Let's explore the meaning of this ritual, and keep in mind that some have reclaimed this rite for all firstborn children.

For some, like Hannah in the Torah and many other matriarchs, a firstborn child arrives after a frustrating, depressing cycle of infertility. Out of gratitude for finally giving birth, Hannah dedicated the life of her firstborn to working in the Temple. When he was old enough, she sent him to be raised in the Temple by Eli the priest.

The other big story in Judaism is in Exodus, when the firstborn Israelite children were passed over and the firstborn children of their oppressors were killed. Tradition teaches us not to celebrate the deaths of such children; the losses of war and struggles for freedom are horrific. Today our children do not perform Temple service, but we can take note and recognize with compassion the other thing a firstborn may be called upon to do—to serve in a war.

The *Pidyon* ritual itself usually involves a meal but is not done on Shabbat. Having ritually washed their hands and said the blessing over bread (see volume II, *Meaning & Mitzvah: Daily Practice for Reclaiming Judaism through Prayer, God, Torah, Hebrew, Mitzvot and Peoplehood*, page 49), invited guests and family, except for the parents and baby, are seated around the dining room table:

RECIPE #18: The Rite of the Firstborn

1. *Option:* Welcoming melody or song—something from Jewish tradition or popular culture can be chosen.
2. *Option:* If those present are unfamiliar with the rite, someone at the table can provide an explanation of the symbols, meaning, and order of events.
3. Parent(s) enter carrying the baby; everyone stands up. If before the ritual there will be more teaching or discussion, it's okay to sit down again.

4. Be sure a *Kohen,* a descendant of the priests who served in Temple times, is present. This person will stand with the parents, who are holding the thirty-one-day-old child.

5. *Option:* Parents or a guest teach a bit about birth order in Jewish tradition and then open a discussion about birth order among those present.

6. The parent(s) turn to the *Kohen* and says, "This is my firstborn (son/daughter) who opened this mother's womb." (Traditional texts quote the relevant Torah portions; please consult a prayer book or rabbi's manual.)

7. The *Kohen* asks, "Which would you prefer, to give me—your firstborn or five silver coins, as is the tradition?"

8. The parent(s) reply, "To redeem this child, here is the money as we are obligated."

9. The parents have two blessings to say, the traditional induction verse, *Baruh atah* … the closing of which for this occasion is *al pidyon ha-ben* [or] *ha-bat,* and the *Sheheheyanu. Option:* Poetry or art relating to such an occasion might be found and shared.

10. The parent(s) then pass the silver to the *Kohen,* who receives it on behalf of the child and on behalf of the Temple workers in order to exempt the child from direct service.

11. The *Kohen* holds the silver above the child's head and says, "This instead of that, this in commutation for that, and this in remission for that. May this child be granted the life, learning, and respect that come from living in awe of creation."

12. *Option:* Pass around a *pushke,* or coin box, for guests to give to charity too; it's okay to insert checks and bills as well.

13. Next, the *Kohen* gives the traditional blessing for the well-being of the child and recites the traditional Priestly Benediction (see "Building the Nest," later in this chapter).

14. *Option:* Closing song or melody.

15. Now let's eat! A *seudat mitzvah,* a meal for the holding of a mitzvah, is generally served following the ceremony.

WEANING

Details of the weaning rituals of Jewish women in antiquity are not available to us, but we know there was a party and merrymaking. Still, it's a huge transition to that first sippy cup; the woman's body has to adjust to the absence of demand for milk, and the hours of intimacy are reduced as the child's independence increases.

What to do? One idea is to gather the family around to watch and applaud/praise the baby with the sippy cup. Now, share some of your favorite memories from nursing this child. This will likely have its humorous side. Given some of our cultural taboos, there are places women find to nurse that are hilarious—between coat racks and behind sculptures, for example.

AGE 3: FIRST HAIRCUT, RITUAL OF *UPSHIRIN*

Day thirty-three of the Omer, the time between Passover and Shavuot, is a traditional time to hold a ritual for a Jewish child's first haircut, which is generally not done until about three years of age. There's no law requiring this; it's just a sweet custom. This is done at a family gathering as a rite of transition, known as *upshirin* (Yiddish for haircut), celebrating the transition from being a curious and challenging toddler to a child capable of classroom learning and increasingly responsible behavior. In some communities, long strands of hair are left by the ears, called earlocks—*peyes* (Yiddish), *peyot* (Hebrew)—as a reminder of the importance of learning to be generous. This is also the customary age for a first written Torah lesson. Some put honey on a laminated card with a Hebrew letter on it and invite the child to have fun licking it off so that the letters of the *lashon kodesh*, the holy language, might always be sweet in his mouth. (For a full guide to *upshirin*, see volume I, *Reclaiming Judaism as a Spiritual Practice: Holy Days and Shabbat*, pages 121–128.)

BUILDING THE NEST

The culture of Jewish family life requires our attention. For the sake of brevity, since the first two volumes of this series focus in depth on the creation of a meaningful daily Jewish life, let's consider four core areas that most advance the potential for a healthy Jewish home:

1. The ability to identify and experience life as abundant in blessings.
2. An emphasis on learning and Torah study, coupled with the value of contributing to the understanding of Torah and the body of human knowledge.
3. Rituals that sculpt personal character and togetherness—time for Shabbat and holidays as well as life cycle rituals and rites of passage.
4. Caring relationships that flow from the qualities that undergird the living of a mitzvah-centered life, such as awe, respect, generosity, and empathy.

In Torah, Jews are often referred to as the children of Israel, *b'nai Yisrael*. Israel, the nation, is named for Abraham's grandson, Jacob, whose sacred name was changed to Yisrael, Israel, after a very difficult sequence of events in Jacob's life. Jacob's story makes for great reading. His character development is complex and illustrates how and why growing up is rich in both enchantments and challenges. Unlike Abraham, Jacob has children early enough and lives long enough for Torah to describe him as acting in the capacity of a grandfather. He has something very important to convey through his grandchildren. In contemporary life, this is illustrated when we bless our children on Friday night.

❧

Zak, age five, is standing, arms akimbo, while asking his parents: "Why do you always say you want us to be like Ephraim and Menashe? Who are they and what did they do that was so great?"

Zak's mom answers his original question: "Zak, the Torah teaches us that the founding fathers of the Jewish people were named Abraham, Isaac, and Jacob. But none of them could seem to be peaceful or get along with their brothers. Jacob's son Joseph learned the hard way about how important it is for brothers to get along. When he showed off his new coat of many colors to his brothers, they got so jealous they sold him into slavery! But Joseph survived and had children of his own, and Jacob saw that two of them, Ephraim and Menashe, got along beautifully with each other. So their grandpa Jacob made an example of their good behavior and gave them his blessing first, even before his own children. That is why to this very day on Shabbat we bless our children to be good like Ephraim and Menashe."

It is Friday night and we are visiting friends at their lovely home in the mountains of Pennsylvania. Shabbat candles, the glowing heart of a Jewish home, are dancing their reflections in the boy's eyes. It was wonderful watching Zak and his four-year-old sister Nili settle into their parents' laps for the Jewish tradition of bestowing a Friday night blessing. For many children, this blessing experience plants a lifelong memory of their parents' lap as the world's safest and most loving place.

I notice that some hold their children, as this couple does, on their laps, while others have the child stand in front of them, and then place a hand on the child's head or shoulder and say:

> Y'sim_hem elohim k'ephraim v'k'menashe
> May your G*d-given nature be
> like Ephraim and Menashe

Being an egalitarian household, they switch hands and heads and continue:

u'k'sarah, rivka, ra-hel v'lay-ah
and like Sarah, Rebecca, Rachael, and Leah.

Since the destruction of the sacrificial system, the table at home is the altar of Jewish life, where holiness happens by how we treat each other and our guests. The home is called the *mikdash m'at*, the little sanctuary. Heads of households are the high priests of modernity, meaning parents are the spiritual leaders of family life.

The couple continues in unison with what is known as *birkat ha-kohanim*, the Priestly Benediction from Numbers 6:24–26. They did the original in Hebrew, but I'm also including a personal interpretative translation.

The Priestly Benediction

INTERPRETIVE TRANSLATION

y'vareh-ha adonai   May you be blessed and
v'yishm'reh'hah   always know you are cared for
ya-eir adonai panahv eilehah   May you be illuminated with awe
v'yihuneka   and experience grace
yissa adonai   May you see the image of G*d raised up
panav elehah   toward you in each person.
v'yasem l'ha shalom   May your life be rich
                            in wholeness of body and spirit
                            and may you know the world at peace.

CLASSICAL TRANSLATION

May G*d bless you and protect you
May G*d's presence shine upon you
and be favorable to you
May G*d's face turn to you and give
you peace.

Traditionally, on Friday night a Jewish husband expresses gratitude to his wife by chanting verses known as the Woman of Valor, the *Eyshet Hayil*. Links to various translations and interpretations are available at ReclaimingJudaism.org. Some have recently written parallel pieces for wives to say to husbands. An alternative or additional tack is to go spontaneous:

RECIPE #19:
Expanding the Blessings of Children and Partners

- Before blessing the child(ren) at the Friday night dinner, each parent contemplates something each child did that week that was particularly meaningful and caring and tells about it. There is a Hasidic tradition of not criticizing people or things on Shabbat; this helps support that practice and builds self-esteem.

- After blessing the children, invite them to remember something their parents—and, if they are present, their grandparents—did that week that was particularly memorable. If there's a nanny or a mother's helper in the home and present, be sure to include appreciations of that person as well. Something like, "Mom, I want to thank you for the special thing you did this week when you read me the poem you found that you wrote when you were little." Or, "Dad, I want to appreciate going out sailing with you on Sunday." Or, "Karen, thank you for picking me up from school all week; it's great how you're always on time and I don't have to worry like other kids do about people remembering to pick them up." Patterns like these reinforce good memories, gratitude, and loving behaviors.

- Adults, especially parents and caretakers, present at the meal can turn to each other and give their own appreciations. "Barry, it meant so much that you offered to shop and make the meals all week so I could focus on finishing my manuscript." "Goldie, thanks for calling my mother in South Africa; she's been so worried about my brother who's ill. I know she appreciated your call of support."

Jewish families are legendary for rearing children who will grow up to contribute major advances in science and medicine, or for earning top awards for accomplishments in literature, education, art, music, and more. As the phrase *children of Israel* emphasizes, parenting matters and grandparenting matters. The structure and flow of the practices in a Jewish life help to build a child into a *mensch*, an ethical, capable, reliable, knowledgeable being. The person a child becomes is determined by more than genetics and more than having a village. There are identifiable characteristics in many Jewish homes that positively and profoundly influence whom a child is becoming.

The experience of life as abundant in blessings is a foundational Jewish perspective for raising a family. This idea becomes a child's authentic experience when Jewish blessing traditions are known and followed. The decision to create a Jewish family requires planning, parental agreement, and focused consciousness. Sending children to Hebrew day school or an afternoon or Sunday Hebrew school to get a Jewish education is a supplemental act; the value and values of Judaism take root only when they are the qualities emphasized and lived with integrity at home.

To keep our eyes wide open with wonder, our people are taught to pause and say unique blessings for experiences like:

- Seeing rainbows and lightning, eating fragrant fruits, and using a fragrant bark, such as cinnamon.
- The first times we are wearing an item of clothing, tasting a fruit coming into season, and holding your own newborn baby, and the first night of candlelighting at each of the festivals and joyful holy days.

- Hearing good news, seeing the first tree of the season in bloom, beginning and ending meals, for washing hands, for the rooster's ability to recognize and sound the dawn, for the ability of the body to function and heal, and many, many more.

Note: Most of us know some who turn such blessings into rote, formulaic experiences. Thoughtful parents and those serious about spirituality don't do that; they understand that Jewish blessing practice is designed to make sure that we do not become inured to, unaware of, or ungrateful for the manifold gifts in this life. This is part of what makes for great scientists, major poets, and delightful children!

Educational methods are always evolving; numerous new dynamic approaches are emerging that thankfully take into account that we all have learning differences. At the same time, some of the most traditional Jewish educational methods shape critical thinking in remarkable ways.

The culture of an effective Jewish family involves encouraging rigorous learning and teaching the patience and persistence necessary to find all possible options. Parents give a lot of thought to public versus private school; the same degree of research needs to go into a child's Jewish education. Don't sit in on religious services only when seeking out a community that responds to your own spiritual yearnings; also sit in on religious school life and youth group options before deciding on a community to join. Enlightened philosophies of education are spreading rapidly, but even so, it is important to check them out personally.

Some families also pay for weekly homeschooling sessions that they often attend with their children so that Jewish life and learning become a family experience. There are Jewish summer camps and retreat centers that offer programs for the whole family and range in options from Elat Chayyim's emphasis on spirituality and inclusiveness to the annual Yiddish culture retreat called Klezcamp to England's Limmud Conference, a model for learning in a context of respectful pluralism that's spreading worldwide, and many more.

Travel in Israel with time-intensive language study is like taking a booster rocket to a Jewish education. Explore, check for quality and what fits with the needs of your family. Scholarships are widely available for those financially strapped, so be sure to inquire while keeping in mind that most nonprofits, such as synagogues and Jewish schools, are almost always financially challenged, too.

RITUAL OF WELCOMING BODILY CHANGE

What ritual cues might we draw upon in our tradition to help a child move mindfully into the body of a young adult with appreciation for the holiness and health of her body, mind, and spirit? There was a European custom in many religious communities of a mother slapping a girl upon the arrival of her first period; some say that upon bringing blood to her daughter's cheek, the mother would then give her a blessing for health and fertility and a warning to guard her "gates" against premarital entry. This transition is far too significant a life marker to leave untouched or to be so addressed in our times. Some have tried creating women's circles to induct daughters into the mysteries of the body, but often daughters find this an uncomfortable scenario. Let us imagine an alternative scenario.

You are a female and get your period for the first time and are told, "Welcome to the sisterhood. May your life as a woman be filled with blessing! When your flow ceases this month, let's do a little ritual that you can do every month to honor the return of your body cycle, to ensure your well-being, and to welcome the restoration of your energy. Let me know when you are ready, and I will draw you a warm bath. We'll put a pan out to collect rainwater to add to your bath. Just as you are made of *mayim ḥayim*, living waters, so it is our custom to immerse in a *mikvah*, a pool of living waters, at the end of a cycle of life, which is the egg that has finished its season in your body.

"We'll put in perfumed bubbles or soothing salts, if you'd like. As you rest in the tub, you can review the month gone by. What is it that has lost potential this month, what are you letting go of? What is developing in fascinating ways that you wish to nurture? What blessings and strengths do you hope to draw on as a new cycle of days begins? Later, you might write these thoughts in a diary.

"You can also shape your thoughts into a prayer and whisper them—that is a tradition that goes all the way back to Hannah in the Bible. Your body is a sacred space and you deserve privacy in your bath. Should you wish to share any thoughts with me, I will listen with deep respect.

"This monthly mini-*mikvah* is also an important time to check over your body, which is developing so beautifully every day. It is good to enjoy and marvel at the woman you are becoming.

"Next month I will teach you another mitzvah, *shmirat ha-guf*—caring for your body and protecting yourself in several ways. Meanwhile, written in washable fabric paint on this hand towel is the *mikvah* blessing. I hope you will recite it and perhaps experience the tradition of the bath as a womb; slip under the water and emerge, reborn, into a new month of living and a new season of your life.

"This month, this *mikvah* is a celebration of your physical arrival as a woman. *Mazel tov!*"

Here are two version of the blessing for immersion that you may want to print on the hand towel.

Baru<u>h</u> atah adonai, eloheinu mele<u>h</u> ha-olam, asher kidshanu be-mitzvotav v'tzivatnu 'al ha-tevilah.

Blessed are you Lord, our G*d, King of the Universe, who has made us holy with your *mitzvot* and commanded us on immersion. (Traditional)

B'ru<u>h</u>a at yah, she<u>h</u>inah, hei ha-olamim, asher kidshatnu b'mitzvotehah v'tzivatnu al ha-t'vilah.

Blessed be G*d, Presence, Life of All Eternity,
we are made holy through Your sacred guidance to immerse.
(Using feminine God language)

The next month and months after might include teaching breast self-exam, contraception, AIDS and herpes awareness, and perhaps, given how early in life menstrual onset can begin, a particular focus on how nutrition influences a woman's long-term health and beauty.

Not every parent is up to such ritual encounters; a friend can be asked, if necessary, to serve as a surrogate aunt or mother. Some fathers have offered their daughters such support and done it beautifully.

Since these monthly bodily experiences are in themselves threshold times, try combining some new phrasing with the ending of the traditional daily blessing for the body, such as a simple blessing for breast or testicular self-examination.

One of the Hebrew names for God is *el shaddai*. *El* is a generic word in Hebrew and Mesopotamian for "God," and *shaddai* means "hills" or "breasts," and is sometimes translated as "Nurturing One."

B'shem el shaddai ekra	In the name of *el shaddai*
meleh ha-olam	I call out
avakesh beri'ut	King of Eternity,
u-shlaymut be-gufi u-ve-ruhi	I request health
b'hayai avareh et adonai	and wholeness in my body
rofei kol bassar	and spirit
u-maflee la'asot.	With my life I will bless G*d (my threshold) Healer of all flesh, Maker of miracles.

We've gone from conception to physical maturation. A season of exponential personal growth is just ahead, with new approaches emerging for becoming bar mitzvah and bat mitzvah.

6

Creating a Meaningful and Memorable Adult or Adolescent Bar/Bat Mitzvah

After serving in the Vietnam War it was difficult for veterans to find work. Especially someone like Randall O'Malley, who went "missing in action" while he was imprisoned and tortured, and who still struggles with memories that interrupt and slow his efforts. One day a man named Jake Weintraub hired Randy to work in his shop. Randy asked why Jake had hired him when no one else would. Jake, of blessed memory, replied, "Because it's a mitzvah."

Randy followed that word *mitzvah* everywhere. Not just in texts but also in people. It led him to the Jewish people. By 1970 Randall O'Malley had become Jewish, intent on living a mitzvah-centered life.

Thirty years later, on his seventieth birthday, Randy stood before his assembled family, friends, and community, chanted Torah, and blew our minds open by what he taught us that day when he became bar mitzvah.

Note: As in the author's extensive book on this subject, *Make Your Own Bar/Bat Mitzvah: A Personal Approach to Creating a Meaningful Rite of Passage*, from here on "B-mitzvah" will primarily be used out of respect for ink and trees and gender inclusiveness.

The B-mitzvah experience, when well-conceived, imbues the youth or adult student with a sense of him- or herself as an empowered, capable, knowledgeable, valued member of the family, community, and the Jewish people. The student has a primary assignment on the day of the B-mitzvah ritual: to inspire those in attendance by communicating an aspect of being Jewish—be it cultural or religious—that is relevant and inspiring to all those present. In other words, the student becomes a teacher to the inner circle of his life.

You don't have to give a speech to teach. Composing a ballad, a film, a play, or a serious artwork that inspires others are fine ways of teaching, too, depending on a student's community. The ways of communicating a Jewishly meaningful message are virtually boundless—with the caveat that interpretations of Shabbat observance and customs vary widely between communities, especially with regard to issues such as use of electricity and musical instruments.

TYPES OF B-MITZVAH OPTIONS

There are a number of B-mitzvah rites and study settings.

OPTION #1: CONGREGATIONAL

Today, a classic B-mitzvah ritual is one in which the student symbolically reveals Jewish life skills by chanting from the Torah scroll and then offers an inspiring interpretation of the weekly Torah portion during a religious service. Congregations often have additional expectations of the B-mitzvah student, such as chanting from the prophets; wearing of a *kippah* (skullcap), tallit (prayer shawl), and, on weekdays, *tefillin* (meditation boxes with straps); as well as lighting Shabbat candles; leading parts of a Shabbat, Monday, or Thursday service; regular service attendance; and organizing a social action initiative to help others materially or physically. Some communities reserve some of these elements for males only. Many congregations welcome innovation and creativity by the student in formulating the ritual. Be sure not to assume local norms; bring your questions to the presiding rabbi or cantor.

OPTION # 2: INDEPENDENT

In the twenty-first century, almost half of all B-mitzvah are being undertaken independently, rather than in conjunction with an existing Jewish institution or organization. These rites tend to be held in backyards, retreat centers, community centers, botanical gardens, hotels, Israel, and so on. Social action initiatives are often involved as well. Educators are engaged for private study, and ritual styles vary from the classical form of a Shabbat morning service to cultural gatherings. Among new B-mitzvah preparation phenomena are small, independent Jewish study groups formed by a group of individuals or families who hire a talented educator to work with bar/bat mitzvah students and their families in the home.

OPTION #3: CULTURAL OR VALUE-BASED

You don't have to be religious to be Jewish. Judaism is much more than a religion; it is a civilization comprising values, languages (Hebrew, Yiddish, Ladino, Aramaic), regional cuisines, music, literature, art and artists, dance forms, politics, and more. Communities that prefer a cultural or value-based B-mitzvah model also gather to experience the B-mitzvah student offering a presentation that demonstrates her depth of Jewish learning and maturation. This presentation might be based on a Torah portion, or on some other major Jewish literary, historical, ethical, or social justice action material, but it generally does not include the prayer components of a religious service.

Another effective model among nonreligious Jewish groups is for the student to select a topic of interest to study in depth and then to lead an intensive morning or afternoon session on the topic that is attended by members of the community. The session would include breaks for Jewish cultural sharing and appreciative toasts/comments by family and teachers. These kinds of B-mitzvah are fairly common among nonreligious Israelis and are also available through Jewish schools and groups such as Folkshul, Shalom Aleichem clubs, Secular Jewish Humanists, and, in Great Britain, a group called the Red Herring Club. The usual bar/bat mitzvah sequence is as follows:

1. Learning and living a baseline of Jewish values, cultural and religious traditions, sacred texts, and basic history of the Jewish people.
2. Planning, which involves gathering your B-mitzvah organizing team together to plan a process grounded in Jewish values that will lead to an emotionally satisfying, intellectually expanding, and spirited experience for the initiate and those in attendance.
3. Personal preparation by the student for his rite of passage that involves:
   - Designing a meaningful teaching based on the Torah portion that corresponds to the date of the rite, or on an aspect of Jewish life and learning about which the student is passionate.
   - Selecting and preparing a meaningful religious or cultural event that will resonate with the student's community of reference or preference (congregation, organization, school, or gathering of family and friends).
   - Formulating and undertaking, as a commitment to our Jewish future, a significant social action project, this year or next year, because being Jewish means caring about others less fortunate as well as caring for the planet.
4. Celebration, which fulfills the mitzvah of caring for our guests by ensuring a communal meal and seeing to their needs while they honor the B-mitzvah student's accomplishment and partake of Jewish cultural and secular forms of expressing joy, such as dance, song, and skits.

5. Expressions of appreciation by the initiate by means of:
   - A public statement of gratitude to parents, mentors, clergy, and those preparing and serving food and entertainment on the day of the rite. This is preferably done at the reception and not during a religious service. Better to keep the focus of the service on worship and not on self.
   - Thank-you notes sent in appreciation for gifts and special acts of loving-kindness received during this process.

WHAT AGE B-MITZVAH?

Technically, one becomes B-mitzvah simply by turning thirteen, even if no formal ritual or celebration is involved. Accordingly, it is not a requirement to hold an official rite of passage in adolescence. While many do so starting at age twelve for girls and thirteen for boys, a public B-mitzvah rite is viable at any age thereafter.

Under healthy learning conditions, a person matures because of the B-mitzvah preparation process and becomes response-*able* in new ways. Please don't undertake a B-mitzvah process of learning and planning a ritual and celebration just because everyone else is doing it or because of parental or communal pressure. It is right to undertake B-mitzvah when you are developmentally willing, curious, and have the time to learn new things about being Jewish and about yourself.

Forced B-mitzvah experiences result in trauma that can lead the student to feel negatively about self and Judaism. When a youth is hostile to the idea of becoming B-mitzvah, it is advisable to hold regular study periods with a Jewish mentor so the student is supported in continued development as a person and as a Jew, and to delay any ritual until the student feels enthusiastic and ready. That said, however, the joys of Jewishing are to be found in family life and community, so if B-mitzvah is delayed, it is essential to remain connected by attending religious school, youth group, summer camp, and/or Jewish life mentoring.

One day both mentor and student will feel that the time for a formal rite of passage is nearing. At that point, studies can shift to skills useful for the rite of passage. In the meantime, stay focused on what's important—exploring and creating a meaningful Jewish life that supports the challenging journey involved in growing up.

ADULT B-MITZVAH AND RE-MITZVAH

In the twenty-first century, B-mitzvah has become an important rite of Jewish revitalization among adults as well as a rite of passage from childhood into young adulthood for adolescents. Adults of all ages partake in it, most often those who:

- were not interested in the opportunity to prepare for B-mitzvah when they were younger
- were denied access to this rite by their parents (these are often women born before equal rites for women became available within Judaism or people who grew up in fully assimilated families)
- found their original bar or bat mitzvah experience unsatisfying and now want a "re-mitzvah" to renew their Jewish life and learning through the lens of greater maturity in a time of higher-quality Jewish education.

The term *simhat hohmah*, a Celebration of Wisdom, is sometimes used to refer to such rituals when they are undertaken as rites of maturation by women who are consciously assuming the role as a matriarch, a wisdom-source, and a guide for younger family members. *Timbrels and Torah* is a brief, powerful documentary about the first three such rituals. (For more information, see the Suggestions for Further Reading and Learning section at the back of this book.) However, there's no reason this term couldn't apply to men who are reframing and taking on the role of patriarch as well.

Remember, you're never too old to go up the mountain, to metaphorically stand at Sinai and receive insight from Torah and teach it to the inner circle of your life. There's no upper age limit on bar/bat mitzvah. B-mitzvah celebrations are late inventions in Jewish culture and still works in progress. They are the easiest of all rites of passage to customize in the context of a willing community or independent setting.

Following is a letter that I sent my father about the B-mitzvah of Randy, the veteran we met at the opening of this chapter. Questions to consider while reading it are:

- What touches you?
- What doesn't?
- What resources did Randy use to put his ideas together?
- What literary devices help make the teaching interesting?

You might use a highlighter to note points that capture your interest. Even if you're not on track to become B-mitzvah or re-mitzvah, Randy's teaching demonstrates a unique approach to learning from Torah and tradition in the context of modernity.

RECIPE #20:
Harvesting Pointers from Randy's Mind-Opening Torah Teaching

Dear Dad,

I wish you could have been at the bar mitzvah here today. Remember that Friday night last year after services when you were sharing stories about your war experiences with a fellow who had served in Vietnam? His name is Randy and he teaches at the Vocational School. He's a specialist in learning differences. Well,

Randy's a great example of the power and impact a bar mitzvah teaching can have. Auspiciously, his *parsha*, Torah portion, was titled Eikev: As a Consequence.

Randy asked us, "Wouldn't a boy be traumatized if he watched his people enslaved and beaten, all along knowing he had a secret—that he was one of them, and that this could one day happen to him? Moses was such a boy."

He continued: "Would Moses, who, as a young man, single-handedly killed a horrific slave master, fled his capital crime, and lived in hiding in a strange land in the household of a Midianite priest, not have suffered trauma at taking a life?

"Moses, who, as a man, found the insight and courage to organize a slave rebellion and help redeem his brother, sister, and people, also lived in exile for years not knowing their fate, more trauma.

"Moses was pursued into the sea bed by Pharaoh and his chari-oteers, only to lead his people through the perilous wilderness of Sinai, where enemies attacked and killed at times, where he watched his nephews, his brother's children, be fried to cinders, where plagues decimated his followers and rebellions were not uncommon. Was this not trauma?"

Randy told us he had done an Internet search to explore what intrigued him most: Why did Moses spend forty days and nights on the mountain top? Surely it would have been hard for a leader to leave his group for such a long period of time; it had to be more than a retreat for rest and relaxation. Randy had a theory that the time on the mountain was connected to Moses's trauma. Here's what he found in a traditional commentary:

He was learning Torah but kept forgetting it. Moses said to the Master of the Universe: "Look, I've had forty days and I don't know a thing. What should I do?' So the Holy One of Blessing gave the Torah to him as a present [i.e., carved in stone]. (Tanchuma Buber, Ki Tissa, 12)

Randy explained to us that traumatized individuals can manifest learning differences, temporarily or permanently, including difficulty remembering things. So teachers have to find other tools to help them. In this story, G*d realizes that Moses couldn't remember. He needed it written down.

In his Torah talk, Randy sensitized us to what it is like to be slowed down by a learning difference, and he compared himself to the many Hebrew school students he had observed showing attention deficit behaviors. Students' heads nodded constantly as he spoke. They were riveted; we all were. He also honored his bar mitzvah mentors by having them called up to the Torah during his service. They had gone out of their way to help him learn, to find the tools and techniques that enabled him to chant in the ways of his people, so he could study his portion and Judaism in depth and experience being a first-time teacher of Torah.

Randy's entire class from Vo-Tech attended his bar mitzvah. Many of his students got up to toast him at the party our community gave in honor of his accomplishments. They acclaimed him the greatest teacher they had ever met, their Moses.

Dad, I thought of you as he spoke, of how you overcame your challenges after being wounded while serving in World War II. Like Randy and Moses, you turned trauma into new ideas about living, understanding, and compassion for others. Through the privilege of knowing you both, and because of the Torah Randy taught me, I feel I now understand you both in new ways.

I know your own bar mitzvah was a big disappointment for you, and I was wondering if you'd ever thought of redoing it, of creating a re-mitzvah? I'm here for you.

With abounding love, Goldie

Whatever form of B-mitzvah works for you and the members of your family, the capacity to experience Torah as literature that inspires new ways of thinking and living is a vital part of your Jewish inheritance. Whether you believe it was written by G*d or humans, Torah is a core cultural referent for the Jewish people, which also infuses Western and Middle Eastern Jewish literature. It might make you angry, sad, or joyful; such reactions when deeply mined can yield important insights for the human future. Your reactions help align the Jewish people with the times in which we live in the context of evolving Jewish values. What you see and say matters: you can use the lens of Torah to teach a new way of looking at a social justice issue. This is a classic way of creating a B-mitzvah teaching. The converse is also classic—to find a point in Torah that our ancestors used as an opportunity to teach ethics, and to build a connection to our times from there.

- Key concepts for those preparing a Torah talk, often called a *dvar torah*, include reflecting on those who will be in attendance. What issues are pertinent to their lives? Who will be learning from you? Make your *dvar torah* relevant to your audience, and they will listen.
- Slow down when you speak. If it was worth using your life force to create, it's worth our hearing.

HOW *NOT* TO PREPARE FOR B-MITZVAH

When my father, Samuel Milgram, heard I was working with B-mitzvah students, while just a few towns away his grandson was rebelling against going to Hebrew school, he sat me down and told me the story of his own bar mitzvah, which was held in a *shtiebl*, a tiny local Orthodox congregation, in 1922. Dad's recollections will offer surprises for most readers.

Note: Please highlight the story below as you read in order to note your own points of reaction.

∿

"Daughter dear, I hear you are working on a bar mitzvah revolution. Did I ever tell you about my bar mitzvah?"

Oddly, he hadn't. In fact, none of the elders in the family ever had. I bade him go on.

"I used to go to Talmud Torah (religious school) between Third and Fourth on Catherine Street in South Philadelphia. Mr. Zentner was the principal of the school. It was an after-school thing during junior high.

"One day stands out in particular. I was the second to arrive for class. My friend Leibl Gratz, he says, 'Sam, I can't get this damn desk up in the air. I was going to hang it out the window.' So I say, 'Why do you want to do that?' He says, 'Come on, Sam, you're a good friend.' So I help him hang the desk out the window. The whole time we can see the neighbor lady across the street is watching, smiling, and laughing.

"Mr. Zentner comes running in—I guess the neighbor called him. He took one look and all he did was point and holler 'aroys fum dort dee banditin!' [Yiddish for "Away from there, you bandits!"]

"When I inform my father a few weeks later about this incident, he says to me: 'You are going to learn whether you like it or not.' So they changed me over to studying at home with an elderly rabbi.

"Ritual? Yes, we had a daily opening ritual. The rabbi would open the book and fall sound asleep within the first few minutes. I'd run out back to play and later come in, sit down, and nudge his leg. He'd wake up, and I'd say, "Time to stop, Rabbi." One day my father caught on. So I was switched to studying with another rabbi who lived right across the street. He knew how to apply a ruler to your knuckles and got all the 'bad boys' real good.

"Oh, you want to know about my bar mitzvah?

"We conveniently lived next door to the tiny Otik Moliver Synagogue. We walked next door for the ordinary morning service during the middle of the week. It was always difficult to get a minyan. I remember my cousin Harry came down; he was the only relative other than my dad present. There were eleven of us at my bar mitzvah, including me.

"I said the blessings, didn't read from the scroll—not an expectation back then—and then we went down to the musty basement meeting room. My father brought out a large marinated herring and a bottle of schnapps. All I got was congratulations—not even a shot of the liquor—and then everybody pats me on the head and my daddy says, 'Now you can go out and play in the street.'

"I remember my dad didn't give me a tallis. I'd thought I heard that your father gives you your first tallis, then I thought, 'Well, maybe that happens when you get married' ... well it didn't.

"I took my dad's tallis after he died—never really liked it. I never realized you could wash 'em. The only tallis I ever got was the one you gave me, beautiful. You brought it back from Israel along with that old joke about the Chinese laundry where the bill to launder the tallis is $200 and when asked why, the guy says, 'Do you know how long it took to untie all the knots?!'

"Did I tell you we each had this big book on our desks in Hebrew school, a _humash_ [Bible]? We did find a use for them—they were great for hiding comic books."

CONCEPT #1: SHARING YOUR VISION. One of the primary gifts in Judaism for a B-mitzvah student, whether an adult like Randy, introduced at the chapter opening, or a thirteen-year-old like Samuel, is the opportunity to pass verses of Torah through the lens of the student's life experience so that new insights form. While some of your insights will be personal, many are of a magnitude that merit being taught to others. You may have been born, in part, to bring these insights forward. Your life experience is unique; you have things to teach that no one else can. Don't let the system take this opportunity away from you.

On occasion, parents and clergy overstep their bounds and write the student's presentation for her. If someone tries to do this for you (or your child), just say no. It's fine to accept interesting ideas that might form the basis of your teaching, accept help with grammar and finding relevant Jewish sources, and seek assistance in working with technology. But your insights should be your own.

Every person's insights into living as a Jew are important. Some laypeople, rabbis, or educators might recoil at your interpretation of a biblical story. However, further study might show that the tradition also shared your view. For example, some interpreters view the biblical figures David and Jonathan as having been lovers. Whatever your special qualities may be, don't hesitate to bring your full self to the B-mitzvah experience.

CONCEPT #2: WORKING WITH YOUR LEARNING STYLE. Determined and talented as he was in many ways, Randy, of blessed memory, was simply unable to learn sitting still. He was like that as a child, too. By pacing the room during his studies and posting his study texts in large print on the wall so he could pause and look at them, he was able to learn with enthusiasm. Imagine if Samuel's teachers had known experiential teaching methods and how to work with learning differences! No matter what your age, go with your learning strengths. Don't allow systems to limit you. Explore and explain who you are and what you need. Every B-mitzvah student is different. If learning is hard for you or your student or child, consider getting a professional learning evaluation; the new methods out there might change your B-mitzvah experience and your life.

CONCEPT #3: FINDING JOY IN THE PROCESS. If you went to Hebrew school or religious school and felt as if you were treated like a computer hard drive to be packed with information, understand that it needn't be that way. You get to participate in picking your own mentors. B-mitzvah students need to be assertive in the teacher/tutor selection process. Families can learn a lot by asking about a tutor's educational philosophy. Let your tutor know about your specific hopes and needs. If your teacher doesn't relate to you as a person and clearly care about your development as a Jew, look further for resources and teachers who will work with you. You deserve it. Since mentoring/tutoring sometimes takes place behind closed doors, be sure to do a police background check. Unfortunately, it's worth the effort.

CONCEPT #4: JOINING THE JEWISH CONVERSATION. B-mitzvah is a time for in-depth exploration of the meaning and relevance of living as a Jew; it is exciting to take control of your own learning. You will find that every generation of Jews who have engaged with Torah and Jewish life has left inspiring and interesting evidence of what the experience meant to them. Much of this material is accessible to you on the Internet and in libraries, and since surely every B-mitzvah student merits owning a copy of the Torah, various translations are described in the Suggestions for Further Reading and Learning at the back of this book. Don't hesitate to write in the margins of your personal copy of prayer books, volumes of poetry, history books, and other Jewish texts like the *Tanah*. This, too, is a tradition. One day you'll look back and marvel at your thoughts and questions, as might later generations who inherit your books.

CONCEPT #5: SETTING THE "BAR." Adults get to set the level of the "bar" for their rite of passage. It took Randy forty years after becoming Jewish to feel that bar mitzvah was the next mountain he wanted to climb. He used the forty years Moses and the Israelites spent wandering in the wilderness as a metaphor for his own forty years of navigating learning and health challenges before feeling ready to fully receive and teach Torah.

Many congregations "preset the bar" for adolescent B-mitzvah. It is not clear that this is either helpful or empowering. These pre-sets come from wanting to be fair, to treat all students equally. In reality, unless parents get in the way, most youth set the bar higher than their teachers might, and if it is too high, they and their mentors can gradually modify their learning goals. This isn't a competition.

What is a reasonable baseline of knowledge to be able to stand before your community with integrity as a B-mitzvah, which means you are capable of living a knowledgeable, meaningful, mitzvah-centered life? While many communities establish stringent expec-tations for holding an adolescent B-mitzvah under their auspices, the most important criteria are those the students set for them-selves. Here is a brief exercise to help you "set the bar" for yourself, or to help someone else do so:

RECIPE #21:
What Do You Need to Know to Become B-Mitzvah?

- Imagine that an alien imperial commander has landed on earth and you are the representative of the Jewish people called to the bridge of the alien spaceship. The imperial commander asks you:
    1. To explain what it means to live as a Jew.
    2. How would learning the ways of the Jewish people help my civilization to experience and relate to being alive?
    3. What practices of the Jewish people advance the quality and experience of living for the individual and the world?
    4. What does your tradition teach as priorities for living?
    5. What are your people's ways of relating to people, ani-mals, creation, strangers?

6. How does being a member of the Jewish people help you deal with personal growth, tragedy, and change?

- You will know in your *kishkas*, Yiddish for "guts," when you contemplate your answer to these questions, whether you are ready to head straight into preparing for a B-mitzvah ritual, or whether your season of preparation will involve further immersion in the history, culture, and traditions of the Jewish people.

MATURING THROUGH THE B-MITZVAH PROCESS

There are two major dimensions for youth and adult personal growth during B-mitzvah—one involves maturing as a person, the other growing as a Jew. Some of the points to be considered by adults differ from those to be considered by youth. The two exercises below are designed to help make the differences apparent and the profound opportunities clear.

RECIPE #22:
Is an Adult
B-Mitzvah
the Right Rite
for You?

Check all that apply to help your decision-making process evolve:

❏ You are passionate about certain ideas and ideals. You'd be interested in seeing how Judaism approaches them and would love a way to bring your family and friends together to speak with them about this.

❏ You want to explore the meaning, relevance, and substance of Judaism or Jewish history, culture, or practice in greater depth.

❏ You feel that your understanding or practice of Judaism is more developed in some areas than it is in others.

❏ You had a B-mitzvah at twelve or thirteen but felt it wasn't worthwhile, and you would like to revisit the experience with better mentors through the lens of greater maturity. You would like a re-mitzvah.

❏ You were denied a B-mitzvah when you were younger as a result of your family's perspective or gender discrimination and really want to have one.

❏ You are in a chapter of your life where you would like to take on the responsibility of putting time into new learning and organizing a gathering of friends, family, and community to witness your adult rite of passage.

❏ More secular than religiously inclined? You focus on Jewish culture more so than religion in your studies.

❏ You have talents to bring to your experience, and learning differences, too. You want to create and present a ballad, ballet, play, photo essay, painting series, or movie about your Torah portion, instead of giving a *dvar torah*.

❏ In arranging for study mentors, you think of those who "do Jewish" in ways that attract your attention in positive ways. Could one or more of them mentor you in your B-mitzvah learning and ritual preparation adventure? You also want to enrich your studies with weekend retreats and travel to be mentored by authors and teachers who specialize in your interests.

NEW GOALS AND METHODS FOR ADOLESCENT B-MITZVAH PREPARATION

Everything worthwhile is worth "revisioning" from time to time with an eye toward—as the management world terms it—TQI: total quality improvement. It's high time to focus on new concepts and methods for creating a meaningful and memorable process of B-mitzvah preparation, ritual, and celebration. A healthy process supports age-appropriate shifts in maturity and transforms book and experiential knowledge into meaning for living.

In capable settings, B-mitzvah students engage in weekly or twice-weekly learning sessions at home or in religious school. Jews don't just study; we learn. Learning means knowing how to apply knowledge meaningfully in your life, not just being able to repeat what the text or teacher has said. In order to learn, you need more than coaching or tutoring; you need mentoring. Here is an example of the importance of this process:

Dear Reb Goldie,

I hope you don't mind my writing. I found your e-mail address on the Web. It's hard to believe I'm in college now and my bat mitzvah is so many years behind me. I've been going through such a painful time. I really wish you were here to talk to.

My folks split up last month and last week I lost my position as head of the student assembly. The board said I'm not myself lately, saying the wrong things, making leadership mistakes. I really thought seriously about killing myself, but then I remembered my bat mitzvah lessons with you. You said some things that I didn't fully understand at the time, but with all that's happened since, what you taught suddenly makes total sense.

Remember that we were studying about when Miriam got into big trouble and had to leave the Israelite camp, and Moses was afraid she'd end up like someone half-dead? You said that when times are rough, it can hurt so much that a person might think it would feel better just to be dead. You also said that life over the long run is too glorious to let the hard times wipe out all the future great times. Then I asked, So what does a person do when life hurts too much?

I think you said it can help to get away from the situation for a while, to do what Miriam did, to go on retreat. You said to seek out support from someone not involved, and to come back to the situation later.

So, frankly, I blew off my schoolwork and asked a good friend to go camping with me over the weekend. Out there in the forest I ranted and cried a lot just like you had said it's important to do. Even though I don't think I believe in G*d, I cried out how unfair this all is and how much it hurts, as though there were a G*d who listens.

After a long time in the forest, I eventually felt empty and got very quiet. I was surprised to find that losing the position at school wasn't the big thing for me; it's my parents' divorcing. I realized the board did me a favor; I should have stepped down myself because this isn't a really good time for me to have extra responsibilities. I'm just too sad right now to be in charge of anything. Out there in the forest I thought a lot about how my parents must also be hurting, and now they don't have each other to turn to.

I just can't believe we'll never have a whole family vacation again. I saw on your website that after Abraham almost killed Isaac as an act of faith, he and Sarah never saw each other again. Wow, Abraham and Sarah split!? I don't remember learning about that in Hebrew school. I looked up the verse you cited; it's right there in the Torah. Still, they had a mostly good, long life together. You also wrote that Isaac, Abraham and Sarah's son, really loved his wife, Rebecca. I take heart that Isaac's parents split up and still their child was capable of a loving relationship. So maybe I am, too. There's another reason to live.

I'm sorry this is so long. I'm really writing because I feel you got to know me, to care about me, and so you'll understand what I'm trying to say. But mostly I want to say, thank you. The Torah you taught me helped me hang onto life.

Alicia

∾

The seed of learning planted during bat mitzvah by the mentor of the young woman whose note is reprinted here was watered by life's tears and grew into inner strength for survival and greater self-understanding. That's what is meant here in *Living Jewish Life Cycle* by mentoring versus tutoring.

How can we make the B-mitzvah a forum for healthy growth? The following ideas are intended to help point the way.

RECIPE #23:
Sacred Shifts

Students often lament that they're not likely to be treated any more as adults after their B-mitzvah is completed than they were before their special day. On the other side of the equation, many communities complain that adolescent B-mitzvah students can be distressingly disruptive during class, services, and celebrations. Both sides want a maturation factor to emerge from this process. A B-mitzvah experience that will deeply delight and yield inspiration for everyone requires creative shifts in thinking with regard to preparation, planning, requirements, and celebrations.

Here are some key goals, desirable developmental shifts that, once thoughtfully addressed, are likely to increase the quality of B-mitzvah experience for all involved:

- Parents shift from stressed taskmasters to empowered family B-mitzvah team members.
- Youth go from being cared for like children to becoming young adults, caring for others by learning to recognize, respect, and consider the needs of others, and acting accordingly. They start taking on the mitzvah of helping one another by carrying out assigned hosting tasks at the B-mitzvah services and celebrations of family and friends.

- Youth unaccustomed to responsibility for major tasks are guided into becoming young adults who are trained, supported, and successful in carrying out the major life task of preparing for and becoming B-mitzvah.
- Youth discovering traditional interpretations of Torah are also mentored in how to find personal meaning for living through the lens of Torah.
- Students who are accustomed to passively receiving information are mentored in communicating meaning to others and step up to the plate at their B-mitzvah as empowered first-time teachers of Torah.
- Disempowered parents who engage tutors shift to being empowered parents who seek out meaning-making mentors, including family, friends, and professionals.
- Youth are guided in learning the Exodus story so they understand how people change as they themselves move from childhood into young adulthood.
- Youth move from the twenty-first-century culture of "self" to delighting in the realization that they are an important part of an amazing "tribe" with a rich, diverse culture, effective spiritual practices, and mitzvah-centered life models.
- Youth are mentored to engage their talents and learning strengths creatively throughout the B-mitzvah process so they become young adults preparing to serve as cultural, political, and religious contributors to the Jewish and world future.
- Families accustomed to party-planner-driven B-mitzvah celebrations become advocates for renewal of Jewish culture by bringing Jewish artists, *maggidim* (storytellers), folk dance teachers, *bad̲hanim* (humorists), and such back to the celebratory experience.

- Parents, youth, and educators can be helped to go beyond the written word to expressing and experiencing the prayer of their hearts and the interconnectedness of All Being (G*d) through living a mitzvah-centered life.
- Move the convention of engaging in a B-mitzvah social action mitzvah project to the year after B-mitzvah. Involve all families and students who have just completed B-mitzvah in a semester's collective study of a sequence of mitzvot, selected by the B-mitzvah graduates themselves. As these families grow in Jewish awareness, they can then collaborate and enjoy creating and completing a substantial and satisfying joint mitzvah project during the next semester. Studies show that up to 60 percent of families who attempt mitzvah projects during the year of preparing for a B-mitzvah do not complete them; they just get totally stressed out. Moving this project into a commitment for the year after B-mitzvah allows a maturing young person to experience the profound satisfaction of a job well done in the context of community collaboration that builds the Jewish future.

By identifying and implementing attainable objectives, based on these points, the B-mitzvah experience will become more powerfully engaging, memorable, and meaningful.

Now, having read the list above, create family team meetings to consider how to implement each item. If you are involved in a Jewish afternoon, weekly, or day school, bring these points to the principal and suggest a school board, parent, and faculty meeting process to create and agree upon objectives for each item that makes good sense as a B-mitzvah goal.

FINDING B-MITZVAH MENTORS

Mentors don't have to be experts in the tradition; the best mentors love their lives and their connection to Judaism. Who relates to

Judaism and life in ways you truly admire? Might they be willing to mentor you or your child?

Think.

Example: Well, there's Cousin Brad. He's a journalist. My Torah portion is about a war between the Israelites and the Moabites. Maybe he could help me write about my portion as though I were a reporter on the scene. Why doesn't war go away? I'd like to talk with him about that. And then there's Uncle Bennie, the way he chants the *Kiddush* over the wine, you can tell he loves doing it. I'd love to talk to him about that. Why is he so into it? And …

Who has talents like yours, who relates to Judaism and life in ways you might want to emulate? Who could help you use your talents in service to family and community through a Jewish lens on life?

Think.

Many conventional B-mitzvah tutors are more like coaches; they help the student learn how to chant prayers and Torah. As you saw from Samuel's Orthodox B-mitzvah in 1922, he wasn't expected to lead or chant anything other than the blessings when he was called up to the Torah. That's the way it used to be. Once communities started being able to afford cantors, those rabbis who weren't great at relating to adolescents would pass the B-mitzvah students over to them. Cantors are rarely specifically trained to interpret Torah. They are trained in the beauty and wide repertoire of Jewish music, especially synagogue music, so they train the students to lead services and chant Torah because it's what they do well, not because it was historically central to coming of age as a Jew. The ability to lead a meaningful Jewish life, to understand the rituals, prayers, and ethical responsibilities, is what was meant to be most important.

Are there Jewishly focused poets, chefs, artists, historians, or politicians available to you as mentors?

Think.

Are there graduates of advanced lay Jewish learning programs or students of Judaism at local universities who might become mentors?

Think.

Now call.

B-MITZVAH ISRAELI *HILONI* STYLE

Tali and her brother Gilad were born almost exactly one year apart, and they celebrated their B-mitzvah the same year and weekend. Their family isn't religious; they are *hiloni*, secular, but still very Jewish. They have a Passover seder every year and light a Hanukkah menorah, they picnic on Lag B'Omer and go to the beach on Shabbat, they have the whole extended local family over for Rosh Ha Shannah dinner, and their life has a Jewish rhythm, but going to services and daily prayer is not their way of being Jewish.

When Gilad and Tali needed to decide what Jewish studies to undertake for their rite of passage, they chose thirteen mitzvot to learn about and implement in their daily lives leading up to the day of their B-mitzvah family gathering. Tali and Gilad chose the following mitzvot to study and implement:

1. **Care and understanding of the body, *shmirat ha-guf.*** Changing bodies and voices is a big part of adolescence. The body is considered a gift, a temple for the soul's expression in this lifetime, and it is meant to be carefully cared for. Tali's Aunt Malki wanted her to understand the relationship between her heart and her changing body and so she held a women's wisdom circle for Tali a few weeks before the B-mitzvah. Five women gathered and shared stories about love and feelings both physical and emotional. Their sharings were geared to Tali's age

and yet planted important seeds of understanding for her teenage years and beyond. Each of the women also promised to be available to Tali to talk "confidentially" over the following years. Tali brought two girlfriends with her as companions, and when question time came around, they added theirs.

2. **Receiving and caring for guests, *hahnassat orhim.*** Tali and Gilad considered the traditional sources on this subject and discussed how to treat those around them as their guests in the world, not just on the day of their rite of passage but every day.

3. **The peace-keeping mitzvah, *shalom bayit.*** Both Tali and Gilad had been quite moody and argumentative lately; "hormonal," said their mom. They decided to engage in conscious acts of self-restraint that would make homelife more pleasant.

4. **The stumbling block mitzvah, *lo titeyn mikshol.*** Their grandma had broken her hip the previous year, falling on a rug in their kitchen, so they decided to visit each relative's apartment and give guidance on how to make it "elder-safe."

5. **The animal mitzvah, *tzaar baalei hayyim.*** Jewish values emphasize that no unnecessary pain be visited on living things. Tali and Gilad decided to explore the difference between free-range and conventionally raised animals and eventually convinced their parents to buy only free-range meats and poultry.

6. **The memory mitzvah, *yizkor.*** They were very close to their cousin, Dani, who was killed when a terrorist bomb went off at a B-mitzvah party in Israel. They decided to raise money in his name to fund a scholarship for an Israeli/Arab teen understanding project.

7. **The dangerous desire mitzvah, *lo tahmod.*** Tali noticed that she was sometimes mean to girls her age when she envied something they had that she didn't. Gilad noticed that he envied boys who were better at sports than he was. They decided to focus on being happy for those kids rather than

envying them. On their B-mitzvah day they both spoke about the happiness learning about and practicing this mitzvah had added to their lives.

8. **Deeds of loving-kindness, *gemilut ḥasadim*.** This mitzvah has an associated mitzvah, that of caring for widows and orphans. Tali and Gilad didn't personally know any widows or orphans and wondered what to do. Then they had a thought—what about caring for recently divorced relatives who were sad and lonely? They made a plan to take two relatives in that situation out for walks once each week. Not surprisingly, the aunt and uncle they selected became important mentors during their B-mitzvah process and may never have realized that this came about through an act of reciprocal mitzvah!

9. **The promise mitzvah, *nedarim*.** Taking care to honorably fulfill commitments they made had been a challenge for both Tali and Gilad up to this point. So they made a plan to set their cell phones with reminder rings to see if they could become more trustworthy. It worked beautifully.

10. **The masked mitzvah, *Megillah*.** While both Tali and Gilad had often participated in the wondrous street parades of costumed Purim revelers in Israel, neither understood how the story of Esther might be meaningful to them. They decided to read it out loud to each other. Then they studied some of the commentaries, attended a *Megillah* reading in their neighborhood on Purim and discussed with their mentors ideas about taking risks for freedom the way Esther did.

11. **The community pantry mitzvah, *tanhui*.** Tourism in Israel was way down the year of their B-mitzvah and many large families, especially religious families, were having trouble putting three meals on the table. Tali and Gilad searched on the Internet and found a shelter for battered women that was

short on food in a religious neighborhood only two bus stops away from their apartment. They rallied their family to set aside secular/religious differences and took food and treats to the mothers and children at the shelter.

12. **The time mitzvah, *Shabbat*.** Tali and Gilad learned from one of the religious families to whom they took food that it is not kosher to do homework on Shabbat because it's work. They decided to experiment with adding a touch of Shabbat to their B-mitzvah year. They decided not to watch TV on Shabbat and found that the extra time resulted in a deepening of their friendships.

13. **The reconnection mitzvah, *teshuvah*.** Their dad and his brother hadn't spoken to one another since they were teens. Tali and Gilad really wanted their uncle to be at their B-mitzvah so they asked their dad to consider reconnecting with his brother for their sake. While their dad and his brother didn't become best of friends, their uncle, his wife, and their children were invited and did attend Tali and Gilad's B-mitzvah, and the family healing was appreciated by all.

Tali's mom is Sephardi, and her grandmother loves to cook and bake, so they decided that she and her grandma, along with friends and other female relatives, would cook a buffet meal for the B-mitzvah celebration together. To this day Tali talks about what it was like to go to the market with her grandmother and aunts, to talk about family recipes, and to hear their stories about relatives she never knew. "We were tired but so happy to have made the party ourselves," she recalls.

Gilad's four uncles took him for a different kind of togetherness. They went on a Society for the Preservation of Nature working trip in Israel and not only got close to nature but also to each other. Gilad says that was his favorite B-mitzvah present of all.

At Tali and Gilad's B-mitzvah ritual, they spoke about the thirteen mitzvot they had chosen, and each of them shared one memorable encounter that had resulted. They also held up a picture of their cousin who had died and asked those present to continue contributing to the scholarship fund in his memory in the years to come.

One of their uncles picked up his violin and began to play Israeli dance music as everyone in the room joined in with joyful dancing. Gilad stepped into the center of the circle and taught a new dance created by one of his teachers. It was called *Rikkud Ahavat Olam*, a "Loving the World Dance," and Gilad asked everyone to join him in learning it as a closing prayer for peace. One of his grandfathers stepped forward at that moment and called Tali into the circle too. He then asked all the elders in the family to step up to bless these wonderful young adults.

CULTURE MATTERS

The McDonaldization of the world, as Dr. Steven Dinero of Philadelphia University has termed it, will soon be completely accomplished. Imagine being invited to an adolescent or adult rite of another culture—Native American, Japanese, Chinese, Moroccan, Mexican—and finding that when you walk in there is nothing particularly ethnic about what is going on—no chants, dances, none of the history or culture of the people.

Our people, who are known for their careful study of golf, tennis, theater, opera, organic gardening, historical restoration of homes, preservation of important artworks, and much more, are accidentally losing our own inheritance. Jewish culture abounds in language, music, dance, cuisine, philosophy, art, and literature.

This flattening of the world cultural palate to a predictable blandness is something that every B-mitzvah family can reduce through conscious inclusion of Jewish culture throughout the rite of passage. What elements might this involve?

- Sample some of the hundreds of Jewish folk dances that express love of life, love of the earth, harvest themes, family themes, mountain metaphors, and much more. There are circle dances and partner dances, slow dances and fast dances.
- Hire a Jewish folk dance instructor to come to the B-mitzvah party, or to the buffet after Friday night services, and teach two or three twenty-minute segments.
- Consider incorporating Jewish music in your ritual and celebration.
- Invite a composer of new Jewish music to perform and lead singing during your ritual and celebration.
- Get a klezmer, Sephardi, or Jewish fusion band like Atzilut involved in your ritual or celebration. Cultivate a taste for Jewish music by ordering a new CD or downloading links to Jewish music.
- Tap into our liturgical culture, which has both beauty and meaning. A healthy B-mitzvah learning process makes this clear.
- Infuse a B-mitzvah with meaning by placing the Torah scroll, a primary symbol of Jewish origins, front and center—both literally and figuratively. Most indigenous peoples ask those undergoing a tribal identity–related rite of passage to publicly do some traditional chants. This is also a Jewish tradition.
- Consider explaining to the B-mitzvah guests that the symbols for chanting Torah, generally known by the Yiddish term *trop*, pronounced trope, each represent a set of notes. There are a number of different Ashkenazi, Mizrahi, and Sephardi melody systems for *trop*; each community has its norms and preferences.
- Make your occasion a cause for new Jewish art.

- Commission a Jewish artist to illustrate the booklet of prayers or readings for your rite of passage with Jewish symbols and themes. Or do it yourself.
- If an organization or synagogue is the setting for your ritual or celebration, consider commissioning a mosaic or fabric artist to work with the synagogue youth group or religious school to create a beautiful wall hanging on a Jewish theme.
- Traditionally, a Jewish person receives a prayer shawl, a tallit, from a dear one on the occasion of B-mitzvah. Explore the wide range of finely made woven and silk *tallitot* (plural in modern Hebrew; *talleism* is plural in Yiddish) available, or you or those dear to you can make your own, incorporating sacred symbols, names, and phrases that are meaningful to you.
- In some communities it is traditional for men, and sometimes women, to wear *kippot*, skull caps that indicate that you are engaged in the mitzvah of prayer, or study, or have said blessings of gratitude for eating, and such. Find a word or phrase that you love in your Torah portion or readings and have it embossed in Hebrew, in transliteration, and in your local language, and illustrated on the *kippot* you provide to your guests. This way almost everyone in attendance will carry some Jewish learning home.
- Select a theme from your Torah portion or cultural sharing and have centerpieces made to illustrate it.
- Research some Jewish foods from around the world and consider a food festival of Jewish culture for the *seudah shel mitzvah*, the meal you will be serving your guests.

WHY THE B-MITZVAH GIRL WEPT

The soft crinkled leather of the small, old white book with gold lettering surprised her.

After opening numerous wrapped CD jewel cases of mostly duplicate recordings, five watches, and a pile of checks with mostly duplicate cards, Sandra's B-mitzvah continued to disappoint. Oh, she'd memorized, chanted, and spoken as required by the "bar mitzvah mill," as the cantor at her synagogue calls it. And the party was lavish. But sitting with what her brother called the "loot," she'd been sure she'd missed something important along the way, maybe something about the meaning of being Jewish or feeling the presence of G*d ... something.

But now her heart leapt in joy and amazement at the sight of the little worn white volume resting atop the crumpled wrapping. It was her mother's copy of Edna St. Vincent Millay poems, which she knew better than Torah. The pages were filled with tearstains and memories of her mom's own adolescence and loves longed for, won, and lost.

Sandra suffers from Crohn's disease, and during bouts of pain her mother would always bring out the little book to help her transcend physicality by sharing the moments of memory contained in those poems and written in the margins, often blurred with tears. At these times she spoke about savoring the sensation of a first kiss, surviving the loss of a first love, and even having a parent lose his job and move the family to another state. She spoke about mourning the loss of friends, changing schools, and starting a new, good life all over again, and then yet again.

A note came with the treasured volume:

Dear Sandra,

We have spent more time together than most parents and children are privileged to do these days. I treasure every moment with you. You are such a fine young woman—dignified, kind, determined, life-loving, curious, talented, and creative.

We owe you an apology. You were right to implore us to send you to your friend Lydia's synagogue for bat mitzvah preparation. Hers was indeed the kind of rite of initiation we had hoped for you. But we didn't really understand that until we attended Lydia's bat mitzvah last week and experienced the difference between a rote rite and one that is inspired. We promise we will work with you to plan a more meaningful Jewish future for our family.

After last week, while thumbing through this little book that has been so comforting through my pain and your own, the thought came that this is really the right present. We entrust this volume to you as a legacy and charge you with one day passing it on to just the right bat mitzvah daughter or niece or granddaughter of your own.

Next week, when we walk and talk and things are less frenetic, more gifts will arrive in the mail for you—two volumes by wonderful Jewish women poets of our times, one by Marge Piercy and another by Merle Feld. You are of an age when we're sure both of them will begin to speak to your heart, and now, if you so choose, your memories can also be written into the margins for generations to come.

With abounding love,
Mom and Dad

Touched, honored, feeling fully known and respected, Sandra wept.

In studies now widely available, some 73 percent of B-mitzvah students and families report disenchantment with the rote process of preparation practiced in most synagogues. They are clear about what they were hoping for—meaning; to discover the meaning for living to be found in Jewish practice; to receive the answer to the question, "I'm a good person anyway, so why be Jewish?" They yearn to experience life-touching, family-enriching Judaism by means of their local synagogue.

Meaning-making mentoring matters.
Readers, are you seeing necessary shifts
happening in bar/bat mitzvah preparation?
Spread the information by posting to the
blog at ReclamingJudaism.org.

7

Expanding Jewish Ritual Support
for the Many Stages of Adulthood

A recently popular aphorism states that "sixty is the new forty," the new prime of adult life. Whereas at the turn of the twentieth century a person could reasonably have expected to die at the age of forty-seven, today the average life expectancy in the United States is seventy-nine, and in some countries it's even higher. Children born today who have the benefit of good fortune, good genes, good diet, regular exercise, and state-of-the-art health care stand a decent chance of living beyond one hundred, and, some researchers predict, to 120.

One hundred and twenty! That's neither dog years nor biblical years, mind you. In the Torah, Moses lives to 120, which is the basis for the traditional Yiddish birthday blessing, *zolst leben biz hundert un tzvontzik*—may you live to 120.

One Shabbat morning, a colleague, Rabbi Lewis John Eron, announced that a well-loved resident of the home was about to celebrate a milestone birthday, and he wished that she live to the age of 120. At that moment, a friend of hers raised her voice and corrected him: "No, Rabbi, you should wish her 120 years and three months."

"Why the extra three months?" asked Rabbi Eron.

"Rabbi," she declared, "why should she spoil her last birthday? Don't you want her to enjoy her party?"

For those of us who live in developed countries, being alive in the twenty-first century is dramatically different from living in earlier times. It's worth pausing to consider just how very blessed we are, compared to those living one hundred–plus years ago, despite the environmental and political challenges of our times:

- Maternal mortality in the West was 65 percent higher at the turn of the twentieth century than it is today. The typical American woman had between seven and eight live births in her lifetime and researchers think she lived fewer than forty years on average.
- Antibiotics had not yet been invented, so infections festered in every organ, and surgery would more likely kill you than save you.
- Loss of teeth, due to untreatable infection and ignorance about oral hygiene, meant that people were unable to chew and activate the nutrients in food.
- Pollutants in the home and work environments led to lung, nerve, and skin destruction and early painful death.
- Crop failure was rampant, pest control virtually unknown, and famine a fact of life.
- Poverty was widespread.
- Orphans were incredibly common, usually lived on the streets, and almost always became hardened criminals.

Despite environmental and political challenges and the increase in obesity and diabetes, those in developed countries are healthier and living longer than ever in human history. We also have vastly more time to allocate to leisure pursuits. We have on average six decades of adulthood, contrasted with three at the turn of the twentieth century. How will Judaism evolve in response to expanded needs in an adult lifetime?

Longer life results in many more transitions for each of us. There are increasingly more:

- marriages, divorces, interim relationships, anniversaries, birthdays, and graduations.
- career and residential changes, geographic dispersion of families.
- shifts in health status, diagnosis, treatment, and survival of what were previously body- and mind-destroying diseases.
- opportunities for educational growth, advanced learning, publications, projects, exhibitions, interests, and travel.
- chances for experimentation, mistakes, personal growth, depth of understanding, exposure to diversity, and capacity to be understanding.
- choices in terms of morality.

WHAT DO RITES OF PASSAGE ACCOMPLISH?
(WRITTEN WITH HUBBATZIN BARRY BUB, MD)

As has been demonstrated in the previous chapters, rituals facilitate life cycle events or significant transitions by:

- providing the framework of support for desired or necessary change.
- allowing us to identify losses, something inherent to all transitions.
- acting as speed bumps that invite reflection and integration.
- affirming our identity and our place in the community.

- helping us see the bigger picture, which creates an experiential shift in awareness in the here and now, helping deepen and create meaning from experience.
- helping us to connect with the mystery of existence.
- providing nurturing.
- promoting healing and balance.
- supporting our emerging identity.
- supporting the family and community of the person in transition.
- providing a way to celebrate cycles and seasons.
- honoring and understanding patterns larger than ourselves.

Since our rituals have been determined over the centuries, it is up to us to find creative variations as well as to come up with new forms that become part of our culture.

PHASE I: PREPARATION

The initial idea: You feel the need to enact or commemorate a major event in your life. A thought occurs—how about a ritual? Some questions to ask yourself:

- What is the significance of the transition, what do I want the ritual to support, what do I need? (A guide to seeing points in your adult life that might merit a new ritual appears later in this chapter.)
- What metaphors, myths, or stories from Jewish and local culture come to mind as symbolizing me or my transition?

RECIPE #24:

Phases in the Creation and Enactment of a New or Adapted Jewish Rite of Passage

(written with Barry Bub, MD)

PHASE II: COLLECTING DATA

Gather material and concepts for the ritual process, including, for example, poetry, songs, symbols, and people who have brought you to this place in life. This is best done by writing down freely whatever thoughts arise. To facilitate this process consider the following:

- Who will facilitate and share in the planning of this ritual?
- Will I base this ritual on an existing one from within Judaism or will I design a totally original one?
- Who do I envision being present? Who comprises my inner circle? Who feels safe to have present? Who might be touched by this? (Also see volume I, *Reclaiming Judaism as a Spiritual Practice: Holy Days and Shabbat*, pages 48–49.)
- What symbols would I want for this ritual?
- When should the ritual take place? How much time do I need to plan, design, and send out invitations; prepare myself emotionally; set up; and host this event?
- Where is the most appropriate place for the ritual? How will we create sacred space?
- Who is connected to this transition? How will they be impacted by it? Will they be included in the ritual? How?

PHASE III: DESIGN

Look at each stage of the ritual and determine what form it will take. To do this, draw on the material you have already accumulated as well as new thoughts that will emerge during the process.

THE STAGES

1. Preparing yourself.
2. Preparing the space.
3. Singing or playing a familiar, appropriate melody that those present can join in. This signals that the ritual is about to begin.

4. Offering words of welcome.
5. Declaring the intention.
6. Telling the story.
7. Using symbolic music, poetry, and actions to signify the transition you are commemorating. This can occur anywhere in the ritual. In the middle there are usually specific symbolic actions that highlight the particular transition.
8. Inviting blessings.
9. Closing melody or prayer.
10. Serving the meal.

PHASE IV: LOGISTICS

Each stage of the ritual needs a basic script so that the process goes smoothly, is well-integrated and uninterrupted, yet leaves room for spontaneous expression and genuine emotion to emerge.

A timetable is essential, including who is assigned to follow through with tasks like making room reservations, obtaining ritual objects, text reproduction, décor items, foods, setup, welcome, and clean up. Depending on the nature of the event, you might also assign someone to videotape or photograph the ritual.

PHASE V: ENACTMENT

The process of preparing for the ritual is in itself an essential part of the shift that comes from the enactment. A wealth of memories, emotions, and perhaps awareness arise in those preparing to participate. The enactment is the climax of the process.

PHASE VI: INTEGRATION

In the days, weeks, and months after the ritual, you will begin to savor the unfolding of its effects. Try to avoid microanalyzing the inevitable glitches that occurred, and allow the overall experience to fill your soul.

On the one-year anniversary of the ritual, revisit memories, plans, images, and symbols. What has shifted? Is more needed or did a difficult or precious season of life unfold that now resides comfortably in your past?

RECIPE #25:
Observing
Adult
Birthdays

In the Talmud we read of Rabbis who timed completion of important studies to coincide with their birthdays. They would hold a gathering, offer a meal, and teach a *siyyum*, sharing a summary of their learning. Remember that the Talmud, as well as texts of Kabbalah and H̲asidism, often give credence to astrology, indicating that the time of a person's birth is auspicious for good things to happen.

- Consider using your lunar, Jewish birthdate to celebrate. This is easily found at Hebcal.com, which offers a simple way to type in your secular birthdate and identify your Jewish birthdate.
- Take time for self-reflection and contemplation on your birthday.
- Or consider timing a partner study or group study of a major book to finish as close to your birthday as feasible. This book might be a tractate of Talmud or a volume of *Encyclopedia Judaica*, or something like Viktor Frankl's *Man's Search for Meaning* or another profoundly rich text for a mature adult, such as Dr. Judith Plaskow's *Standing Again at Sinai*, Rabbi Adin Steinsaltz's *The Strife of the Spirit*, or Estelle Frankl's *Sacred Therapy*, or perhaps consider a volume from this *Reclaiming Judaism* series. Prepare a summary of your learning to share with friends. Or you

might look up the Torah portion that was paired by tradition with your actual birthdate, study it, and give a teaching based on it to your friends.

- Organize a session with a *mashpia*, a Jewish counselor regarding matters of heart and soul, as a birthday present for yourself. Someone with this training can help you have a vision for your future, study your Torah portion in a way that will touch your heart and impact your spirit. All staff at ReclaimingJudaism.org offer *mashpia* support via telephone and can also refer you to local professionals with this training.

- For each decade leading up to this birthday, select one photo or symbolic item that stimulates an important memory or reflects the theme from a chapter of your life. Use these as cues to harvest and teach some of your life's hard-earned wisdom as well as some of the most delightful times. Be real. Place the pictures around the periphery of a table around which you set seats for a minyan, ten of your friends, those who really "get who you are."

- Arrange a musical collage of pieces that have touched your spirit during these decades of life. Let the music accompany the stories you tell about each decade of your life. Consider distributing song sheets; people need ways to participate in ritual, not just be witnesses.

- Designate money to a worthy cause in honor of your birthday and ask those in attendance not to bring gifts but to join you in using this auspicious date to expand the good that is possible in the world.

- Invite each friend to take turns sharing memories of seeing you grow and learn, and have them give you an honest blessing that can help you frame your future.

- Serve a nice meal to fulfill the mitzvah of caring for guests.

RECIPE #26:
The Jewish
Way: Finding
New Strength
after Failure

One of the painful realities of an evolving life is the inevitability of failing at something at which we dearly wanted to succeed—school, work, sports, an invention, a hobby, artistic work, and, of course, loving relationships. As it says in Proverbs 24:16, "[Even] the *tzaddik* (the most righteous) will fall seven times and will rise." Any of us who have failed at one or more of these in a big way probably said and did some unfortunate things upon learning of the toxic outcome of our best labors. Judaism's sages offer wiser, healthy, profound ways to relate to this difficult place on the sine wave of life.

When Moses's sister Miriam is demoted from the Israelites' key leadership triangle of Moses, Miriam, and Aaron in Numbers 12:1–16, she is sent out of the camp for a period of time, which, on the surface of things, seems to be in order to heal from tza-ra'at, an outbreak of white scales on her skin viewed as quite serious in the Torah. Toxic shame at being demeaned is dangerous to undergo around those from whom you may later want letters of reference, to coexist with in community, or to see at family gatherings.

This is why businesses want the desk of a person who's been fired cleared out and the person off-premises the very day of the firing—to protect the employee as well as the work site. Perhaps, we can imagine, the prophetess Miriam sublimating her rage at the power of the patriarchy to marginalize her vision, views, voice, and values into her frightening skin eruption, tza-ra'at. (Learn more about this scene and why tza-ra'at is not leprosy, as it has long been mistranslated, in volume II, *Meaning & Mitzvah: Daily Practices for Reclaiming Judaism through Prayer, God, Torah, Hebrew, Mizvot and Peoplehood,* pages 126–129.)

Wisely, Miriam is sent out of the camp, on retreat you might say, to get a grip on herself (and decide whether to hire a lawyer or a therapist—just kidding). She also has time to marinate contemplatively in the stew of what has come undone in her life so she one day returns to her community re-centered and with dignity even if she still profoundly disagrees with the judgment against her.

Accordingly, the spirituality of healthy failure includes promptly getting away from the scene and all the involved players lest we soil that nest irremediably with our negativity. In other words, even if you weren't a good fit for that situation, you might still get a good reference for your good characteristics and outcomes.

After somehow getting yourself away from it all, take time for pure mourning of what was, what was expected, and what isn't going to be the case anymore. Sackcloth and ashes almost seem reasonable when failure hurts so much that it is hard to keep living. This sounds severe, but even when things don't look extreme to an objective observer, they can feel this way to the one who missed the mark for which she was aiming. A safe, quiet place for tears, anger, and grief is essential.

Consider the verse from Torah:

> I will sprinkle pure water upon you and you will be pure from all your errors and all your idols will I purify you. I will give you a new heart and I will give within you a new spirit and I will turn the heart of stone from out of your flesh and I will give you a heart of flesh. (Ezekiel 36:27)

This verse reminds us that our human spirit must go through the process of weeping in order to soften and process our rage and pain, lest we move forward into life wounded and at risk of compounding our failure, instead of emerging from a difficult time a bit older and far wiser.

Eventually grieving and blaming others, rightly or wrongly, leads to acceptance of "what is" and we begin to look inward to see how we may have contributed to the situation. This is the most spiritual part, when we let go of ego and self-righteous indignation. Fossil fuel for a better future, energy for living, comes as we break down our old assumptions and sense of self and probe deeply for what can be learned from this experience, and possibly related ones, about who we are and what we might want to consider upgrading about ourselves. After a time, surprisingly, we will be ready to try again, in a different time and place, with "new eyes" for how to proceed in healthier, more effective ways. Judaism understands that this kind of descent into despair is going to happen to humans repeatedly, that it is inherent in the very design of creation. This is beautifully articulated in a phrase from Hasidic literature: *yeridah l'tzoreh aliyah*—a descent necessary for ascent.

1. Metaphorically speaking, what "idols" have led to your own failures?
2. How does pure water (tears? *mikvah*? loving-kindness to self?) help keep a heart from hardening?
3. How can the process in these verses and this recipe lead to "a new spirit"?

As our awareness of our own role or overlooked cues in some situations builds, we have apologies to make. When the light of new awareness dawns, the ascent back to community, family, joy of life happens quite naturally. It will be alright. It helps to have gone through this once; the next time it's still no fun, but you can tolerate the process knowing great good comes from this.

Take profound care during such times. Get massages. Limit social engagements to very best friends and only those who can keep a confidence, so bitterness doesn't cause you to spill your sorry tale more places than you'd want it to be known if you were in your right mind. Learning that you are going to be divorced or fired from a job, for example, when you didn't see it coming, can result in an actual acute stress reaction and lead to some of the characteristics of post-trau-matic stress disorder. Muscles and bones may ache, or you'll have sleep disturbances and no energy, flashbacks to when you heard the news, and a tendency to constantly replay scenes that might have clues to why, why, why? Let others drive, be careful on steps, avoid medicating your pain with drugs or alcohol—this is an important time to feel deeply, to trust your body's process. If you feel suicidal, make sure someone stays with you and that you get professional help. Don't take chances with the gift of life; all things pass eventually. Because it will not only be alright, it will soon be better than it was before. All of us have been there, too.

The day comes when there will be those with whom you need to do *teshuvah*, relationship repair, those we blamed unfairly for our descent, those we said hurtful things to in our exhaustion or pain. A transformed person can do this without feeling shame as much as joy at the potential for a different kind of connection and a correction of something about the "other" that may have left her wounded emotionally. It's all good.

SURVIVING A LIFE-THREATENING SITUATION

The traditional reasons for saying the blessing known as *benching gomel* are found in Psalm 107, which speaks of one who

crossed a desert (v. 4–5)
was released from prison (v. 10–12)
fell seriously ill and recovered (v. 17–18)
returned from travel at sea (v. 23–27)

The *gomel* prayer, "blessing beneficence," conveys the sense that you feel you have made it through a difficult or frightening life passage by sheer grace. *Gomel* is typically recited in synagogue after the Torah reading in a call and response mode. The spiritual dynamic involves your community's being simultaneously informed that you've been through something serious and uplifted by dint of your presence or the news of your recovery. Expanding the traditional times to say this to include surviving birthing, car accidents, cancer treatment, military service, major surgery and terrorist attacks is another example of how Jewish rites can be stretched to offer support in changing times (Shul<u>h</u>an Aru<u>h</u> Ore<u>h</u> <u>H</u>ayyim 219:9).

Birkat ha-gomel is as follows:

The person recovering says:

> *Baru<u>h</u> atah adonai elohenu mele<u>h</u> ha-olam*
> *n'varke<u>h</u> et m'kor ha-<u>h</u>ayyim ha-gomel l'<u>h</u>ayahvim tovot*
> *she<u>h</u>-g'mah-lah-ni kol tov.*

Let us bless the Source of Life that bestows goodness,
> for having bestowed such goodness upon me.

And the community responds:

> *Ameyn. Mee-she<u>h</u>-g'malay<u>h</u> kol tov,*
> *[hu] yeegmalay<u>h</u> kol tov. Selah.*

Amen. May the One who dealt goodly to you [continue to] bestow all [possible] goodness upon you. So may it be!

DAILY PRAYER FOR HEALING AFTER SURGERY

The integration of new knowledge in medicine with Jewish tradition can be introduced within prayer, not only within ritual. Here is an example jointly composed with my hubbatzin, Barry Bub, MD, written for those whose surgery involves the healing of bone.

Praised be the Source of Life, present in the miracle of human being, for the healing powers of body, mind, and spirit.
Grant me ever-renewing faith, courage, and comfort.
May each osteoblast, the cells that heal bones, be like the angel Gabriel, bringing strength and healing bonding.

May each white corpuscle, the cells that conquer infection,
Be like the angel Uriel, carrying healing light to the site of surgery,
    rapidly closing each wound.

May each medication be supported by Your messenger Raphael,
    the angel of healing. Let each droplet of medication be a
    healing dew for me, Your creation.

May the presence of Your angel Micha-el lovingly
    support the talented staff at this special hospital.
    May Your presence, Holy One, light up my spirit,
    nurturing me and my loved ones now and forever more.

Blessed is the Source of Life. Amen.

MOVING TO A NEW LEVEL OF PHYSICAL AWARENESS, CHANGE AND MATURATION

Surviving domestic violence or sexual abuse, graduations, retirement, job changes, coming out as gay or lesbian, sex changes, publishing a book, hysterectomy, mastectomy, and other major physical changes are among the many changes and transitions in adulthood for which there are already a number of adapted and innovative rites of passage available.

Some have also created major menopause rituals, but the genre has not really caught on. The process tends to be quite gradual unless it's induced by surgery or medication. It's a season most postreproductive women seem to welcome, and, as with *birkat ha-gomel*, something as simple as a blessing or sacred phrase can have the necessary impact.

There is a verse in Jewish prayer that names G*d as *m'shaneh itim u'mahaleef et ha-z'manim*, "who changes the seasons and transforms the times." Let this sacred phrase become a mantra that calms and comforts you and supports familial resilience, for, indeed, this too shall pass.

HONORING THE SHIFT FROM DAUGHTER/SON TO CAREGIVER

My mother has Alzheimer's disease. One day while I was combing her hair, Mom pointed in the mirror to me or to her own image—I wasn't sure which—and asked in an alarmed manner, "Who is that?"

Confused, I pointed to myself and asked, "Do you mean me? I'm your daughter. My name is Goldie, Mom."

"No," Mom protested. Visibly agitated she placed her finger to her own image in the mirror. "Who is that woman? Why is she here? What is her name?!"

My mother, physically healthy save for incontinence, had lost another layer in the relentless progress of Alzheimer's; she had finally lost her self. I stepped out of the room to weep and rail against heaven's way.

Becoming a caregiver to an elder parent is a major life transition, as is becoming dependent upon your children and/or spouse for care. The latter stages of the aging process are rife with rites of passage—assigning power of attorney and health care proxy; beginning to sign checks and documents for Mom or Dad; emptying and selling the family home; helping parents bathe, toilet and dress; organizing home health care; moving to various types of elder communities, rehabilitation, or skilled nursing facilities; surrendering the car keys; ceasing to cook for yourself; the shift to diapers, plastic mattress covers, and perhaps a walker or wheelchair; and for most, some degree of memory loss.

We read in Torah, "Before an elder, rise and pay honor to the face of age, be awestruck regarding *Elohim, I am Adonai* (Leviticus 19:32). Sometimes grief-struck can be a form of awestruck. How to respond or manage this difficult transition? I recommend doing so in community by means of a ritual that allows us to remember and honor the people who can no longer remember us while also acknowledging the burden we try to manage honorably.

RECIPE #27: Memories of Those Who No Longer Remember

- Gather participants in a group, encouraging each to bring a picture of the person they are caring for in a state of full vitality, illuminated by the fullness of personality.
- Allow time for each participant to share his or her story of life with this person before and now.
- Invite each participant, if they wish, to bring something symbolic of their parent as a way to stimulate sharing. I brought a ring my mother gave me for my bat mitzvah. She had bought it from a Native American craftsman in New Mexico on her first adventure away from her Orthodox home enclave in New York. She'd told me the ring carried the blessing for me to "see the world." Her blessing proved most effective.
- Lead participants in reading Jewish quotations or a text on aging, perhaps the Hosea text (2:19) in relation to parents and partners.
- Each participant who wishes to can say, "I forgive myself for … [not visiting as often as I know I should, for yelling when I don't mean to, for holding on to old gripes that we can never resolve, for …]"

- Without reciting the whole prayer (that time hasn't come yet), perhaps include the refrain from the *Kaddish*, which blesses the Great Name, the Unity of All Being, which surely includes that of parent and child.
- Pass an envelope around for those who wish to give funds for Alzheimer's research and also send around a letter for those present to sign voicing appreciation to the geriatric center staff who care for our family members.

If you choose to hold such a ritual, you might also consider meeting annually or quarterly, as is the case with *Yizkor*, the memorial service that is part of each of the festivals.

May you be blessed to add to the tradition with your own ideas and rites for life's inevitable and sometimes unanticipated adult passages. Now, in the next chapter, we come to ritual processes well-perfected over time. The dying, death, funeral, and mourning practices of the Jewish people are deeply effective and quite substantial.

8

Leaving Life
Dying, Death, Burial, Mourning, and Memorial

A year after the death of Sue's teenage daughter, I asked, "How did the shiva *experience feel for you?" "Like softly gloved hands were helping me through the tunnel of necessary grief. I became pure mourning, held by the rhythm of the evening services in our home, rarely rising from the ocean of tears cleansing my shattered world except to say* Kaddish, *marking time, integrating loss while the life I loved dissolved. As the week progressed, I realized those hands were connected to faces; friends, family, and yours, Rabbi. Now, each time someone new rises to say* Kaddish, *though I am now seated, my heart rises with that person."*

Jewish dying, burial, and mourning practices offer a system of support for getting through the death of a family member or other significant person in your life. There are specific spiritual practices for leaving one's own life with depth and dignity. There is also a beautiful and powerful depth of culture involved that requires transmission from one generation to the next. Many did not receive that transmission following the traumas of World War II, so mentoring will be provided here.

PART I: CONSIDERATIONS BEFORE DYING

Write and regularly update a *legal will*, an *ethical will* (see pages 211–215), a *living will*, and *power of attorney for finance* and *health care*; be sure to specify in your living will your intention regarding organ donation.

ACQUIRING THE DEED TO YOUR *KEVER*, GRAVE

"For you are dust and to dust you will return" (Genesis 3:19). Jewish tradition views humanity as created from earth, so we are responsible for the rapid return of our body's remaining nutrients to the earth to support the cycle of all living things. Most traditionally, this is done within twenty-four hours. It is customary to prearrange a grave for yourself; many do this in late midlife. Arranging for a family plot with a prepaid perpetual care contract reduces stress on future generations and creates a genealogical cluster of grave markers that may become meaningful to those who come long after you.

A cemetery, *beit olam*, "eternal home," becomes sacred ground because of the dedicated use the community selects for it. Used Torahs, prayer books, anything written that is no longer of use because of damage or obsolescence that contains the most sacred, unpronounceable name of G*d (the *Yud Hey Vav Hey*, termed the tetragrammaton and usually pronounced *Adonai* in prayer and *HaShem* during study) must also be buried in a Jewish cemetery so that these items will return their material value to the earth and won't be treated like garbage and desecrated through any public, institutional disposal mechanism. The grave for such items is called a *genizah*, from the root word that means "hidden." Burying a human body, which is also a manifestation of the image of G*d, serves the same function. Jewish tradition compares a body to a Torah scroll so worn it can no longer be restored for use. These must both be treated with respect for their term of sacred service, and their physical substance returned to nourish the earth.

Before moving forward, let's first examine the remarkable evolution of the Jewish view on organ donation.

SURPRISING NEWS: WHAT JUDAISM SAYS ABOUT ORGAN DONATION

Depending on your age, you might remember the Jewish view of organ donation as being very different from what it is today. Now that organ transplantation has become a highly successful, lifesaving procedure, it is deemed an obligatory act, a *mitzvah hiyuvit*, by every major branch of Judaism, with only a few rabbis dissenting. In our time, not to bequeath your organs has become a transgression of the mitzvah of *pikuah nefesh*, "saving a life," a primary Jewish value. At any given moment, more than forty thousand people are on the waiting list of the United Network for Organ Sharing. Since taking the medical steps necessary to save your life if at all possible is also obligatory under Jewish law and custom, *accepting* an organ transplant when it would be the most effective way of extending your life has become obligatory as well.

Three verses from Torah frame the contemporary view on acceptance of organ donation: "You shall not stand by the blood of your neighbor" (Leviticus 19:16), "You shall surely heal" (Exodus 21:19), and "You shall restore" [a lost object, which includes someone's health] (Exodus 23:4).

There were, however, issues to work through. The freshest organs often are the most viable, but important Jewish texts and prevailing traditions seemed to call for both heartbeat and breathing to have stopped in order for a person to be officially declared dead. And a donor heart must be kept pumping after brain death if it is to remain viable for transplant. So what to do?

Authorities in Jewish medical law delved into the sources and practices condoned by *gedolim*, great teachers of traditional life such as Rabbi Moshe Feinstein, and determined that the actual Jewish legal criterion for death was not cessation of heartbeat, but rather the permanent loss of the independent ability to breathe—which could be noticed around the chest, mouth, or nose. These scholars also undertook to learn about new technologies and determinations of death unknown to prior Jewish authorities, such as reliable tests for brain stem death. As a consequence, all Jewish denominations now have initiatives in place to encourage the mitzvah of organ donation.

Our tradition also treats a cadaver as sacred space, not to be viewed or invaded once the soul has moved on and can no longer animate that body in its own unique way. For this reason, autopsy is allowed only under very restrictive circumstances—to save a life (in proving the facts in a murder investigation, to determine a devastating genetic disease pattern, or to restore mental health to an extremely distraught family member). The primacy of the integrity of a body is most definitely trumped by the mitzvah of saving a life.

So what about donating an organ while you are alive—is that also a mitzvah? As long as it will not endanger your own life, donation of bone marrow and organs such as a lung or a kidney by a living donor is a *mitzvah kiyumit*, praiseworthy, but not obligatory, since with all surgery there is some risk and for some, great fear.

RECIPE #28:
Ensuring That
Your Wishes
Will Be
Followed

Emotions are complicated and decisions get confusing when a loved one dies. Misplaced zeal and misinformation all too often lead families to block a soul's chance to fulfill the postmortem mitzvah of organ donation. There are special organ donor cards, teaching videos, and excellent articles available on this subject for every kind of Jew and Jewish family.

- Be sure to brief your family in advance about your decision.
- Sign the back of your driver's license to indicate that this is your intention, or, if you are following the guidance of

a rabbi who maintains specific hala<u>h</u>ic criteria for organ donation, place a card such as that available at www.hods.org (Halachic Organ Donor Society) in your wallet with details.

- Include information about your desires and specific guidelines from your rabbi in any legal health proxy you sign, and add a note indicating that "this decision is part of my commitment as a Jew to fulfill the mitzvah of *pikua<u>h</u> nefesh*. It is permitted."

> May you be blessed to examine your intentions,
> to take the time to honor and overcome
> any inner fears or conceptual obstacles
> to making the mitzvah of organ donation.
> Remember, "If you save one life
> it is as if you saved an entire world" *(Mishnah Sanhedrin 4:6).*

RECIPE #29: In Your Own Words: Creating an Ethical Will

What values do you hope your children or students will carry on? An ethical will allows you to give voice to what you have learned in a form that can be transmitted to future generations. While there are whole books written on the subject, here is a simple guide, plus an example, to let you try out the process of creating an ethical will. This can be done at any age. Things to consider for your ethical will:

- What values are most important to you?
- Where did you miss the ethical targets you've aimed for that merit inclusion in this document?
- What teachers, experiences, or qualities of self have had the greatest impact upon your life and relationships?
- What literary sources or images can you draw on? Will you illustrate this piece? Record it? Write it?

- What remains unsaid or under-said that needs to be expressed?
- How can you show your significant others in a positive way that you "get" who they are, that you appreciate their qualities and how they navigate their challenges?
- In Torah, receiving the blessing of a parent is a poignant and powerful experience. What blessings do you want to give?
- Do you want to allow visits while you are alive to pass along some of this personally, rather than in writing?

As an example, here is my ethical will, which I have upgraded three times so far; there will hopefully be more.

Dear Parents, Husband, and Children,

Revisiting an ethical will after a major car accident certainly intensifies the importance of this effort. I often find myself deeply regretting not being available to my family when I am on the road for teaching assignments or immersed in writing, art, or study. My dear husband and children, you have been more gracious about these absences than is reasonable to expect. Mark, you once told someone when you were about eight years old that your mommy was away teaching in Russia on assignment from G*d. While I was relieved to hear your creative rationalization, nothing can make up for what has been lost. As my beloved hubbatzin Barry says, writing an ethical will can also be a wake-up call.

The need to discover how to live meaningfully through a Jewish lens was borne inside from my earliest years. No amount of trying to stray from being a teacher of Torah and Jewish spiritual practice into secular pursuits has ever worked out for me; it is the path I was born to. This is a happy convergence—Jews hoping to learn and teach emerge in every corner of creation. When we teach, our students offer and elicit new understandings. It is exhilarating and wondrous to watch students evolving. That's what Torah can do in healthy hands and hearts—help us to evolve, to raise the cake of civilization in every possible emergent ethical way. As one who believes not a whit in messiahs, I believe that humanity's only great hope is that we can evolve physically, emotionally, intellectually, and spiritually.

A dear colleague, Rabbi Rami Shapiro, teaches that a primary principle for his life is "First do no harm," the great axiom undergirding the medical profession. While aspiring always to keep to this path, I pray those who have experienced my errors in judgment and style will be able to heal. A better aphorism for my life would be from our tradition: "Those who have not sampled all the permitted things this world has to offer will be held accountable in the world to come" (Talmud, Yerushalmi Kiddushin). Of Rabbi Samson Raphael Hirsch it is said that after returning from a visit to the Alps, provided to him as a gift from his students, he realized that humanity is accountable for more than Torah study and dealing honestly with others. He imagined a G*d who could ask: "Have you seen my Alps?" Loving life so, like a butterfly drawn to every gorgeous flower, I tend to flit about the world, not only teaching but also touring, fulfilling the mitzvah of *yirah*—awe. I pray that you, too, will continue the family legacy of both exploring and caring about the world, nature, and humanity. Nothing can motivate a person to live in harmony with creation as much as experiencing its fullness.

My sons, Adam and Mark, you, too, are born teachers, as are your stepsiblings Jonathan, Juliette, and Jeremy. May you be blessed to continue being nourished by profound teachers and mentors, as I have been so blessed. Adam and Mark, may you fulfill your career aspirations to become professors and any further healthy goals that emerge. Like a fine wine, may your burgeoning knowledge mature into wisdom. From this wisdom may you nurture healthy, satisfying relationships with family and students, and may you be blessed with your own children and grandchildren. Juliette, may your ability to connect art, science, and spirit erupt into ever more awesome levels of awareness. Jonathan, may your dedication to Torah bring you surprising insights that you add to the repertoire of the generations. Jeremy, may the kindness you so generously bestow on all come back to you a thousandfold in this life.

The ability to function as an effective change agent, to fulfill the mitzvah of *tikkun olam*, "repair of the world," has also been an ethical imperative in my life, as it is in any serious Jewish life. There are things to change everywhere—to increase inclusivity and care for the environment, to try to help reduce the suffering of those sore of spirit, promote possible pathways to peace, and make advances in the field of experiential education. I notice you, my beloved family, do not shy away from your ethical awarenesses; you move into thoughtful, effective, inclusive action, and I am very proud of you. Justice, fairness, kindness, and improving the quality of life for all sentient life forms starts with each of us.

Beyond knowledge is what Rabbi Zalman Schachter-Shalomi calls the G*d Field. Here the Unity of All-Being comes to teach us that we are all interdependent. I pray you will live with the attitude inherent in the mitzvah of *haḥnassat orḥim*, to treat every person around you as your guest, wherever you may be. This may be the secret to sustainable love, even peace.

I hope you are also reading my relationship with Barry like a book. By stretching one another in the dimensions where we each fall short, he and I have generated not only conflict but also profound joy and growth. I have never felt so well met and infuriatingly well-challenged as with my beloved hubbatzin. You who are all children of divorce maybe find it hard to trust that an intimate relationship can evolve and endure. My parents taught me that the hard times are the truest test of love; the easy times are the reward. I am infinitely grateful to my parents, yet alive, thank G*d, Samuel and Leona, for their perpetual unconditional support, for transmitting their passion for art, music, literature, kindness, generosity, and a harmonious human future through me to you.

To our burgeoning flock of grandchildren—Jason, Natalia, Simon, Simcha Naftalie, David Hayyim, and Benyamin Zev—don't believe everything your parents tell you; there is more to the world than any parent, myself included, ever realizes. As our tradition teaches: "Find a friend, make yourself a teacher, go and learn!" One of my life goals has been to be a true and good friend. Among a minyan or more of precious close friends, I have been blessed with extraordinarily loyal, loving best friends and extended family. It is hard to imagine an existence, if there is a next life, without you.

Barry, if you are alive to read this, know that even from my travels into Mystery I will be blessing you to bring your capacity for love, joy, and growth into a future loving relationship. Let someone new walk this life with you; she will be very fortunate. May the tears of this time shine through the light of your love and yield a rainbow of new possibilities. If there is something after this, I hope it will be many, many years before I have the joy of welcoming you on the other side.

With abounding love,
Goldie

PART 2: THE DIGNITY OF DYING: A CORE JEWISH PRINCIPLE

The time of dying is an important time of healing. The individual who is dying does not cease to have experiences that are transformative. The potential in this lifetime exists until death. For family members, many of whom may have been distant, absent, with words unspoken, slights never fully resolved, this is an opportunity to set aside differences and find room for connection.

Everyone, not only the dying, is on a journey. One specific task of the loved ones, with the help of health care and spiritual care team members, is to set the stage for the soul's departure. This means keeping comfortable but not infantilizing, and caring without impeding the inevitable.

When physically possible, dying is a process of consciously completing a mitzvah-centered life. The Jewish approach to dying involves several major life tasks including:

TESHUVAH. Engage in all possible healthy efforts to heal open wounds in relationships before your death. If there are wounds that you are responsible for keeping open, do everything in your power to release the person involved from responsibility and make sure she is informed. Leave this world with a clean slate; your ability to do this mitzvah, called *teshuvah*, will affect the wellness of future generations. (To learn more, see volume I, *Reclaiming Judaism as a Spiritual Practice: Holy Days and Shabbat*, pages 15–33.)

GOSES. At the point when your doctors report that you are likely to be within three days of dying, you are considered to be a *goses*, one who is not to be disturbed. In order for families to implement this practice, it is important that they understand it in advance. Tell them, and in your living will leave instructions, that when this point is reached, people should disturb you as little as possible. This does not, however, mean leaving you unattended or in pain; a dying person should not feel abandoned (Shulḥan Aruḥ, Yoreh Deah 339:4). That said, nothing should be done that might interfere with your soul's work of preparation and departure.

VIDUI. This is a traditional piece of liturgy in which you take responsibility for what you've done in your life. Some elect to add to the liturgy from their own life's specific journey. Those who are uncomfortable with G*d language may also create their own simple, free-flowing statements. Often translated as "confession," a process-based approach to this idea is termed "life review." Those clergy with clinical pastoral counseling training can be wonderful guides through an end-of-life review process.

Here is an interpretive version of the shorter of the several traditional *Vidui* options. Items in brackets are my options, not traditional ones:

> Here, as I face the Threshold of life, I acknowledge that I am not in control of my recovery or death. May it be that a total recovery will take place, but, if I die, may my death atone for my errors, wrongful actions, and willfully missed opportunities [for good in this life]. May my portion [if there is an afterlife] be edenic. May I merit the quality of afterlife that [one would hope] is available to the righteous. (Continue with the *Shema*.)

SHEMA. This is the sacred phrase we say when going to sleep, waking up, and leaving this life.

Shema yisrael adonai eloheynu adonai eḥad.

No translation effectively conveys the meaning of this phrase,
which reads like an Aha! moment: "Listen! G*d is One."

AN EXAMPLE OF DYING WITH DIGNITY

Midwifing a soul's departure is subtle, holy work, and while some clergy may prove helpful, everyone is involved. This account is told by Gary Cohen, in memory of Edward M. Cohen, Eliyah Meir ben Feivel v'Sarah.

We get embedded in a fabric. The fabric of all includes when Reb Goldie came to Boston to do a *hanukkat ha-bayit*, a gathering to dedicate a new living space by hanging a mezuzah on the front door of my new home. This was surprisingly moving to my dad. You see, my father was embarrassed and squeamish about ritual. That it was a mezuzah, and not Shabbos candles, at that moment must have fit his state of consciousness. In a twelve-year struggle with prostate cancer, he was unable to acknowledge that he was himself in the "doorway" space and that he was going to be "crossing over" from one space to another. Every time I rehang my mezuzah, I think of how moved my dad was as we nailed it into the doorpost of my home.

Then my dad moved to hospice. In his room, on the wall opposite his bed near the doorway, was a gold crucifix with Jesus on it. That particular hospice is a sensitive Christian organization, and they'd asked him when he checked in if he wanted it taken down. His response was "I can use all the help I can get. Leave it there."

On one of my visits, my brother was in town and Mom was there, too. For some reason I'd noticed the car mezuzah Reb Goldie had given me in the glove compartment and thought maybe I needed to bring that upstairs to his room. I did so, and asked if he had any interest in our putting the mezuzah up in the room. And he said, "Absolutely, yes. Put it up next to Jesus." That whole room was a gateway, for sure.

So I said yes to that. Realizing I was a wee bit fuzzy on the right *bra<u>h</u>ah*, blessing, I went to the nurses' station to use the Internet to print out the tune and words for the mezuzah-hanging blessings.

Sitting at the computer terminal was a young doctor we had come to know and like. He had a Jewish-sounding family name, so we asked him if we could use the Internet and chatted with him about why. I told him about the *hanukkat ha-bayit* Reb Goldie had led and her teaching about using the mezuzah as a consciousness-shifting reminder as we move from one space to another, which seemed deeply applicable to a hospice room.

So the doctor said, "Can I join you for the ceremony?" He came in and we recited the blessing—my mom, my brother, my dad, the doctor, and me. I affixed the mezuzah with double-sided tape and it stayed there for two and a half months.

The evening my dad died, they took his body to the funeral home. The mezuzah was the last thing I pried off as I left the room. And I sent it to the doctor with a note that read: "Keep listening."

To understand the *Shema*, you have to understand the shhh sound, a reminder to be quiet for a second. A mezuzah is a fundamental listening totem, a reminder I'd think for physicians especially. You have to wonder why physicians, in addition to a stethoscope, don't carry a portable mezuzah and stick it on the door of every hospital and exam room when they walk in. How much better would American health care be if they did this, especially in a hospice? Since physical healing isn't possible at that point, what more can you do than make the person comfortable and listen?

Not all Jewish families would have felt comfortable leaving the crucifix at the Christian hospice on the wall. Some would have sought out a more traditional kind of mezuzah for the hospice room. It is pertinent that the new custom of the car mezuzah has the traditional prayer for travel inside, certainly appropriate for a soul anticipating departure. And all of us can learn to listen better. Even professional listeners, when confronted with the loss of a loved one, can become anxious and forget to maintain the healing power of a pure listening presence.

> When someone is in the throes of dying
> we don't implore them to stay,
> paper their final minutes with chatter,
> or deny their reality.

Our role is passive:
to allow this soul the space it needs to depart.
While those left behind must suffer
and grow beyond the loss,
the soul may be moving on
to adventures we cannot predict.

An important, often told talmudic story is that of Rabbi Akiva's dying. His room was filled with his students who were praying, imploring G*d to keep their great teacher in life. His housekeeper went to the roof and threw off a pot so it shattered on the ground, attracting the students' attention to the window. In the seconds of their distraction, his soul was given the necessary space to leave this world. Jewish tradition favors the housekeeper's wisdom as _hesed_, pure loving-kindness. Even though it meant the end of her employment, she wanted nothing for herself; she lived a mitzvah-centered, rather than a self-centered, life.

RECIPE #30:
Listening at
the Threshold

In addition to the listening of those visiting, there is a special form of listening for the one departing. This exercise takes you through the _Shema_ one word at a time. Deepening your relationship with this sacred phrase in life increases its power when we say it at death.

> **Shema**—Listen

Listening is such a central Jewish principle that tradition teaches a dying person to leave life, as he does when going to sleep, by saying the sacred phrase that begins with this word, _shema_, "Listen!" A dying person is not meant to be listening to the sounds of distressed family, nor the incessant beeping of hospital equipment. Dying is a time to listen at the gateway that leads out of life, beyond the threshold of the body. You might listen for the voice of G*d or for whatever experience might be awaiting you after embodied life ends.

Shema **yisrael**

Yisrael was the name given to Jacob, and by association it is the terminology for all his descendants and those who have joined his lineage, the Jewish people. This phrase was first said by Moses— you are hearing it across space and time, repeating an instruction of Torah en route to the mystery beyond.

Shema yisrael **adonai**

Dying is a time of "threshold," *Adonai* consciousness. The root letters of *Adonai—aleph, daled, nun—*spell *eh-den*, "threshold." A huge sacred shift is taking place, from attention to affairs in this life to listening into the Beyond.

Shema yisrael adonai **eloheynu**

Eloheynu, our G*d-sense, this threshold place of mystery—what is it?

Shema yisrael adonai eloheynu adonai **e<u>h</u>ad**.

E<u>h</u>ad means "One." Judaism teaches that life begins when the baby's head emerges from the birth canal and the first breath is drawn. That is when our soul enters, when our individual G*d-spark, what makes us in the image of G*d and fully human, arrives. At the end of life, we exhale our last breath, and the soul crosses the threshold of the body as a song leaves a cello to fall on ears Beyond, to be appreciated and to reconnect its energy with its Source. Like a mobius strip, a soul's life before, during, and after is all a manifestation of the One.

LOVING AND LEAVING

In traditional prayer services, the *Shema* is bracketed by prayers that are about love. On the threshold of leaving this life, look back on the truth of your life, concluding with those you have loved and those times you loved, remembering.

- A traditional *Vidui* is appropriate.
- By saying the *Shema* when you are aware that death is imminent, you are putting a mezuzah up at the threshold of your life. Your soul may be about to move beyond your body. If tradition has it right, you will be pleasantly surprised.
- Should you not have time to do this, know that it will be done for you if a Jewish hospice or chaplaincy program or a family rabbi is involved in your dying and death process.

(Additional *Shema* teachings can be found in *Meaning & Mitzvah: Daily Practices for Reclaiming Judaism through Prayer, God, Torah, Hebrew, Mitzvot and Peoplehood*, pages xi–xii, 13, 15, 32–33.)

PART 3: DEATH

In 1986 the chief rabbinate of Israel ruled that death would be determined by these factors:

1. Clear knowledge of the cause of injury.
2. Absolute cessation of natural breathing (not breathing that requires a respirator).
3. Clinical proof that the brain stem is indeed dead.
4. Objective proof, such as the BAER test, that the brain stem is dead and proof that numbers two and three continue for at least twelve hours under full and normal treatment.

These criteria are widely cited and applied in health care settings involving Jewish patients, though there are rabbis and *poskim* who do not rule in accordance with them.

IS THERE A WORLD TO COME?

Many options exist within the range of traditional Jewish sources on this question:

SOME SAY: The world to come is the world we leave to our children.

SOME SAY: The body will be physically resurrected into renewed life when a messiah or messianic age dawns.

SOME SAY: Souls travel disembodied through many levels in another realm of being until they rejoin the pool of all souls or cluster to create a wisdom pool called the "World's oversoul."

SOME SAY: There is a form of reincarnation, *gilgul*. You may be surprised to learn this means that souls that have not yet reached the level of *tzaddik*, the highest level of an ethically pure life, will be reconditioned and "recycled" after being in an interim space called *sheol* for about a year. These souls are said to reenter life as the soul-sparks of a newborn in order to evolve more completely. This can happen repeatedly, even with rebirth as an animal or plant. Many soul-sparks can combine to comprise the soul of any one person.

SOME SAY: Souls are able to touch this earthly plane of being with messages in dreams or by the process of *ibbur*, wherein an elevated soul chooses to enter and help you with the mission of your life.

SOME SAY: There is also the process of *dybbuk*, wherein a soul that was meant to depart enters someone quite randomly and clings to that person, requiring professional intervention to help the soul accept that its term here is over.

Scholarly documentation of these diverse approaches to life after death is widely available; please see the Suggestions for Further Reading and Learning at the back of this book.

IT HELPS TO HAVE SOMETHING TO SAY

Upon hearing of a death, we say:

Baruh dayan ha-emet

Blessed be the True Judge.

(Mishnah Berahot 9:2; B. Ber. 54a; O.H. 222:2)

Traditionally, these words are uttered when we learn of a death. It is said at all deaths as a universal expression of humility and acceptance, meaning that we don't understand the Big Picture but accept it as being out of our control.

WHEN MEETING A FIRST-DEGREE MOURNER (PARENT, SIBLING, LIFE PARTNER, CHILD)

Few moments are as tender as coming into contact with someone whose loved one has just or recently died. "I'm sorry" doesn't really work. The sacred phrase to say for this occasion, as the funeral concludes and up through the thirtieth day after burial, is:

Ha-makom yinaheim et-hem betoh she-ar aveilei

tziyon v'yerushalayim.

May "Ha-Makom" comfort you among the others mourners of [our people] Zion and Jerusalem.

Ha-Makom, one of the mystical names for G*d in Judaism, means "The Place," as in a meeting place or a gathering place, a holy place, an emanating place of creation, or the connecting point of the Unity of All Being. Note how this phrase gently connects this mourner to all who are in the same condition at this time around the world.

After thirty days, when meeting a person in his or her year of mourning you can say, "May you experience no more pain" (Shulhan Aruh, Yoreh Deah 385:2).

PART 4: _HESED SHEL EMET_—ULTIMATE KINDNESS

This is the category of all things done to respectfully prepare and return the soul's body to earth because in _emet_, truth, this involves mitzvot we cannot do for ourselves. These practices comfort the living as well as the soul that has died, so anything you do that is part of _hessed shel emet_ is a double mitzvah. These practices include:

KAVOD HA-MET. Respect for the corpse. This becomes the core mitzvah of this time. Most dying persons take comfort in knowing that the traditional Jewish rituals of preparation such as washing, being dressed in a soft shroud, sitting with the corpse, and burial of the body will take place according to tradition. Souls on their journey are said to hover until burial because they need others to do these final mitzvot for them.

TAHARA. Pure. A courageous and tender trained group of volunteers called a _hevra kaddisha_, holy friends, respectfully and gently wash and dress the body in _tahrihim_, the soft white linen garments, including the flowing pants, a tunic, a robe, and head and foot coverings that make up the Jewish version of a shroud. This is not done in the case of a violent death, wherein the person's blood is mixed with her garments (Shul<u>h</u>an Aru<u>h</u>, Yoreh Deah 364:4).

Why do Jews traditionally dress everyone at burial alike and discourage burial in fine clothing (Shul<u>h</u>an Aru<u>h</u>, Yoreh Deah 352:1)? The principle is that all are equal in death; as with the coffin (see below), the clothes that defined social status no longer apply. There are no class distinctions in death—that is not the Jewish way. As in Job 1:21—"Naked I came from my mother's womb, and naked shall I return there"—the tradition is for everyone to go out much as we arrived, first bare, then cleaned and swaddled.

You have to actively request this service when speaking with the funeral home; it won't be provided automatically. There is sometimes a nominal fee for supplies. For many who are dying, knowing that such gentle care will be given to the body they will leave behind is a source of comfort.

Note: A baby who dies before thirty full days of life receives *tahara* if requested by the family. The baby is given a Jewish name by the parent(s), and a Jewish funeral, but there is no official mourning period stipulated by the tradition as the sages recognize the mourning will have its own organic season.

A *TAHARA* EXPERIENCE

Long before I became a rabbi, a young social work colleague of mine, a mother of three, was dying of a particularly virulent form of breast cancer. She called me one day to ask if we could meet privately because she had something to share and a favor to ask.

We met on the king-sized bed in her bedroom. She looked skeletal. Strewn upon the bed were details of all of her volunteer projects, tasks she kept up with until virtually her last breath. She wanted to share some of the wisdom and methods she'd gathered in her years as a social worker. What a profound honor; her ideas were very thoughtful, and I use her methods to this day. Then came the "favor." She asked me, "When I die, would you do me the honor of serving on the <u>h</u>evra kaddisha, the team of women who will prepare my body for burial?"

I had thought funeral homes did all that. I was mistaken; in fact, they only arrange to bring in a local nonprofit *tahara* organization for those who request it. Susan wanted someone who knew her, and who wouldn't be as traumatized as a family member might be, to help prepare her body for burial. The idea gave her comfort. Fearful, but wanting to do her honor, I promised to show up when that final call came.

On the sad day that Susan died, our <u>h</u>evra kaddisha team, all women to protect her modesty, met in a room at a Jewish funeral home specially designed for this purpose. There Susan's body lay completely covered in a soft white sheet. I felt scared to be this close to death, and for a while no degree of trying to exercise mind over matter got me to stop trembling.

Guided by an experienced member of the ḥevra kaddisha, we drew the traditionally prescribed amounts of lukewarm water for the washing. It is customary, out of respect, to pull the sheet away one small area at a time, wash, and restore the covering to that area before moving on. I was amazed at how clear it was that Susan's soul was no longer in her body. She seemed as empty and light as the shell of a cicada I'd found on a tree as a child. We did as instructed, gently cleaning her nails and any other areas needing attention.

Next, the team leader hydraulically tilted the table several degrees, and twenty-four quarts of warm water were washed over her. Some funeral homes have a mikvah, a ritual bath, specifically for this purpose. Water symbolizes flowing loving-kindness, ḥesed. Our chanting flowed with the water.

As is traditional, while working, we softly sang psalms, surrendering to the awesomeness of what we were doing. In Hebrew the term for awe, yirah, combines the senses of fear and amazement. Jews are taught to experience awe of G*d; we are yirei Ha-Shem. This feeling soon replaced the paḥad, pure fear, I'd felt earlier.

I had thought the shroud would be made of coarse monk's cloth, and shaped like a body bag. Not so. Taḥrihim are rather ethereal, soft, hand-sewn, white gauze-like garments: mitznefet, hood; miḥnasayim, pants; ketonet, chemise; kittel, robe; and avnet, a belt, followed by sovev, a full gauze sheet. We dressed her ever so gently. Since the body cannot cooperate, dressing required assistance from several of us. We added her tallit, her prayer shawl, one fringe cut away to make it pasul, unusable, and to symbolize her soul's departure from this body. We set the separated fringe upon the tallit near her heart.

We then lined the coffin with the sheet and sprinkled a sachet of earth from Israel. Lifting the body all together, we gently set her inside the coffin.

Finally, we placed broken fragments of pottery over the area of cloth above her eyes. These are called *sherblah* in Yiddish. *Sherblah* seem to symbolize a broken wine amphora, a metaphor for the body as a vessel no longer able to contain a soul or life force.

We now asked forgiveness of her soul for the intrusion of our efforts. Why? Tradition teaches that her soul could still be hovering, refraining from its journeys into the realm of mystery while awaiting our completion of this one mitzvah a soul cannot possibly do for itself. Finally, we placed the lid on the coffin, tidied up, and went out to gather and reflect on our experience in almost total and inward silence. Two *shomrim*, "watchers," from the *hevra kaddisha* relieved us; they would take turns with others sitting with the body until the burial.

I lived alone at the time and made the mistake of going home. It was an uncomfortable night for me, taking in what we'd done, the surprisingly awesome beauty of this caring act and the emotional difficulty of it. I would have been wise to spend the night with someone from the *hevra kaddisha* who would have understood. Subsequently, when needed, I help out with the *hevra kaddisha* where I live. *Tahara* ceased to be scary, but the awe only grows stronger. One thing is for sure: When I die, I hope my women friends will do *tahara* for my body. It is pure holiness.

SHMIRA. Guarding. A candle is placed at the head and/or foot of the body. A flame is the primary Jewish symbol for the soul, in this case meaning that the flame of memory will not go out. Traditionally, one or two members of the Jewish burial society, friends, or nonimmediate family members chant, study, or contemplate comforting psalms in shifts while sitting with the body until burial. This simple mitzvah feels both very holy and less scary when you are actually doing it. The practice offers comfort to the living that the body is being treated with respect, as well as to the departing soul.

Note: Lit candles are not allowed anywhere in a hospital as they are a fire hazard. Electric candles may be used.

ARON. "Coffin." The same term is applied to the cabinet in which a Torah lives in synagogue and to the "ark" Noah built. About nineteen hundred years ago, Gamliel, a prominent rabbi, refused to be buried in his honorary robes of office, setting an important standard of modesty for Jewish funerals. Voluntary simplicity remains the spiritual practice for Jewish funerals. Only basic all-wood coffins, held together with wooden pegs, are appropriate. No family need suffer dishonor because they can't compete in honoring their beloved with an elaborate funeral. Because every family applies the same standard of simplicity, no one ends up humiliated.

CLOSED CASKET. The person is to be remembered as in life and the body given privacy in death. The eyes are closed and a sheet drawn up over the entire body immediately after death. Out of respect, there is no further viewing, now or at the funeral, since the soul no longer has the power and autonomy to animate the body it once inhabited (Babylonian Talmud, Moed Kattan 2a). The body is the family's province only to return to the earth.

BURIAL AS SOON AS POSSIBLE AFTER DEATH (Yoreh Deah 357:1). This interval can be stretched when a murder investigation is involved or to accommodate a first-degree family member who must travel a long distance to attend. Otherwise, those who won't be able to arrive for days go directly to the *shiva* at the family home. They can visit the grave and hold a memorial service in their home community when they return. Be aware that airlines offer so-called compassionate travel fares, for family and clergy. The airline may ask for a copy of the death certificate. You will need official copies for estate matters later in any case, so request at least ten of them.

NO AUTOPSY. This holds true unless it might help solve a murder or yield vital medical information that could save lives in the family with a known disorder where data could make a meaningful difference. Otherwise, autopsy is considered disrespectful. Consult a rabbinic authority for assistance in figuring out the right thing to do; each circumstance is individual.

NO CREMATION. Just as we would not burn a worn-out Torah scroll that can no longer be read, so we do not burn a human body. Cremation was adopted by a small percentage of Jews in the twentieth century, most of whom erroneously believed that it was protective of the environment. However, recent studies have shown that crematoria contribute significantly to global warming; some countries are considering banning them as a result. For these reasons, some Jewish cemeteries will not accept ashes for burial, and some Jewish clergy will not officiate at such burials.

NO EMBALMING. While Joseph is described in Genesis 50:26 as having been embalmed in Egypt, embalming did not become a Jewish practice. The integrity of the body is carefully guarded. Because the process is invasive and designed to profoundly delay decomposition, Jews are not embalmed except under rare circumstances when it is required by civil law. Should this become an issue with authorities, call on a local rabbinic authority to intervene.

PART 5: FROM DEATH TO BURIAL—*ANINUT*

From the moment the soul leaves until the body's burial, the family enters a status called *aninut*, which means, literally, "lamentable." No duties in life need be addressed by such a person except to be occupied with the anguish or fact of loss, thoughts of how to honor the departed soul, and making arrangements for the body and the funeral. So distracted a time is this, that we learn "Before burial, the mourner cannot be counted in a quorum for prayer" (Kitzur Shulḥan Aruḥ 196:2).

We do not speak words of comfort at this time. Those who are present to the family are meant to be quietly helpful and self-effacing. While mourners tend to eat little out of lack of desire, mourners with disorders that require them to take medication are expected to do so, and with food as indicated. Life comes first.

KRIAH. Rending your garment near your heart immediately upon hearing of the death of a first-degree relative (2 Samuel 1:11; Genesis 37:24), just before the funeral, or, in Sephardi families, upon returning home from the funeral, symbolizes the tearing open of your heart. Tradition teaches that "garments ought be torn opposite the heart ... for the mourner has to expose the heart" (Kitzur Shulḥan Aruḥ 195:3–4).

These days, it is customary to tear or cut a black button holding a small black ribbon as a symbolic substitute. Just before the funeral, men sometimes cut into a tie and rip it. Before tearing, we say: "*Baruḥ atah adonai eloheynu meleḥ ha-olam baruḥ dayan ha-emet*, Blessed is the Source of Life, Governing Principle of Eternity," the traditional blessing formulation plus the phrase used upon hearing of, or witnessing a death: "*Baruḥ dayan ha-emet*, Blessed be the True Judge." In the word *truth*, *emet*, is the word *met*, dead.

The *kriah* button is worn on the left side for the death of a parent, on the right side for the death of other immediate relatives. We wear this as a symbol of mourning until the thirtieth day after burial. People appreciate that you give them this visual cue because it reminds them of your emotional fragility and helps them to remember to tread lightly (Kitzur Shulḥan Aruḥ 195:3–4). In most communities, the *kriah* button is not worn on Shabbat.

PART 6: THE FUNERAL

The order of the funeral service varies from one community to another and depends on whether a service is also being held in a chapel before burial (which is a convenience, not a necessity). Under rare circumstances, usually for major Jewish leaders and teachers, the deceased can be eulogized in the synagogue and the coffin brought up to the front of the sanctuary for the chapel service. One who knows they are descended from the *Kohanim*, the priests of Temple times, traditionally does not enter a room with a dead body or a cemetery, though this is primarily observed in Orthodox communities (Leviticus 21:1).

Note: The order of the events described below varies widely from community to community and among the denominations, and may even be done differently by different rabbis within the same denomination.

LEVAYAH. This is the mitzvah of accompanying the body and the family to the cemetery by attending the funeral. Do bring children. Sheltering them from knowledge of death is a mistake that makes later losses even harder. Let them frolic among the stones if they wish. Their presence adds hope for the future and helps them begin to accept the idea that the person is gone from their life.

When a funeral takes place in a person's hometown, some have the hearse stop in front of seven key places from the life of the deceased. The rear door is opened and those at the place being visited may step out on the front stoop and wave for a moment to honor the memory of the departed. Pall bearers may also stop seven times on certain days when walking the coffin to the grave because the number seven has numerous mystical meanings in Judaism.

APPROPRIATE PSALMS. These are usually chanted by a clergy person or a caring friend who often walks in front of, or sometimes behind, those carrying the coffin from the hearse to the grave.

THE COFFIN IS PLACED INTO THE GRAVE. The tradition of keeping the coffin suspended during the service is not a Jewish one. Some American funeral operators are accustomed to keeping the coffin hanging on straps and both lowering and filling a grave after the funeral. Be sure to explain that you expect the coffin to be lowered at the beginning of the ceremony when initially making arrangements with the cemetery or funeral home.

HESPED. Eulogy. It is traditional for the living to recount the best aspects of the person's life without exaggeration (Berahot 62a). Clergy generally visit immediate family members to gather stories and perceptions in order to reflect them back at the funeral. Ecclesiastes 7:2 explains the purpose of this practice as, "So that the living shall reflect" (also, Semahot 3:5–6). For some families, when a person of advanced age dies what some might call a "good death"—that is, one that is timely and not agonized—family or friends might wish to give or add to the eulogy. If the eulogy has not already been given in the chapel, it can be done at the graveside. In classical settings, eulogies are omitted during certain times and on certain days of the calendar.

TZIDDUK HA-DIN OR PSALM 16. Traditionally, certain days of the week have special qualities regarding self-reflection that make one of these prayers appropriate. The *Tzidduk ha-Din* prayer is customarily recited in Ashkenazi communities and is based on verses from Deuteronomy 32:4, 1 Samuel 2:6, Psalms 119 and 137, and Jeremiah 32:19. The essence of *Tzidduk ha-Din* is awe at the magnificence of creation and recognition of how fortunate we are to experience life at all. A sense of the Big Picture is given in Psalm 92:15: "In G*d consciousness nothing appears out of alignment." Psalm 16 affirms the path of life.

EL MALEH. This funeral prayer wishes for the soul to have an edenic experience in the afterlife under the wings of the *Shehinah*, a metaphor for G*d as sheltering presence. Rich in imagery, this prayer also describes the shimmering of holy souls in the firmament and includes a commitment to give to charity in honor of, and to increase the merit of, the soul of the deceased. The Jewish sacred name of the person is used in this prayer and will also appear on the grave marker like this: *Eliyahu* [person's name] *ben* [son of] or *bat* [daughter of] *Shlomo* [father] *v'Rayzl* [mother]. (Learn more about sacred names in chapter 5).

BURIAL. It is a mitzvah to participate in the act of burial by shoveling some earth into the grave. Not everything healing feels good while it's happening. Both observing the lowering of the coffin and remaining to help fill the grave are actually important elements of the first stages of healing and transition for the living. In some communities, it is appropriate to place a few shovels of earth upon the coffin while others completely fill the grave, taking turns among those present. It is customary not to hand the shovel to the next person waiting to engage in this mitzvah, but rather to place it into the mound and step away so another can approach. Some will place just a handful of earth in the grave, others will fully engage their rage, love, pain, and care, letting each thrust of the shovel become a spoonful of acceptance and finality.

KADDISH. This "holiness" prayer takes several forms, including one for mourners and funerals. It is said for the first time at the graveside after the coffin has been lowered and covered with an initial layer of earth. *Kaddish* unites those mourning in the rhythm of this comforting Aramaic recitation that never mentions death but rather emphasizes the interconnectedness and unity of all Being.

Every step of Jewish burial and mourning practice is visceral, hands-on, wrenchingly real, designed to prevent denial and support the process of successful transformation of the pain of loss into memory.

PART 7: THE MOURNING PROCESS—TAKING ONE DAY AT A TIME

It is our people's practice to engage in a process known as *shiva*, refraining from work and school for up to seven days after a death, three where severe economic adversity would result. Some shorten this further. *Shiva* has immense therapeutic value and is best undertaken for as many of the seven days as possible.

AN INTRODUCTION TO *SHIVA*

Sonia's beloved husband, Al, had died. She served on the board of the local Jewish Federation while I was the executive director, and she could always be counted on to show up for others. But back then, at age twenty-five, I didn't know how to show up for her.

"Why didn't you come to the house after the funeral?" Sonia asked. "I've missed you; this has been such a difficult month."

"Sonia, I'm so embarrassed to tell you that I've never been to a house where *shiva* is being observed. I wouldn't know how to act." I said. "I was afraid I'd do something embarrassing or wrong, so I just sent a fruit basket to let you know I care."

"How awkward for you not to know these things; of course you are forgiven. Would you like me to take you with me on a *shiva* call the next time someone in the community dies?"

Almost thirty years ago, Sonia, of blessed memory, helped fill a gap in my Jewish preparation for life. When the son of a board member died in a tragic car accident, Sonia and I went to the family's home together. Here, as best I can recall, is the way she prepared me for the visit.

We are primarily going to the mourners' home to make sure there is a gentle flow of continuing life in their house. We let them know not so much by our words as by our presence that they are not alone in their loss, that they are part of a family and a community (Shulḥan Aruḥ, Yoreh Deah 393:3). It is our people's custom not to let mourners isolate themselves. It's not healthy, their feelings will fester, and a deep depression may set in. *Shiva* is from the root word *sheva*, "seven," in Hebrew, and also encompasses the root letters for *shev*, "sit." Our custom is to sit at home for seven days after the death of an immediate family member, though some shorten the amount of time. Shortening is done at our own peril. Healing takes time and simply can't be rushed.

The traditional way to enter a house of mourning is without actively engaging the mourner. Don't go running over to give a hug or shake hands, don't say shalom or hello (Shulḥan Aruḥ, Yoreh Deah 385:1). You can sit in a seat near the mourners in solidarity for a while, if you wish. Should one of the mourners make eye contact with you and speak, you can reply (Shulḥan Aruḥ, Yoreh Deah 376:1). In some communities it's customary to touch your heart to show your caring, should a mourner catch your eye. In some communities it is not unusual to hear someone softly say something like, "I'm here for you, to listen or do. Just ask." In South Africa, Great Britain, and Australia, it is customary to wish the mourner "long life" during a *shiva* visit.

Mourners go through a natural, intense inner process that is necessary for the kind of healing and recovery that leads to renewed living. Be sensitive, say little, show up often during *shiva* week, and don't neglect the mourner afterward, either. This is a focused time for him or her to feel, contemplate, and begin to integrate the loss. So, though you may be anxious or uncomfortable, don't get chatty.

Note the pitcher of water, the basin, and the towel on the stoop by the front door, just as sometimes these appear at the cemetery. For each transition of the soul, we symbolically wash or immerse in water, our symbol for compassion, flow, Presence, and loving-kindness. Our people do this at marriage, meals, conversion, death, and returning from a funeral to family life. Rinse your hands and let the images from the funeral be washed away. Remember their son, Ron, not for how he died but as he lived.

When we enter, you may see that some seats are lower than others. Traditionally the first-degree mourners—spouse, parents, or siblings—sit on a low chair, a stool, or a couch with the seat cushions removed. Back in Germany before the war, we would sit on the floor. It felt good to do that, sort of cocoon-like down there. I remember that when my little sister died of whooping cough, I didn't want anyone touching me, hugging or asking questions because I was too stunned to answer. Being seated lower, I felt safer, reserved. So if you see a low seat in the room when you walk in, don't sit on it. This tradition is wise; it gives space to those grieving without leaving us totally alone. Some homes of mourning want shoes off; let's watch when we enter to see what's expected here.

My family stopped short of sackcloth and ashes, the way it used to be, but we each did tear a corner on the right side of the clothing we wore that week. Today people are more practical; they pin on a small black ribbon and tear or cut it a bit. Tearing is a good thing to do. I discovered I was feeling very angry when I tore the corner of my smock. I found I really wanted my obnoxious little sister back. I didn't really want her dead, even though sometimes I used to wish it.

I remember my sister Etta's death like it was yesterday. I was eleven. She was five. They tell me I had a brother who died from polio when I was one and a half, but I don't have any memories of him. When we sat *shiva* for Etta, the guests buzzed above us, catching up on community news in their softly held discussions. Plates of food would seem to just arrive near us, glasses of water and hard-boiled eggs. Eggs symbolize life. The soul breaks out of the eggshell of the body and perhaps, who knows, continues to a different plane of being. We ate, we drank water and hot tea full of sugar, unconsciously, but we did. We slept in our own beds, but I remember my grandfather saying his family used to put the mattresses of mourners on the floor.

We didn't use mirrors; they were covered. Tradition teaches that this is not the time for being self-conscious or fashionable; the first visitors covered the mirrors for us. Mourners are guided not to attend to their appearance, and men let their beards grow out for the year of mourning. Poppa and my brother didn't shave, but who could think about it anyway? We mostly got up for bathroom breaks and *Kaddish*, the mourner's prayer. Though I was allowed to run or play, I just didn't want to. Poppa read a bit of Mishnah, a section of that text about generosity, out loud at the services in honor of Etta. These days, in communities where those coming to services weren't at the funeral or didn't know the deceased, sometimes one of the mourners who is emotionally able to do so will say a few words about the person. Poppa was too broken up to speak about Etta, though at the funeral the rabbi did so beautifully. Have you noticed it's rare for a Jewish mourner to give a eulogy? The tradition understands that it is an imposition to ask a mourner to speak, though some who do so find it healing. When a person is in mourning, it is best to witness and take in what is said. This also guards against breaking down and weeping and not being able to continue.

On the thirtieth day after the burial, there always used to be what we'd call *shloshim*, meaning "thirty," a gathering where people could recount memories of the person. By then, usually, the mourners would be ready to speak. For parents, *Kaddish* is said for eleven months; for other family members, the official mourning period concludes at thirty days. We still have *shloshim* as a tradition here in our community; it is a very good thing to do.

The guests who came to us for Etta's *shiva* were like some kind of nest that surrounds you until you can remember how to fly. I remember my uncle Benny asked me at one point during *shiva* week if I wanted to make a drawing, and I did, a nest of a bird family, with my sister falling through a hole in it and flying away toward a garden in the sky. Momma, Poppa, and I sadly huddling inside. I drew the people from the town bringing string and reeds to rebuild the nest to keep it strong. When I visit mourners and the family has children, I invite them to draw in a similar way if they wish. It helps, I know from my own experience. I also remember I would put my head into Momma's lap, but I don't think she realized I was there very much.

On about day three my favorite uncle, Mendel, arrived. He'd been doing business in France; I remember when he came in, he told us to call him Maurice from now on, but I never seemed to remember to do that. I asked him to go for a walk. Mourners are supposed to ask if they want to talk, or need something. Visitors don't traditionally ask them, because then the mourner might feel obligated to the visitor. On our walk, my Uncle Mendel waited for me to speak. I remember asking him questions like "Do you feel the cold when you're dead?"

My uncle didn't laugh. He told me that life and death are full of mystery, just like Poppa said. He said, "Would a baby inside a mommy ever imagine a world where you have to cry to get fed and everything doesn't come to you just naturally? So, who knows what it's like on the other side when we leave this world? It's probably more miraculous than anyone could ever guess." I've always loved that notion. I asked if he was scared of death, and he said something like, "No. I'm in no rush to leave—believe you me, I love life. But I sure am curious what's around that particular corner."

Missing a week of school for me, and a week out of the shop for Momma and Poppa, did mean a lot of catching up for all of us, but by going deeply into grief we began to heal. Today some people make idols of school and work, putting them ahead of loving and healing. Imagine if I'd been sent to school and the family and community had not created that safe nest for us. Jewish law does allow someone to go to work after three days' *shiva* if staying out will destroy their business, but we weren't that poor. Judaism typically leans toward what's healthy for the living.

Day four of our *shiva* was Shabbat; you don't stay home during *shiva* on Shabbat; you go to synagogue instead of the community coming to you. We waited to enter, as is traditional, until after the joyful Friday night psalms. If a major Jewish holiday arrives during the *shiva* week, *shiva* ends as the holiday begins, even if it has only been one or two days.

When we got up from *shiva* after morning services on the seventh day, Momma's eyes were clear again and she started fussing over me like she always did. For the first time, that made me happy. Friends who were visiting walked with us around the corner, the tradition that ends *shiva*. It took a long time to stop missing my sister, but we did have strength by then to go to school and work. That's what *shiva* does; it gives you the strength to go on.

Sonia is long gone, but I am eternally grateful for the gift of her guidance. From her role-modeling, the Reclaiming Judaism mentoring approach was born. I learned a lot and also discovered that attending a house of mourning is one of the building blocks of a meaningful community, where people show up for each other and know others will one day be there for them or their loved ones.

SHIVA RITUALS AND PRACTICES

GEMILUT HASADIM. Deeds of loving-kindness, such as bringing foods appropriate to the degree of kashrut the family keeps, are essential in a house of mourning. Tradition teaches: "At the first meal after the funeral, mourners are not to eat their own food. It is a mitzvah to prepare food for the mourner" (Shulhan Aruh Yoreh Deah 378:1). Also, do slip into the bathroom and kitchen to see that they stay in order, note whether there is laundry to be done, diapers to be fetched, dogs to be walked, pets to be fed, and the like. Some deaths result from accidents in which others were hurt. In such a situation, you may provide rides to treatment. See what's needed and quietly get it done—without acknowledgment. It is a mitzvah and essential also to visit those sick or wounded, but know that visiting the *shiva* home to engage in *mena<u>h</u>em aveil*, the comforting of a mourner, with your presence comes first, as it is a double mitzvah—one for the living and one for the deceased (Maimonides, Laws of Mourners, 14:7). That's what community means; each of us is responsible for the others.

CHILDREN AT A HOUSE OF MOURNING. Children will often vacillate between play and grief or acting out. If they seek you out, play with them quietly, ask what they need, and help them determine how to get it. Suggestions for Furthur Reading and Learning at the back of this book lists books on death to read with children. A conversation-starter might be to find a dead insect in the grass and bury it together. Let the child give the insect's eulogy; what needs to be vented may well come out.

THE MEAL OF CONDOLENCE. The first meal after the funeral, this is always meant to be provided for the family. Healthy congregations and organizations make it a priority to have a group of volunteers who coordinate care for the mourners. In some communities an annual call goes out, asking if members would like to contribute to the purchase of platters of food that keeps well sitting out to arrive daily at *shiva* homes. Later, the family will contribute to the funeral fund in honor of the deceased's memory so that other families will receive the same loving attention. Hard-boiled eggs are usually available in a house of *shiva* because they symbolize the cycle of life.

SHIVA MINYAN. A daily service is held in the home of the family sitting *shiva*. Friends and family gather for those unaffiliated with a synagogue. You need not be a clergy person to lead the simple service, which can be held in the morning, afternoon, or evening. Secular Jews may invite those coming over for *shiva* to share a poem or give a teaching instead of holding a religious service.

SHIVA CANDLE. It is not an inherently Jewish custom to blow out candles. Jews have come to consider the flame to be a symbol for the soul, something that never goes out. We have Hanukkah, Shabbat, holy day, and memorial candles, and all are allowed to burn down at their own pace. After the funeral, when arriving at the house of mourning, a tall candle intended to last for the full week of *shiva* is lit.

ON *SHABBAT* DURING *SHIVA*, BOTH MOURNERS AND *MINYAN* GO TO SYNAGOGUE. Many congregations have reclaimed the practice of having the mourners enter after the conclusion of the seven joyful psalms welcoming Shabbat. Seats toward the center of the room are held for mourners so that there is no confusion or excess focus upon where they sit. Typically, the community remains standing at the end of *L'ha Dodi*, and a member of the community goes out to guide the mourners into the service, in respect and support for their loss. Mourners do not take *aliyot* or even have to pray; they just rise and lead the community in the Mourner's *Kaddish*.

IF *SHIVA* IS NOT OVER BEFORE A MAJOR JEWISH HOLIDAY BEGINS, IT ENDS AS THE HOLY DAY BEGINS. While it is difficult when this happens early in *shiva*, the message from tradition is the overarching importance of entering the major cycle of the seasons with your community so that life goes on. There are nuances to this; check with a rabbi who knows the local norms.

AS THE WEEK OF *SHIVA* ENDS. It is customary for the rabbi, cantor, or another supportive presence to walk the mourners out of the *shiva* house and around the block. While the mourners are out walking, community members uncover the mirrors and the family continues into the rest of *shloshim*, the less intense phase of the first thirty days. In Sephardi communities there may be a special meal and a *mishmara*, a "study session" including another eulogy, held as *shiva* ends, and mourners are encouraged to do *teshuvah* with whomever possible.

MOURNING, WEEKS 2 AND 3

A downshifting of intensity of mourning begins in the second week. Mourners are expected to go to work as well as to keep up the home environment and their personal appearance, although men traditionally allow their beards to grow for the full year when mourning for a parent.

SHLOSHIM GATHERING. Thirty days postburial, mourners, friends, classmates, and/or coworkers may gather to further honor the soul of the deceased with memorial prayers and *Kaddish* followed by the telling of stories about the life of the deceased. Some people sing songs the deceased was known to love or recite his favorite poetry or stories. Sephardim do this as another *mishmara*, in the cemetery, while dining beside the grave. At thirty days, mourners stop wearing torn clothing or the black *kriah* ribbon, and daily saying of *Kaddish* for relative(s) other than parents also ends.

KAVOD. "Honor." In some Jewish communities it is traditional to refrain from attending large social gatherings and cultural events for the first thirty days after the death of a sibling, partner, or child, and for a year after the death of a parent to memorialize the deceased and deal more deeply with loss.

PART 8: MEMORIAL—TURNING LOSS INTO SACRED MEMORY

HEADSTONE. A traditional metaphor for G*d is rock, and each of our own small souls is a stone cleaved from the One. A headstone represents the soul of the person whose body is buried beneath. At the top of many Jewish tombstones is the abbreviation פנ which stands for *po nikbar* or *po nitman*, "here lies." At the bottom of many Hebrew tombstone inscriptions you will find תנצבה, which is an abbreviation of "May [this person's] soul be bound up in the bond of eternal life" (Samuel 1 25:29). The person's Hebrew name is usually engraved as well as the person's secular name. The date of death is also listed according to both Jewish and secular calendars. (A link to a one-hundred-year Jewish calendar can be found at www.Hebcal.com). By all means, add poetry, artwork, phrases from Psalms, Torah, or prayer, or other descriptive terms if you wish. The stone can be flat or standing depending upon cemetery style. There are local norms, so check with a rabbi if you are unsure of what would be acceptable in your community.

UNVEILING. The stone is usually placed within twelve months after burial in Western countries; after three months in others. This is a day marking the completion of responsibility for respectful interment. There is a small veil over the stone that is now peeled or cut off—hence the term *unveiling.* Seeing a loved one's name on the gravestone for the first time is a striking event. Standing there, seeing that monument, you can't help but reflect back on the process up to this point. After the veil is removed, the *El Maleh* prayer can be chanted and *Kaddish* recited. Some may want to share memories. Just as the headstone represents the soul that has departed, for those who visit the grave it is traditional to leave a small stone atop the headstone to indicate that your soul visited as a way of honoring the memory of the deceased. As small stones accrue, people who see them are often heard to say, "Look how much this person is remembered and loved."

This responsive prayer that I composed for my Aunt Sylvia's stone unveiling has proven helpful to many families.

LEADER: Your memory is sacred to us.

ALL: We will never forget you.

LEADER: May the ongoing journey

ALL: of your soul be joyful.

LEADER: We will never forget you.

ALL: We will tell stories of your life.

LEADER: We will never forget you.

ALL: Send us blessings when you can.

LEADER: We will never forget you.

KADDISH AND YARTZEIT. Jews celebrate the anniversary—*yar* = year and *tzeit* = time in Yiddish—of a person's death by reciting the prayer called *Kaddish* with a minimum of ten Jews, a minyan, usually in synagogue. Having an *aliyah* to the Torah, where the funeral prayer, *El Maleh*, is chanted naming your loved one, is also an option. For the homebound, online and conference call *minyanim* (pl.) are now available and often offer optional dialogue time for safely sharing feelings and memories, as do grief support groups at Jewish community centers or with private grief counselors. The virtual minyan is an emergent practice of envisioning those who live in distant cities whom the mourner feels close to, and bringing them to mind as part of creating your minyan experience, though not all authorities view a virtual minyan as valid.

YARTZEIT CANDLE. Every year on the *yartzeit*, or anniversary, of a first-degree relative's death, a candle that burns for one full day is lit. *Yartzeit* candles are usually white, symbolizing transition. By lighting a candle we keep the flame of memory burning for those we have loved.

YARTZEIT CEMETERY VISIT. This is good day to visit the cemetery, if possible. Check on the quality of perpetual care, weed, leave a stone as a reminder that someone cares about this person and visits.

TZEDAKAH. In keeping with the tradition of emphasizing simplicity and equality in death, it is not customary to send flowers to a Jewish funeral, unveiling, or memorial anywhere except in Israel, where flowers are plentiful. Families and friends who can afford to create physical testaments that honor the dead do not do so with elaborate burials or funerals but by dedicating charitable works in their names. Edifices, scholarships, public art, and other philanthropic efforts around the world dedicated to the memory of someone who had an impact on the life of the donor are testaments to the Jewish practice of honoring the dead by bringing something good to life. This can be done at any time and is especially appreciated by family members shortly after the person's death and on the *yartzeit*.

YIZKOR. Four times a year, on Yom Kippur, Shemini Atzeret, Passover, and Shavuot, a memorial service is added to the holiday religious services. *Yizkor* comes from the root *za<u>h</u>or*, "remember." After the first full year following a death, the family can say *Kaddish* at these services as well. It is traditional to light *yartzeit* candles at home at the beginning of each *Yizkor* eve, one for each person who has died in your immediate family. At this time some families tell stories about those who have died, honoring their lives by making sure the next generation remembers them. (Learn more in volume I of this series, *Reclaiming Judaism as a Spiritual Practice: Holy Days and Shabbat*, pages 37–42.)

RECENT DEVELOPMENTS

There have been a few innovations to traditional practice that relate to various aspects of Jewish death and mourning rituals.

SHIVA

The tradition is not to engage a mourner in discussion unless he or she initiates it. A colleague did just that when his thirty-four-year-old brother died of a sudden heart attack while playing ice hockey with friends.

On the third night of sitting *shiva* for his brother, my colleague returned to his home community and invited us to attend the next four days of *shiva*. As the evening *shiva* service concluded, he spoke honestly about trying to conceive of a world without his brother's calls, without his warm willingness to help out, and without his frightening fits of temper and long periods of icy noncommunication. He then posed a question to everyone present and invited us to take turns responding as he gazed around the room. "What does being a sibling really mean? What have you noticed in the lives of others or in your own life? I ask you not for a sugar-coated answer, but for what is true for you."

Many in the room were stunned. It seemed unprecedented to turn the focus onto our experience, and yet it would be rude not to reply. Silence reigned for long minutes and then virtually every person gave a thoughtful, fascinating, and honest reply. The preciousness, pain, power, and poignancy of being a sibling soon filled the room. Some would later say that their relationships with their own siblings changed for the better because of what they learned that day.

KADDISH

The best known of all Jewish mourning practices is called "saying *Kaddish*," the rhythmic mantra-like prayer that marks and supports the process of integrating a death. Folk tradition teaches that a soul cannot fully release its hold on this realm until at least one member of its family says *Kaddish* and thereby honors the Source of Life to the merit of the deceased.

Kaddish helps you to keep transforming the pain of loss into sacred memory. And then, when a full month, or, for the death of a parent, eleven months have gone by, most people find that the *Kaddish* has fulfilled its role of keeping them connected to *kedushah*, "holiness," by affirming the flow of life.

As with other key life cycle prayers, there are both classic and more interpretive understandings of *Kaddish*. The first volume of this

Reclaiming Judaism series, which was written in 2005, endorses the idea of G*d not as a supreme being but rather as the infinite potential for change. This interpretation is based on the Great Name of G*d in Jewish tradition, the letters יהוה. These four letters can be combined to make up all the forms of the verb "to be." Embedded in the *Shema*, this name is on our lips as we die. We can read that name as symbolic of the G*d idea discovered by Moses in his burning bush experience, a G*d called, "I am becoming what I am becoming."

In a 2007 lecture given at the University of Pennsylvania, Dr. Stuart Kauffman, director of the Institute for Biocomplexity and Informatics at the University of Calgary, suggested that humans can reclaim a sense of the "sacred" by means of awe at the extreme possibilities for change in creation. Using physics, math, and logic, he demonstrated the impossibility of predicting all the things under the sun that could combine to create new things. He suggested that we call this quality in creation G*d. Perhaps remembering this option for the Great Name helps when faced with the inexplicable.

An early form of *Kaddish* was associated with study done in honor or memory of someone. Not until the horrific death toll of the Crusades did there emerge a modified *Kaddish* explicitly for mourners. All forms of *Kaddish* affirm the awesome/fearsome mystery implied by the Great Name. The funeral form is just somewhat longer, with more adjectives and mentions of death.

Some believe that saying *Kaddish* helps a soul on its travels beyond embodied life. Dr. Laura Vidmar writes: "At the end of saying *Kaddish*, I look at Dad's picture and say, 'May you be helped on your journey,' and I find myself adding, 'And may I be helped on mine.'" Some believe that saying *Kaddish* gives merit to the souls of Moses and Aaron for mistakes they made in their leadership. Whatever their theology, however, most who take on the discipline of saying *Kaddish* find that healing happens not through the meaning of the words but through the rhythm of time set apart in this way and the connection with community that grows when it is said at a formal service, wherever you may be. For your convenience, traditional and interpretive versions of the Kaddish can be found in prayer books and in a file you can easily print out in multiple copies at www.ReclaimingJudaism.org.

SUICIDE AND *KADDISH*. *L'hathillah*, from the outset, suicide has not been a spiritual option in Judaism, since life is viewed as infinitely precious. *B'di-ahvahd*, after the fact, whenever at all supportable, the cause of death will be ruled by the rabbis as mental illness. Most agree that *Kaddish* is to be recited for a full twelve months for those who committed suicide, in hopes of helping the loved one's evolution in the next world, atoning in the face of much survivor guilt, and because this is one of the hardest losses for a family to integrate. Suicide leaves deep tracks on remaining family. Studies show that in families where there is a suicide, it becomes more imaginable, and hence more likely, for other family members to take their own life.

For many generations, funeral rites in the case of suicide were limited to those showing respect for the living. Since a eulogy is meant to honor the dead, one would not usually be given for an adult who announced their intent to suicide. But, a child was not considered culpable but rather definitely ill to do this. In those days, burial would often be outside the sacred ground of the cemetery in a special area designated for those who dishonored the Source by taking their own life. Today, however, we recognize that almost every suicide is an act of mental illness, and all rites are, therefore, accorded (Semahot 2:1; Yoreh Deah 345:1–3).

This version of the traditional *Kaddish* is designed to be said by a physician, a staff member, or any other combination of professional caregivers—chaplain, home health aide, nurse, therapist, neighbors, members of synagogue committees who visit the sick, and the like.

RECIPE #31:
A Caregiver's Kaddish

The preciousness of a life is so great that it is healthy for some to consider pausing during a busy day in a health care setting to remember those who have died.

> We gather for just a few minutes to acknowledge and mourn the passing of _____ , whom we cared for in this practice/facility. As his/her caregiver, I have a few memories of him/her to share. I also invite those of our staff to engage in this mitzvah of zah̲or—remembering.
>
> [Allow time for sharing memories of the person who has died, then continue below.]
>
> Those who are comfortable doing so, please join me in a version of my tradition's memorial *Kaddish* prayer. Also, feel free to express your own words of prayer afterward:
>
> *Yitgadal, v'yitkadash.*
> Ever expanding in our awareness is the miracle of life.
> That connects every cell to the others and every life to one another.
> Yet, in all the worlds of possibility, only certain paths do cross.
> Let us say, *ameyn.*
> *Y'hay shlamah rabbah min shamaya*
> How surprising and what a blessing it is to serve
> And, when required, to help escort a soul past its ties to the body.
> Let us say, *ameyn.*
> *Oseh shalom bimrohmahv*
> May the Source of ultimate wholeness
> support us in creating peace and healing for all—
> mind, body, spirit, and planet.
> Let us say, *ameyn.*
> May our memories of _____
> always be for a blessing.
> Let us say, *ameyn.*

Hold onto some silence here. Try not to rush right back to work. Let holiness happen.

APPENDIX I

The Legacy of Your Footprint:
Caring for the Environment on Your Special Day

Tens of thousands of life cycle events take place worldwide weekly. Because each little act of environmental consciousness is multiplied so many times during life's major events, the mitzvah called *bal tash-ḥit*, no wanton destruction of the planet, merits our focused attention.

LIFE CYCLE ENVIRONMENTAL OPTIONS

❑ **Quantity:** Holding smaller, intimate events reduces not only numbers and costs but also the impact on the environment.

❑ **Flowers:** Seek out and patronize organic flower growers or friends' organic gardens. Alternatively, consider potted plants. Greens that are rooted and growing contribute oxygen and recycle carbon dioxide; they are natural air purifiers. Be aware of people who have pollen allergies; consider silk flowers from a nonlabor-exploitive setting. It is customary to give a charitable gift to a congregation or another caring organization as part of your own life cycle event. Consider purchasing large plants or shrubs for the sanctuary or chapel from a florist or nursery and arranging for them to be maintained for at least a year.

❏ **Candles:** Avoid petroleum-based products; they are "tapping out" our resources. Beeswax candles are a great renewable resource choice. Select containers that are made of recyclable materials.

❏ **Paper products:** Ask caterers and printers to make sure their bids are for recyclable and recycled paper products. E-vites are catching on (and track responses automatically). When you use them, others will think, "Well, if she's doing that, then it's fine for us to save trees and not go to paper for our invitations!" Be an ecological trendsetter; it's a mitzvah.

❏ **Waste disposal:** Ask whether caterers and facilities separate and recycle waste. Let them know that you can't use them if they don't do this—only a few families have to say this before a facility will change its practices rather than lose business. Is the site a congregation? Tell them you'll purchase recycling bins for them if they promise to use them. Take it to the board level, if necessary. You are a leader now. What a mitzvah!

❏ **Leftovers:** Make sure before signing a contract and giving a deposit that the facility and the caterer (if you are using one) have an agreement with a charity to pick up or accept delivery of leftovers. Insist on that or walk. Let the vendors' ethical actions speak through you. Find your prophetic voice; don't give in to the status quo.

❏ **Materials:** Avoid craft foams for centerpieces and cups; these release toxins during production and when unwrapped. One hundred percent recycled paper napkins are readily available. If the packaging of a particular product is not recyclable or biodegradable, ask the vendor to find an alternative. There are also biodegradable trash bags, utensils, and disposable chinaware available. Best is using real dishes and biodegradable soap for washing them. Going potluck? Appoint a volunteer recycling coordinator to be part of the cleanup team. Consider projecting poems, menus, and songs onto screens, walls, and ceilings rather than giving out paper copies to your guests.

❏ **Produce:** Plan a menu that includes as many locally grown and produced in-season ingredients as possible.

❏ **Ethics:** Serve meat and eggs from sources known to be cruelty-free. Ask about labor practices and require bids based on fair trade practices for items such as fruit, coffee, and chocolates. Kosher organics, including wines, are now a growth industry. Ask if the kosher kitchen is supervised by someone trained in eco-kashrut (www.Aleph.org) and look for Hecksher Tzedek ethical kashrut practices and symbols on products.

❏ **Fuel consumption:** Holding a ritual and reception in the same building eliminates the fuel consumed driving between venues. Using a bus or carpooling is the next best option. Ceremonies held in warm but not hot temperatures won't use much fuel for air-conditioning or heat. Consider a carbon footprint offset donation to an environmental charity to compensate for what you use if your event takes place in an extra-hot, extra-cold, or distant locale. Ask vendors to donate as well. Since you're not asking for yourself, the asking will be easier.

❏ **Rent versus buy:** Oftentimes, renting tables, chairs, and props costs as much if not more than buying in bulk. Check with area schools, camps, and other nonprofits to see if they are short on some of the things you could buy in bulk and donate to them (with the donations being tax-deductible in the United States, by the way). Win-win.

❏ **Inspire:** Consider setting up workshops in congregations and organizations to discuss creating environmentally friendly rites of passage and demonstrate products. Offer a carbon footprint analysis form (available on the Internet) to everyone and give a prize for the life cycle event held on site each year that creates the smallest carbon debt.

GLOSSARY

Abraham (Hebrew, Av-rah-hahm): Patriarch from whom, along with his wife Sarah, the Jewish people descended and through whom, according to tradition, the Jewish people's monotheistic orientation originated.

Agudath Israel: Umbrella organization of Orthodox Jewish communities committed to educational outreach. Visit www.agudath.org.

agunah (ah-gue-nah): Jewish woman who is unable to remarry under Jewish auspices because she cannot obtain a *get*, a formal Jewish divorce document from her husband.

ALEPH: Alliance for Jewish Renewal. Umbrella organization for groups, retreats, and clergy engaged in learning how to cultivate a spiritually vital, ethically inclusive Judaism. Visit www.aleph.org.

aliyah (ah-lee-yah): "Going up." The act of moving to Israel, termed "making *aliyah*,"—as when Moses went up to Sinai. Also, the parallel action of going up to witness the reading of the Torah of Moses in any synagogue or service.

Amidah (ah-mee-dah): Peak point of a Jewish service, when everyone stands and each prayer serves as a springboard to finding and expressing the prayer of your heart.

aninut (ah-nee-nute): Acute mourning status of one whose recently deceased family member's burial has not yet taken place.

Aramaic (ar-uh-may-ik): A Semitic language spoken by most Jews during the original developmental period of the talmudic text, which is largely written in Aramaic. Aramaic also appears in many Jewish mystical writings, such as the Zohar, and in some traditional prayers, such as the *Kaddish*.

aufruf (auf-ruf): Special blessing for being called up to the Torah about one week before your wedding.

baal teshuvah, baalat teshuvah: One who has passionately done a *shuv*, "turn" toward personal renewing of one's Jewish life and learning.

badhan (bahd-han): Comedian specializing in spoofing Jewish life, and life in general, who would perform at rites of passage and festival gatherings.

bal tash-hit (bal tahsh-heet): Commandment to engage in no wanton destruction of the resources of the planet.

bar mitzvah (bar mitz-vah): Rite of passage; typically for an adolescent Jewish male; now a rite also undertaken by Jewish men of any age from age thirteen and upward.

bat mitzvah (baht mitz-vah): Rite of passage; originally for an adolescent Jewish female; now a rite also undertaken by Jewish women of any age from age twelve and upward.

b'di-avahd (b'dee-ah-vahd): After the fact.

bedeken (b'deh-kn): Yiddish term for rite of veiling a bride after husband-to-be checks to ensure the right woman is under the veil.

beit din (bet dihn): Term for a court that follows Jewish law; it is made up of three extensively trained and respected individuals.

beshert (b'shert): Yiddish term for feeling you have discovered the one you are meant to marry at this point in your life.

brit bat (breet baht): Covenantal ritual for a baby girl.

brit milah (breet milah, bris milah): Circumcision. A covenantal rite for boys. Colloquially termed a *bris*.

b'tzelem Elohim (b'tzeh-lehm eh-loe-him): Humans are said, in Torah, to have been created "in the image of G*d."

Eihah (ey-hah): Hebrew name for the biblical Book of Lamentations, taken from the first sentence of the text which literally means "How?"

Essenes (eh-seens): Ascetic sect of Jews living in the first century, most of whom were believed to live near the Dead Sea.

ezrat holim (ezraht ho-lim): Helping the sick with visits, shopping, and such; it is a sacred obligation (mitzvah) in Jewish tradition.

Folkshul: A nontheistic approach to Jewish community, offering family programs and youth education that transmit the values of social justice and human responsibility in an environment that nourishes critical thinking and provides a strong sense of Jewish identity. Visit www.folkshul.org.

geirut (gay-rute): Conversion; from *ger*, meaning convert or being a "resident."

Gemara (g'more-uh): Part of the Talmud that contains rabbinical commentaries and analysis of the Mishnah.

gemilut hasadim (g'meelute ha-sah-deem): Deeds of loving-kindness. A core Jewish principle is to seek out opportunities to offer deeds of loving-kindness to others.

get (geht): Jewish writ of divorce. Undoes a Jewish wedding, just as a civil divorce undoes a civil wedding. A *get* is required for remarrying under Jewish auspices.

hahnassat orhim (hah-nah-saht ohr-him): The mitzvah of hosting, welcoming, and paying special attention to caring for the needs of guests.

halahah (hah-lah-hah): The general term for Jewish law. This has evolved differently among the various denominations—some consult, some follow explicitly, all must obtain or create interpretations in every age due to changing times.

Hallel (hah-lell): Psalm-set found in most holiday services that has joyful melodies. *Hallel* is the root of *hallelu-yah*, meaning "praise G*d."

Hasid, Hasidim (pl): Students of the nineteenth-century teacher Israel Baal Shem Tov became dynastic leaders of ultra-observant, ecstatic eastern European Jewish sects; some continue to this day.

hatan (ha-than): Groom.

hatimah (ha-tee-mah): Most Hebrew blessings have a similar opening format; what makes the blessing unique is the way it is "sealed" by referring to what is being blessed, as in "....who brings forth bread from the earth."

havurah (hah-vue-rah): A member- rather then clergy-led collective study, prayer, or other interest-focused Jewish group that meets regularly.

hesed (heh-sed): Quality of overflowing loving-kindness; considered to be one of the attributes of the Divine, emanated into the range of human capability and meant to balance with healthy boundaries to result in compassionate action.

heshbon hanefesh (hesh-bone ha-neh-fesh): Jewish spiritual practice of doing an "account" of the "soul"; an ethical life review.

hevra kaddisha (hevrah k'deeshuh): Volunteer group that does the ritual preparation and accompaniment of a Jewish person's body for burial.

hiddur mitzvah (hee-door meetz-vah): Elaboration on the beauty of a mitzvah and the symbols and music associated with a mitzvah, such as creating a beautiful wedding canopy or kiddush cup; it is considered a good and holy thing to do.

hod (hoed): Quality of containment of self-expression toward deeper development; considered to be one of the attributes of the divine, emanated into the range of human capability and meant to balance with drive for accomplishment to result in readiness.

hohmah (hoh-mah): Wisdom.

hora (hore-uh): Simple, joyful Jewish circle dance.

huppah (hoo-pah, huh-puh): Wedding canopy symbolic of the Jewish home being created by the couple.

intermarriage: Marriage of a person from one religious or tribal tradition with someone from a different religion or tribe.

Isaac (Hebrew, Yitz-hak): Son of Abraham and Sarah; second of Judaism's three founding patriarchs.

Jewish Reconstructionist Federation: Umbrella organization for communities; originally based on the naturalistic philosophy of Rabbi Mordecai Kaplan.

Clergy are trained as facilitators who empower communities and individuals to learn, practice, and grow in relationship to consciously forging a contemporary, inclusive Judaism. Visit www.judaism.jrf.org.

kabbalat panim (kah-bah-lat pah-nim): See *tisch.*

Kaddish (kadeesh, kah-dish): Holiness prayer with several forms; said at various services and life cycle events to reflect upon the Great Name that unifies all.

Karaites (ka-rites): Prominent at the time of Maimonides, this fundamentalist-type Jewish sect did not accept the Talmud and instead tried to live as close to the word of the Torah as they could. Ultimately they became a separate religious group, numbering 10,000 to 20,000 today, with the majority living in Israel.

kashrut, kashrus (kahsh-rute, kashrus): Kosher; Jewish dietary laws and customs.

ketubah (keh-tue-bah): Jewish wedding document.

Kiddush (kee-doosh, kih-dush): Holiness prayer, said over wine, regarding the gift of the vitality of life so deeply appreciated through the joy of holidays and Shabbat.

kiddushin (kee-due-sheen): Holiness section of a Jewish wedding ceremony.

kippah (kee-pah): Modern Hebrew term for a yarmulke or scull cap worn either during prayer, or at all times, except while bathing, to indicate intent to live a mitzvah-centered life.

kittel (kih-tl): Robe component of a shroud that is also available in versions appropriate for spiritual and symbolic wear by those of any gender at one's wedding and on the High Holy Days.

kodesh (koe-desh): Holy.

Kodesh Baruh Hu (koe-desh bah-ruh hoo): A traditional way of referring to G*d as the "Holy One Blessed Be He."

Abraham Isaac Kook (1865–1935): Author, mystic, scholar, and the first Ashkenazi chief rabbi of the British Mandate for Palestine; the founder of the Religious Zionist Yeshiva Mercaz.

l'hathillah (l'haht-hee-lah): From the outset. Before a significant event; in contrast to *b'di-avahd.*

maggid (mah-gihd, mah-geed): Professional Jewish storyteller who communicates Jewish values through story.

mashiah (mah-shee-ah): Messiah. In Jewish sacred literature, a person who would lead the Jews to freedom in their own land. In Jewish cultural literature, someone who has the qualities it takes to bring world peace. In recent Jewish philosophy, a quality inside every person that makes us capable of contributing to world peace.

mazel tov (mazl tove, mazelle tov): Good luck. An expression from astrology meaning, "May the star under which your event occurs be auspicious for good outcomes."

menahem aveil, neihum avelim (meh-nah-hem ah-veyl (s), neehume ah-vey-lim (pl)): Mitzvah of visiting those in mourning to comfort them, so that they know they are not alone in the world and that people care.

midrash (mid-rahsh): Genre of rabbinic literature that imagines what characters in *Tanah* might say or do that sheds light on how Torah was understood or used to regulate Jewish ethical life in different generations and regions of *midrashic* writers. That the fruit Eve gave Adam is an apple, for example, is not written in the Bible. It is a later *midrashic* interpretation that, because it has become so popular, is believed to be true.

mikvah (mik-vuh): Also written *mikveh*; practice of immersing oneself in living waters such as lake, river, ocean, sea, and rain water, or in indoor "kissing waters," like tap water with a conduit to include fresh rain water, for the purpose of transitioning from one stage of life to another. Undertaken for conversion or marriage, after menstruation or a wet dream, and in preparation for Shabbat or a major holiday. More recently, some utilize *mikvah* in preparation for major medical treatments.

minyan (min-yahn): Ten is the number needed to hold a Jewish prayer service, and that number is called a minyan. Some communities require ten males; for some a mixed group of Jewish men and women is fine. A new trend is to wait for ten men and ten women to arrive.

Mishnah (mish-nuh): The first normative, postbiblical compilation of Jewish law; together with subsequent rabbinic discussion called the Gemarah, these form the foundation of the Talmud.

mitzvah (mitz-vuh, meetz-vah): A traditional guideline for ethical living of which 248 are positive to engage in and 365 are things to refrain from. Some apply only to Israel and others are moot because we no longer have an active sacrificial system.

mohel(im)/mohelet (moyl, moyl-eht): Professional title for the person who is trained to perform a circumcision.

moshiah: see mashiah.

National Council of Young Israel: Umbrella organization for a large number of Jewish communities that live according to Jewish law. Visit www.youngisrael.org.

National Havurah Committee: An umbrella organization for sharing of methods and meetings of the *havurah* movement. Visit www.havurah.org.

netzah (neh-tzah): Quality of drive for success; considered to be one of the attributes of the Divine, emanated into the range of human capability and meant to balance with restraint and development in order to result in readiness.

niddah (nee-duh): Practice of refraining from sex and physical contact with your partner during menstruation and prior to going to *mikvah*.

niggun, niggunim (pl) (nih-guhn, nee-gune, nee-gu-nim): Wordless melodies; a Hasidic prayer form.

Orthodox Union: Umbrella organization coordinating programs such as supervision of Kosher food for Jews who live religiously according to Jewish law. Visit www.ou.org.

panim el panim (pah-nim el pah-nim): Face-to-face.

Pharisees: Second Temple–period Jewish sect from second century BCE to second century CE. Held a minority of the seventy seats in the Sanhedrin; viewed as the founding sect of rabbinic Judaism.

pluralism: Many kinds of peoples safely sharing the same space during a conference, experience, training, etc.

Purim (poor-im, poo-reem): Rite of reversal festival involving the chanting of the *Megillat Esther*, and clowning in ways that spoof or reverse roles of oppression in society.

Rashi (1040 to 1105): Major scholar; Talmud and Torah commentator who survived the first Crusade in Europe; born in Troyes, France.

Rosh Hodesh (roesh hoe-desh): Monthly celebration of the new moon; traditionally a day off from labor for women; often a time of Jewish women's gatherings, when life's journeys are shared in confidence and Jewish practices are studied and reframed for contemporary times.

Sabbath, Shabbat (shah-baht): Sabbath. Starts at sundown on Friday nights and ends Saturday evening when three stars are visible in the sky. Traditionally, a day of withdrawing from engagement with commerce and finance, and refocusing energies on family and spiritual community.

Saducees (sad-uh-seas): Second Temple period Jewish sect whose philosophies included rejection of the existence of the doctrine of the resurrection of the dead.

Sarah (Sah-rah, Surah, Sah-ruh): First of the four Jewish matriarchs; mother of Isaac and Ishmael; wife of Abraham.

sephirah (seh-fir-uh): Term for each of the nodes on the kabblists' Tree of Life; each has a unique quality that in their model is holographically emanated from Beyond and can be cultivated within.

seudah (s'ue'duh): Meal.

seudah shel mitzvah (sue'duh shel mitz-vah): Meal held for a major mitzvah such as a wedding, circumcision, or bar/bat mitzvah.

shadhan (shahd-hahn): Matchmaker.

shaliah (shah-lee-ah): Messenger. Also a practice of some rebbes to send emissaries to represent them; the role of the State of Israel's representatives to communities worldwide.

shamor v'zahor (shah-more v'za-hore): Sacred liturgical phrase meaning "guard and remember" [Shabbat].

Sheheheyanu (sheh-he-<u>h</u>eh-yah-nu): "That sustains us." Title and central word of the prayer to celebrate reaching major festivals and certain major lifecycle events.

Shehinah (shuh-<u>h</u>ee-nah, shuh-<u>h</u>ee-nuh): One of the many names of G*d, this one signifies the experience of Presence. A masculine word in rabbinic literature; subsequently has taken on a feminine quality in contemporary times.

shema (sh'mah): "Hear," "listen." Also the title of the central Jewish prayer that is said upon going to sleep and at daily services; it is found in the mezuzah and *tefillin* scrolls; original source is Torah.

Sheva Bra<u>h</u>ot (sheh-vuh brah-<u>h</u>ote): Seven blessings that conclude a Jewish wedding ceremony that are also chanted during the first week of marriage by friends at whose homes the couple are invited to dine.

shidduh (shih-du<u>h</u>): A match of two people toward marriage.

shli<u>h</u>ut (shlee-<u>h</u>ute): Being sent as an emissary on behalf of a teacher, tradition, or the Israeli government; also to deliver and obtain a legal signature for divorce.

shomer (show-mehr): One who watches over— as in one who attends a bride or groom before their wedding, or who watches over the Sabbath by observing it.

Shul<u>h</u>an Aru<u>h</u> (shul-<u>h</u>an ah-ru<u>h</u>): Code of Jewish law, compiled and published by Joseph Caro in 1567, that remains highly influential in traditional Jewish life.

Sicarii: Violent extremist Jewish group that acted against those Jews who were assimilating into Roman society.

sim<u>h</u>ah (sih<u>m</u>-<u>h</u>uh, seem-<u>h</u>ah): Happy life cycle occasion.

sim<u>h</u>at <u>h</u>ohmah (seem-<u>h</u>aht <u>h</u>oh-muh): Eldering ceremony with wisdom sharing by honoree; often Torah is read and taught and a prayer service is led either by honoree or friends.

Society for Humanistic Judaism: Umbrella organization for Jewish community groups that are nontheistic in philosophy and that function as congregations, or havurot. Visit www.shj.org.

Society of Jewish Science: Also known as Center for Applied Judaism. Founded in the early twentieth century, umbrella organization for Jewish communities that seek to intensify the spiritual consciousness of Jews, and to reveal Jewish resources for health, serenity, success, and peace of mind. Visit www.appliedjudaism.org.

Song of Songs: In Hebrew, *Shir HaShirim*. A lengthy love poem and sacred text that is read on the Sabbath and Passover specifically and is often studied for its beauty and power.

striemel (stry-ml): The black fur-wrapped hat worn by senior members of some <u>H</u>asidic groups.

ta<u>h</u>ri<u>h</u>im (ta<u>h</u>-ree-<u>h</u>im): Refers to the gauze-like garments that comprise a shroud.

tallit, tallis (tah-leet, tah-liss): Prayer shawl.

Talmud (tahl-muhd): Compilation of postbiblical rabbinic studies and development of ethics, practices, stories of sage's teachings, dreams, and legal decisions. Basic texts are the Mishnah and Gemarah; they are set in a way such that columns of commentary by subsequent generations surround them.

tameh (tah-mey): State of ritual impurity—such as after touching a corpse.

Tanah (tah-nah): Acronym for the sacred texts in the Jewish canon.

tenaiim (t'nae-im): Conditions agreed to by a couple-to-be-wed regarding quality of life and handling of finances for a marriage.

teshuvah (t'shoe-vah): Spiritual practice of honestly admitting culpability and listening to the experience of another undefensively in order to begin to *shuv*, "return," a relationship to a healthy status.

tisch (tish): Literally means "table"; the practice of gathering around a table on Shabbat or at a wedding to listen to a teaching.

Tosafot (tow-sah-fote): Medieval Talmud commentaries that typically appear as one of the columns on the page of Talmud.

tzaar baalei hayyim (tzah-ahr bah-ah-lay hah-yim): Principle that one should not cause unnecessary pain to sentient beings.

tzedakah (tz'dah-kah): The principle, or mitzvah, of giving money to help others in need and to support research, education, and the arts.

Union for Reform Judaism: Umbrella organization for Judaism's Reform movement, with some 900 congregations dedicated to egalitarian Judaism and enlightened approaches to Jewish living and learning. Visit www.urj.org.

United Jewish Communities: Umbrella organization for the Jewish Federation movement that organizes funds and programming to support Jewish education and social welfare agencies in the United States, Israel, and abroad. Visit www.ujc.org.

United Synagogue of Conservative Judaism: Umbrella group for synagogues and programs that are simultaneously progressive, and seriously dedicated, to enlightened traditional Jewish living. Also known abroad as the Masorti Movement. Visit www.USCJ.org.

vort (vohrt): Yiddish for "a word." A Torah teaching given on special occasions such as the Sabbath, at a meal, or at a life cycle ritual; often called "giving a vort."

yihud (yee-hude): Time of at-one-ment immediately after the marriage ceremony when a couple has private time together.

Yizkor (yiz-core): Service held on holy days to honor the memory of those who have died.

zahor (zah-hor): Remember.

SUGGESTIONS FOR FURTHER READING AND LEARNING

RECLAIMINGJUDAISM.ORG, BLOG, AND E-MAIL MENTORING

The website for this book series, ReclaimingJudaism.org, offers hundreds of pages of additional teachings and extended bibliographies that are available at no cost. You can also register for high-quality, low-cost, conference call, webcam, and retreat opportunities for study. Those on staff at ReclaimingJudaism engage in researching and developing methods of experiential Jewish learning and also provide support for the creation and facilitation of customized Jewish rites of passage, including special attention to bar/bat mitzvah preparation and community retreats.

The opening blog at ReclaimingJudaism.org shares new teachings and travel experiences of staff, and invites ideas and comments from the general public. Readers can also sign up at ReclaimingJudaism.org for one free e-mail mentoring session in any of the concepts and practices covered in the *Reclaiming Judaism* trilogy. Simply type the book's title in the subject line of your e-mail and a response will come, generally within a week's time.

RITES OF PASSAGE IN GENERAL

Adelman, Penina. *Miriam's Well: Rituals for Jewish Women around the Year.* New York: Biblio Press, 1996. Learn the primary *midrash* about Miriam's well along with important approaches to Jewish ritual.

Beck, Renee, and Syndey Barbara Metrick. *The Art of Ritual: Creating and Performing Ceremonies for Growth and Change.* Berkeley: Celestial Arts, 2003. Still a classic that makes it easy to conceive of the steps and types of ritual and what might work for you.

Eliade, Mircea, and Willard R. Trask. *Rites and Symbols of Initiation: The Mysteries of Birth and Rebirth.* Woodstock, CT: Spring Publications, 1994. Seminal work on rites of passage.

Gottlieb, Lynn. *She Who Dwells Within: A Feminist Vision of a Renewed Judaism.* New York: HarperCollins, 1995. Groundbreaking work by one of the first women rabbis, showing how to connect ecology, spirituality, equality, and Judaism through meaningful rites of passage and by personalizing Jewish practices.

Mahdi, Louise Carus, Steven Foster, and Meredith Little, eds. *Betwixt & Between: Patterns of Masculine and Feminine Initiation.* Chicago: Open Court Publishing, 1987. These scholars visited indigenous cultures worldwide to observe, explore, and write about their rites of passage.

Mahdi, Louise Carus, Nancy Geyer Christopher, and Michael Meade, eds. *Crossroads: The Quest for Contemporary Rites of Passage.* Chicago: Open Court Publishing, 1996. These scholars attend to modern cultures and the emerging and creative ways people are expressing major life transitions through ritual.

Orenstein, Debra. *Lifecycles, Vol. 1: Jewish Women on Life Passages and Personal Milestones.* Woodstock, VT: Jewish Lights Publishing, 1998. Creative approaches to rites including some not addressed by tradition.

Waskow, Arthur Ocean, and Phyllis Ocean Berman. *A Time for Every Purpose under Heaven: The Jewish Life-Spiral as a Spiritual Path.* New York: Farrar, Straus and Giroux. 2002. Inclusive and reflective of lives richly immersed in reclaiming spirituality within Judaism, with a focus on rites of passage.

WEB SITES

Itim.org.il. A talented traditional team demystifies Jewish rites of passage and opens up options for readers.

jafi.org.il/education/lifecycle/jewishlc/index.html. The Jewish Agency offers a wide range of accessible, well-documented guides to Jewish rites of passage on this richly informative website.

Jofa.org. Jewish Orthodox Feminist Alliance; offers resources for deep, creative ritual responses.

ReclaimingJudaism.org. Companion site to this volume, rich in ever-expanding teachings on every aspect of Jewish life.

Ritualwell.org. Jewish feminists from every walk of Jewish life the world over contribute creative entries for every stage of life.

ADULT ISSUES

Addison, Howard, and Barbara Eve Breitman. *Jewish Spiritual Direction: An Innovative Guide from Traditional and Contemporary Sources.* Woodstock, VT:

Jewish Lights Publishing, 2006. The first comprehensive resource for spiritual direction in the Jewish tradition.

Berrin, Susan. *A Heart of Wisdom: Making the Jewish Journey from Midlife through the Elder Years*. Woodstock, VT: Jewish Lights Publishing, 1997. Compilation of essays that facilitate a conscious shift from feeling old to feeling wiser, empowered, and valuable.

Biale, David. *Eros and the Jews from Biblical Israel to Contemporary America*. New York: Basic Books, 1993. Fascinating review of major sources and trends in sexual morality within Judaism across the ages.

Frankel, Estelle. *Sacred Therapy: Jewish Spiritual Teachings on Emotional Healing and Inner Wholeness*. Boston: Shambhala, 2005. Exceptionally insightful guide to reflecting on your life, taught by a psychotherapist with an extensive Jewish background in sources, principles, and practices.

Friedman, Dayle A. *Jewish Visions for Aging: A Professional Guide for Fostering Wholeness*. Woodstock, VT: Jewish Lights Publishing, 2008. This rich resource probes Jewish texts, spirituality and observance, uncovering a deep, never-before-realized approach to caring for the aging.

———. *When Someone You Love Needs Long-Term Care*. Woodstock, VT: Jewish Lights Publishing, 2000. Written by a professional who is wise and profoundly experienced in working with elders of advanced age and their families, this pamphlet helps families consider difficult options with understanding and compassion. Part of the LifeLights: Help for Wholeness and Healing Jewish pastoral care pamphlet series from Jewish Lights Publishing.

Gendlin, Gene. *Focusing*. New York: Bantam Books, 2007. Teaches the powerful technique he developed for forming an authentic, inner spiritual connection that helps clarify how to move life-forward.

Greenberg, Steven. *Wrestling with God and Men: Homosexuality in the Jewish Tradition*. Madison: University of Wisconsin Press, 2005. Important, thoughtful, and inclusive teachings for those who wrestle with the range of Jewish understandings and practices of this topic.

Lev, Rachel. *Shine the Light: Sexual Abuse and Healing in the Jewish Community*. Boston: Northeastern University Press, 2002. Wonderful collection of essays on the many ways that communities and individuals acknowledge and recover from abuse.

Schachter-Shalomi, Zalman, and Ronald S. Miller. *From Age-ing to Sage-ing: A Profound New Vision of Growing Older*. New York: Grand Central Publishing, 1997. This book helped start a movement to vanquish the term *elderly* and replace it with *eldering* and *saging*. Deep, wise, important.

Schachter-Shalomi, Zalman, and Daniel Siegel. *Integral Halachah: Transcending and Including*, Victoria, BC: Trafford Publishing, 2007. A bridge for those wanting not to throw the baby out with the bath water or to hurt others. This little book shows how to bridge Jewish life and contemporary life with integrity and creativity.

Twerski, Abraham J. *Happiness and the Human Spirit: The Spirituality of Becoming the Best You Can Be*. Woodstock, VT: Jewish Lights Publishing, 2007. Uses simple, accessible language and clear examples to show you how true happiness can be found within you. Includes easy-to-follow exercises.

————. *I'd Like to Call for Help But I Don't Know the Number: The Search for Spirituality in Everyday Life*. New York: Henry Holt, 1996. Dynamic and encouraging in ways that lead to meaningful personal change. Most everything this author writes touches the core of active spiritual growth.

WEBSITES

focusing.org. Resources, dialogue groups, and conferences.

ncjh.org. National Center for Jewish Healing. Jewish healing defined and explored; many links and resources.

sharsheret.org. Jewish organization addressing breast cancer; resource clearing house.

shiraruskay.org. Annotated list of resources and links for support of the seriously ill and caregivers.

BAR/BAT MITZVAH

Abrams, Judith Z. *Torah and Company: The Weekly Portion of Torah Accompanied by Generous Helpings of Mishnah and Gemara, Served Up with Discussion Questions to Spice Up Your Sabbath Table*. Teaneck, NJ: Ben Yehuda Press, 2005. Questions to discuss about each week's Torah portion at dinner time. Easy way to help families get rolling for the bar/bat mitzvah process by putting everyone on to the same page of curiosity and sharing.

Adelman, Penina, Ali Feldman, and Shulamit Reinharz. *The JGirl's Guide: The Young Jewish Woman's Handbook for Coming of Age*. Woodstock, VT: Jewish Lights Publishing, 2005. A first-of-its-kind book of practical, real-world advice using Judaism as a compass for the journey through adolescence.

Baskin, Nora Raleigh. *The Truth about My Bat Mitzvah*. New York: Simon & Schuster, 2008. For 10–12 year olds, discover what's possible.

Davis, Judith. *Whose Bar/Bat Mitzvah Is This, Anyway? A Guide for Parents through a Family Rite of Passage*. New York: St. Martin's Press, 1998. Focuses on developmental issues in the family. Helpful for those parenting or working with adolescents.

Elper, Ora Wiskind, ed. *Traditions and Celebrations for the Bat Mitzvah*. Jerusalem, Israel: Urim Publications, 2005. Lovely collection of essays where traditional community leaders discuss how to embrace and adapt to the practice of females undertaking to prepare for and engage in a ritual of bat mitzvah.

Gold, Shefa. *Torah Journeys: The Inner Path to the Promised Land*. Teaneck, NJ: Ben Yehuda Press, 2006. Will help parents find a deep connection to each Torah portion so that they can help lead the way for others.

Jacobson, Burt. *Crossing the River: Bar/Bat Mitzvah and the Journey toward Adulthood.* Berkeley: Kehillah Community Synagogue, info@KehillaSynagogue.org.

Milgram, Goldie. *Make Your Own Bar/Bat Mitzvah: A Personal Approach to Creating a Meaningful Rite of Passage.* San Francisco: Jossey-Bass, 2004. Chock-full of ideas, activities, and stories that reframe bar/bat mitzvah to allow for an emotionally satisfying, intellectually expansive, and spiritually profound experience for adult and adolescent *b'nei mitzvah*. Appropriate for individuals, families, and congregations/*havurot*.

———. *Meaning and Mitzvah: Daily Practices for Reclaiming Judaism through Prayer, God, Torah, Hebrew, Mitzvot and Peoplehood.* Woodstock, VT: Jewish Lights Publishing, 2005. Provides the framework for understanding the powerful and often unexplained intellectual, emotional and spiritual tools that are essential for a lively, relevant spiritual practice.

Rosenbloom, Fiona. *You Are SO Not Invited to My Bat Mitzvah.* New York: Hyperion, 2007. Probably too mature for twelve year olds, but great for fourteen and up. A quick fun read that addresses the maturity issues faced by adolescents as they become teens. Important for parents to read along and discuss. Other books in this series are similar in scope. Valuable.

Salkin, Jeffrey K. "Appropriating a Liturgical Context for Bar/Bat Mitzvah." D.Min. Dissertation, Princeton Theological Seminary, 1992. Lays out extensive helpful sources and thinking on the subject.

———. *Putting God on the Guest List: How to Reclaim the Spiritual Meaning of Your Child's Bar or Bat Mitzvah.* 3rd ed. Woodstock, VT: Jewish Lights Publishing, 2005. One of a number of books by this seminal author that encourage a healthier bar/bat mitzvah process.

Vogel, Gila, and Shunit Reiter. "Spiritual Dimensions of Bar/Bat Mitzvah Ceremonies for Jewish Children with Developmental Disabilities." *Education and Training in Developmental Disabilities* 38 (Sept 2003) 3:314–22. Israelis show the way; twenty-one examples discussed and studied.

WEBSITES

Bmitzvah.org. Noncommercial, richly resourced with ways to make bar/bat mitzvah more meaningful and memorable.

Ziv.org. Danny Siegel's site dedicated to every possible way he can think of to help you find a mitzvah to do for others.

PREGNANCY, BIRTHING, ABORTION, MISCARRIAGE, ADOPTION

Berman, Robin E., Arthur Kurzweil, and Dale L. Mintz. *The Hadassah Jewish Family Book of Health and Wellness.* San Francisco: Jossey-Bass, 2006. Offers a wide range of guidance. Be sure to check out chapters on genetic disorders and circumcision.

Cardin, Nina Beth. *Tears of Sorrow, Seeds of Hope: A Spiritual Companion for Infertility and Pregnancy Loss*. 2nd ed. Woodstock, VT: Jewish Lights Publishing, 2007. Beautiful, heart-centered, valuable companion through difficulty into hope and transcendence.

Falk, Sandy, Daniel Judson, and Steven A. Rapp. *The Jewish Pregnancy Book: A Resource for the Soul, Body and Mind during Pregnancy, Birth and the First Three Months*. Woodstock, VT: Jewish Lights Publishing, 2003. Wonderful, comprehensive, flowing guide to Jewish spirituality for those yearning for meaningful Jewish practices during pregnancy.

Frymer-Kensky, Tikva. *Motherprayer: The Pregnant Woman's Spiritual Companion*. New York: Riverhead Books, 1995. This groundbreaking biblical scholar of blessed memory took ancient texts of Middle Eastern cultures and crafted them into a beautiful spiritual guide to navigating pregnancy.

Gold, Michael. *And Hannah Wept: Infertility, Adoption, and the Jewish Couple*. Philadelphia: Jewish Publication Society, 1988. Especially relevant today on matters of understanding and embracing adoption in a Jewish life.

Rosner, Fred. *Biomedical Ethics and Jewish Law*. Hoboken, NJ: Ktav Publishing, 2001. A great teacher and scholar of Jewish bioethics teaches Jewish law and its applications to major health care issues.

WEBSITES

Resolve.org. National infertility association.

starsofdavid.org. Jewish adoption information and support network, not a placement agency.

NAMING

Cohen, Debra Nussbaum. *Celebrating Your New Jewish Daughter: Creating Jewish Ways to Welcome Baby Girls into the Covenant—New and Traditional Ceremonies*. Woodstock, VT: Jewish Lights Publishing, 2001. Ideal for those wanting to customize ceremonies for their daughter.

Diamant, Anita. *New Jewish Baby Book*, 2nd Edition: *Names, Ceremonies and Customs—A Guide for Today's Families*. Woodstock, VT: Jewish Lights Publishing, 2005. A complete guide to the customs and rituals for welcoming a new child.

Kolatch, Alfred J. *The Complete Dictionary of English and Hebrew First Names*. Middle Village, NY: Jonathan David Publishers, 1984. Comprehensive, clear; a true reference book.

Sidi, Smadar Shir. *The Complete Book of Hebrew Baby Names*. San Francisco: HarperOne, 1989. Inexpensive and convenient.

CIRCUMCISION

Barth, Lewis M., ed. *Berit Mila in the Reform Context*. New York: Brit Mila Board of Reform Judaism, 1990.

Hoffman, Lawrence A. *Covenant of Blood: Circumcision and Gender in Rabbinic Judaism*. Chicago: University of Chicago Press, 1996. Great mining of Jewish sources to reveal evolution of circumcision in Judaism.

Krohn, Peysach J. *Bris Milah: Circumcision*. Brooklyn: Mesorah Publications, 1999. Covers the first eight days of life with precise attention to Jewish law and traditional sources.

CHILDREN AND FAMILIES

Danan, Julie Hilton. *The Jewish Parents' Almanac*. Northvale, NJ: Jason Aronson, 1996. Chock full of great ways to fill Jewish family life with meaningful, engaging activities for every day, holidays, life cycle. If out of print, call your local synagogue; they'll likely have it in the library.

Fuchs, Lawrence H. *Beyond Patriarchy: Jewish Fathers and Families*. Hanover, NH: Brandeis University Press, 2000. Raises important questions, teaches history, points to new opportunities for meaningful fathering.

Fuchs-Kreimer, Nancy. *Parenting as a Spiritual Journey: Deepening Ordinary and Extraordinary Events into Sacred Occasions*. Woodstock, VT: Jewish Lights Publishing, 1998. Offers more than one hundred inspiring examples from a great diversity of families.

Musleah, Rahael, and Michael Klayman. *Sharing Blessings: Children's Stories for Exploring the Spirit of the Jewish Holidays*. Woodstock, VT: Jewish Lights Publishing, 1997. Such a fun, colorful, relevant, and inviting a book merits a place in every Jewish home.

Pitzele, Peter. *Our Fathers' Wells: A Personal Encounter with the Myths of Genesis*. New York: HarperCollins, 1995. The father of bibliodrama, as a method for raising awareness, offers sources and methods for gaining insight into our assumptions. What have you drawn from your father's well?

Weiss, G.N., and Weiss E.B. "A perspective on controversies over neonatal circumcision." *Clinical Pediatrics* 33 (Dec 1994) 12:726–30.

CONVERSION

Berkowitz, Allan L., and Patti Moskovitz. *Embracing the Covenant: Converts to Judaism Talk about Why and How*. Woodstock, VT: Jewish Lights Publishing, 1996. A delightful compendium of the many ways people find their way to deciding to be Jewish and to enter a process of conversion within the Jewish community that speaks to them.

Lamm, Maurice. *Becoming a Jew.* Middle Village, NY: Jonathan David Publishers, 1991. Covers the traditional approach to converting to Judaism.

Lester, Julius. *Lovesong: Becoming a Jew.* New York: Arcade Publishing, 1995. The son of a Southern black Methodist minister becomes Jewish. A powerful, well-written story of his journey to Judaism.

Scalamonti, John David. *Ordained to Be a Jew: A Catholic Priest's Conversion to Judaism.* Hoboken, NJ: Ktav Publishing House, 1992. Remarkable story of how a Catholic priest found his way to Judaism.

DYING, DEATH, MOURNING, RECOVERING

Address, Richard, F., and Commission on Jewish Family Concerns, eds. *A Time to Prepare.* New York: UAHC Press, 2002. Reform movement guide.

Angel, Marc D. *The Orphaned Adult: Confronting the Death of a Parent.* Northvale, NJ: Jason Aronson, 1997.

Brener, Anne. *Mourning and Mitzvah: A Guided Journal for Walking the Mourner's Path through Grief to Healing.* Woodstock, VT: Jewish Lights Publishing, 2001. Deeply profound and user-friendly guide to grieving so that healing happens and life can go on in the healthiest way possible.

Brenner, Daniel, Tsvi Blanchard, Bradley Hirschfield, and Joseph J. Fins. *Embracing Life and Facing Death: A Jewish Guide to Palliative Care.* New York: CLAL, 2005. Advances understanding of Jewish practice across the spectrum of Jewish faith.

Broner, E. M. *Mornings and Mourning: A Kaddish Journal.* New York: HarperCollins, 1994. Saying *Kaddish* can be challenging for women in some communities; a view through one woman's powerful experience and growth.

Buscaglia, Leo. *The Fall of Freddie the Leaf: A Story of Life for All Ages.* Thorofare, NJ: Holt Rinehart & Winston. 1982. Lovely small book to help children relate to the death of a loved one.

Dorff, Elliot N. *Matters of Life and Death: A Jewish Approach to Modern Medical Ethics.* Philadelphia: Jewish Publication Society, 1998. A leading middle-ground thinker coming out of the Conservative movement. Highly readable, caring, with a solid presentation of sources.

Eilberg, Amy. *When Someone You Love Is Dying.* Woodstock, VT: Jewish Lights Publishing, 2000. Lovely booklet from a wise professional who is also a deep spiritual guide. Part of the LifeLights: Help for Wholeness and Healing Jewish pastoral care pamphlet series from Jewish Lights Publishing.

Goldstein, Sidney. *Suicide in Rabbinic Literature.* Hoboken, NJ: Ktav Publishing, 1989. A painful subject taught through the lens of a traditional rabbi who suffered himself.

Greenberg, Irving. *Dignity Beyond Death: The Jewish Preparation for Burial.* Jerusalem, Israel: Urim Publications, 2005. Families and volunteers describe the meaning and importance of this practice in their experience.

Kay, Alan A. *A Jewish Book of Comfort*. Northvale, NJ: Jason Aronson, 1997. A compilation of readings from throughout the tradition to keep on a bedside table for perusing in moments when comfort is needed.

Lamm, Maurice. *Jewish Hospice: To Live, to Hope, to Heal*. Woodstock, VT: Jewish Lights Publishing, 2000. Informative, comforting and personal pamphlet. Part of the LifeLights: Help for Wholeness and Healing Jewish pastoral care pamphlet series from JewishLights Publishing.

———. *The Jewish Way in Death and Mourning*. Middle Village, NY: Jonathan David Publishers, 2000. Teaches the basics clearly.

Levy, Naomi. *To Begin Again: The Journey toward Comfort, Strength, and Faith in Difficult Times*. New York: Ballantine Books, 1999. Brings comfort, supports strength, encourages faith. True to title.

Raphael, Simcha Paul. *Jewish Views of the Afterlife*. Northvale, NJ: Jason Aronson, 1996. Fascinating and comprehensive discussion of a wide range of Jewish perspectives and literature on death, reincarnation, dybbuks, life after death.

Reconstructionist Rabbinical College. *Behoref Hayamim: In the Winter of Life: A Values-Based Jewish Guide for Decision-Making at the End of Life*, Wyncote, PA: Reconstructionist Rabbinical College Press, 2002. Offers an empowering approach to understanding Jewish perspectives and forging your own.

Riemer, Jack, and Nathaniel Stampfer. *So That Your Values Live On: Ethical Wills and How to Prepare Them*. Woodstock, VT: Jewish Lights Publishing, 1994. Wonderful assortment of traditional and contemporary Jewish ethical wills.

Rose, Dawn Robinson, and Mona Decker. *Jewish Ethics of Speech: Disclosure to the Terminally Ill*. Wyncote, PA: Reconstructionist Rabbinical College Press, 2001. A great help to navigating difficult emotional terrain.

Schloss, Sima Devora. *Taking Care of Mom, Taking Care of Me: How to Manage with a Relative's Illness and Death*. New York: Judaica Press, 2002. Helpful for those feeling overwhelmed by caring for parents.

Shapiro, Rami M. *Last Breaths: A Guide to Easing Another's Dying*. Miami: Temple Beth Or, 1993. How to be there when being there feels difficult.

Spitz, Elie Kaplan. *Does the Soul Survive? A Jewish Journey to Belief in Afterlife, Past Lives and Living with Purpose*. Woodstock, VT: Jewish Lights Publishing, 2001. Eye-opening, quick read that's full of interesting and inspiring texts, stories, and perspectives.

Tendler, Moshe David, and Moshe Feinstein. *The Responsa of Rav Moshe Feinstein: Translation and Commentary. Volume I: Care of the Critically Ill*. Hoboken, NJ: Ktav Publishing, 1996. A great scholar tackles traditional sources to reconcile compassion and integrity in twentieth-century Jewish medical ethics for those on the threshold of death. His great student translates and explains for us. Important, amazing work.

Wieseltier, Leon. *Kaddish*. New York: Vintage, 2000. Engaging narrative of this thoughtful and deep man's grief and learning.

Wolfson, Ron. *A Time to Mourn, a Time to Comfort: A Guide to Jewish Bereavement*. Woodstock, VT: Jewish Lights Publishing, 2001. Clear step-by-step guide by a master teacher of Judaism.

Zweig, Gedalia. *Living Kaddish: Incredible and Inspiring Stories*. Jerusalem, Israel: Targum Press, 2007. Inspiring collection of stories from people world-wide who committed to saying *Kaddish* for a loved one and who felt changed by the encounters and learning this choice created for them.

WEBSITES

hods.org. Halachic Organ Donors Society.

nijh.org. National Institute for Jewish Hospice.

WEDDINGS, MARRIAGE, DIVORCE

Diamant, Anita. *The New Jewish Wedding, Revised*. New York: Scribner, 2001. Teaches traditional and innovative approaches; lovely translation of *Sheva Brahot*.

Fuchs-Kreimer, Nancy, and Nancy H. Wiener. *Judaism for Two: A Spiritual Guide for Strengthening and Celebrating Your Loving Relationship*. Woodstock, VT: Jewish Lights Publishing, 2005. Guide offers inspiration for Jewish couples who want to live with greater integrity, depth, joy, and wisdom.

Netter, Perry. *Divorce Is a Mitzvah: A Practical Guide to Finding Wholeness and Holiness When Your Marriage Dies*. Woodstock, VT: Jewish Lights Publishing, 2002. An indispensable guide to what Judaism says about ending a marriage and how its teachings can help you make hard decisions.

Saxe, Susan. *Points to Consider in Counseling Same-Sex Couples for Marriage/ Commitment Ceremonies: A Resource Manual*. Philadelphia: ALEPH, 2000.

Wasserfall, Rahel R., ed. *Women and Water: Menstruation in Jewish Life and Law*. Hanover, NH: Brandeis University Press, 1999. Scholarly collection of essays; very interesting and informative.

WEBSITES

mayyimhayyim.org.

ENVIRONMENTAL ACTIVISM

Benstein, Jeremy. *The Way Into Judaism and the Environment*. Woodstock, VT: Jewish Lights Publishing, 2008. Nice introduction to the topic.

Bernstein, Ellen, ed. *Ecology and the Jewish Spirit: Where Nature and the Sacred Meet*. Woodstock, VT: Jewish Lights Publishing, 2000. This is a wonderful treatment of how to get personal on the issue of Judaism and the environment.

Elon, Ari, Naomi Mara Hyman, and Arthur Waskow, eds. *Trees, Earth and Torah: A Tu B'Shvat Anthology*. Philadelphia: Jewish Publication Society, 2000. A wealth of material is covered in this useful work.

Tirosh-Samuelson, Hava, ed. *Judaism and Ecology Volume*. Boston: Center for the Study of World Religions, Harvard Divinity School, 2002. Richness of thought, text, and options here.

WEBSITES

Coejl.org. Seeks to expand the contemporary understanding of such Jewish values as *tikkun olam* (repairing the world) and *tzedek* (justice) to include the protection of both people and other species from environmental degradation. Also serves as an umbrella organization connecting many groups and resources.

Hazon.org. Seeks to build community and raise environmental awareness among Jews from various backgrounds and age groups, raise money for Jewish environmental initiatives, and promote renewed engagement with Jewish tradition.

Shalomcenter.org. Programs include thinking and initiatives that pursue environmental quality and stability.

svivaisrael.org. Fosters a sense of concern for others by creating a humane and caring community based on traditional Jewish environmental ethics learned through study of texts and the modern principles of sustainable development, learned through action.

ACKNOWLEDGMENTS

The *Reclaiming Judaism* trilogy was conceived during a session with Eve Ilsen, a practitioner of the methods of self-awareness developed by Colette Aboulker-Muscat, *z"l*. Using Colette's guided imagery process, in just under three minutes, Eve brought forth from within me a blue leaf-covered porch, which I then swept in my imagination, only to find a trap door with a latch, that, when opened, led me down to a room with a lit candle on a table and beside it a thick open book. The pages were blank. "What is on the cover?" Eve inquired. I closed the book, and behold, on the cover was written: *Reclaiming Judaism as a Spiritual Practice* by Rabbi Goldie Milgram. At the time I was suffering a breakup with a wonderful boyfriend, so perhaps you can imagine my surprise that what was revealed had nothing to do with the breakup. Within the year, my teacher Rabbi Dr. Nancy Fuchs-Kreimer had, unbeknownst to me, directed her agent to my website and the opportunity to find a publisher for the book was under way. Ann Edelstein took things to the next level in her capacity as an agent as best she could until, it seems, my dear colleague Anne Brener suggested to Stuart M. Matlins, publisher of Jewish Lights, that I become one of his authors. A decade later, here is the last volume of the trilogy! There are so many good people in the world who help others with profound generosity of spirit. My gratitude to those mentioned in earlier volumes, and, in accord with the mitzvah of *hakarat ha-tov*, seeing what is good and recognizing it aloud, let's continue.

In anticipation of this volume, Stuart Matlins wondered aloud what one more person could possibly have to say about Jewish life cycle rituals. This question proved the perfect stimulus for ever more creative research and writing. Stuart, for your guidance and support, and for the privilege of being a Jewish Lights author, please accept my deepest thanks.

The *Reclaiming Judaism* trilogy has also been made possible by a grant from the Nathan Cummings Foundation and the support and encouragement of Dr. Ruth Durchshlag. Ruth showed up in my office one day when I was serving as co-dean at the Academy for Jewish Religion with a question: What projects are you thinking about working on next? We went for a walk and talk, and quickly she not only arranged for support for this work, but also formulated a planning grant for the formation of what has become the Reclaiming Judaism 501(C)(3) nonprofit, and initial funding for in-depth research into reframing bar/bat mitzvah as a rite of spiritual initiation. Ruth came along in the unexpected and unsolicited way of a biblical *malakh adonai*, angel of G*d. Ruth, your arrival affected the course of my life in amazing and ever unfolding ways. I am deeply grateful.

The teaching in this book draws heavily upon the largesse and understanding of friends, family, students, clients, and former congregants who have agreed, *l'shem shamayim*, for the sake of Heaven, to have their rites of passage described in such a public way. I pray that the magnificent medium of storytelling employed herein will work its magic as a teaching tool to uncover Judaism as a profoundly meaningful spiritual path.

Generous souls hailing from every walk of Jewish life have put in dozens of hours reading various chapters and communicating with me to help ensure that the content and style of this volume are both congenial to learning and accurate, all the while keeping an eye on the series's important intention of fostering inclusiveness within a context of respectful pluralism. Your honesty, creativity, and emotional support throughout the complex process of trying to put on paper not only facts but also spirit have been a phenomenal gift—there is no way to thank you sufficiently. My infinite gratitude goes out to focus-group readers Suzy Garfinkle, Gary Cohen, Sarah Harwin, Sheri L. Jacobson, Elyse Josephs, Joan Klagsbrun, Tzeitl Locher, Uri Nodelman, Paul Oppenheimer, Rabbi Joyce Reinitz, Carola de Vries Robles, Marty Rubin, Rabbi Robert Scheinberg, Perry Pinchas Spring, Laura Vidmar, and Rabbi Shohama Wiener.

Two professional editors partnered me in this volume. Judith Kern's professional copyediting brought my content to a level that is conducive to joyful learning. Emily Wichland of the Jewish Lights editorial staff stayed the course over the many years it takes to write and lay out a teaching series. These editors maintained utter professionalism and patience, and ensured, through careful attention to detail, that each volume could stand on its own just as well as within a series that is formatted to fit together. The design and marketing teams at Jewish Lights are also an exceptional pool of talented professionals whose creativity adds additional excitement to the already exciting process of the writing.

One person ultimately gave the most of himself so that this project could come to fruition, my beloved hubbatzin Barry. Your capacity to stay present while I obsessed over this manuscript long into the night is saintly. You partnered me in every possible way—as a sounding board and critic as well as by coauthoring some segments and co-creating some rituals—and you selflessly took over responsibility for food shopping, meal preparation, helping with my elderly parents, and the laundry. With you, all that I've always hoped a Jewish home could be has more than come to fruition. You challenge me in holy ways, steadily opening new doorways of consciousness almost every day. I am so blessed.

The following individuals are among many who supplied information, contacts, experiences, and guidance that proved of great service to the formation of sections of this volume. I mention these individuals by name because their e-mails or depth of contact remain as memory aids to help trigger gratitude. Dino Aristides, Juliette Aristides, Ania Bien, Richard Bien, Jonathan Bub, Jeremy Bub, Lauren Bub, Leah Bub, Ellen Bernstein, Rabbi Howard A. Cohen, Zoe Cohen, Shulamit Day, Rabbi Gail Diamond, Dr. Marsha Bryan Edelman, Renee Fields, Yoram Getzler, Blu Greenberg, Trudy Gordon, Rabbi Ayla Grafstein, Judith Hauptman, Judy Heath, the Hitman family, Gloria Hoffman, Eve Ilsen, Debra Kolodny, Rabbi Judy Kummer, Arthur Kurzweil, Rabbi Yitzchak Mann, Rabbi Itzchak Marmorstein, my mother and father, Leona and Samuel Milgram, Rabbi G. Rayzel Raphael, Dr. Simchah Raphael, Liore Milgrom-Elcott, Charles Rich, Susan Saxe, Hazzan Neil Schwartz, Corey Shdaimah, Rabbi Daniel Siegel, Rabbi Margot Stein, Dr. Sharon Ufburg, Dr. Saul Wachs, Rabbi Melissa Wenig, Rabbi David Zaslow, and Rabbi Meryam Zislovich. I apologize if there are those who have been accidentally omitted.

A generation of pioneers in the field of new, renewed, and expanded Jewish rites of passage have published major works before me. It is upon their shoulders that this volume stands; their exceptional efforts have inspired me and given me the courage to add to their legacy with this volume. With apologies and prayers to not have accidentally overlooked someone, here is a comprehensive but probably not exhaustive list of authors in this new field: Penina Adelman, Rabbi Phyllis Berman, Susan Berrin, Anne Brener, E. M. Broner, Rabbi Nina Beth Cardin, Laura Davis, Barbara Diamond, Anita Diamont, Rabbi Amy Eilberg, Sandy Falk, Merle Feld, Irene Fine, Tamar Frankiel, Rabbi Dayle Friedman, Dr. Tikva Frymer-Kensky, z"l, Rabbi Laura Geller, Rabbi Elyse Goldstein, Rabbi Lynn Gottlieb, Blu and Rabbi Yitz Greenberg, Gail Anthony Greenberg, Rabbi Daniel Judson, Rabbi Gabrielle Kaplan-Mayer, Dr. Deborah Lipton Kremsdorf, Rabbi Irwin Kula, Aliza Lavie, Elizabeth Resnick Levine, Rela Monson, Dr. Vanessa Ochs, Rabbi Kerry Olitzky, Rabbi Debra Orenstein, and also Marge Piercy, Riv-Ellen Prell, Steven A. Rapp, Nessa Rappaport and Rabbi Jack Riemer, Rabbi Jeffrey Salkin, Rabbi Sandy Eisenberg Sasso, Rabbi Zalman Schachter-Shalomi, Marcia Cohen Spiegel, Nathaniel Stampfer, Rabbi Arthur Waskow, Rabbi Shohama Wiener, and Rabbi Sean Zevit. There are also numerous recording, ceremonial item, and graphic artists, as well as Jewish newspapers, magazines, and websites too numerous to list whose focused and creative efforts have accepted and produced articles and images essential to the evolution of Jewish rites of passage. An annotated bibliography containing works by most of these wonderful authors is available at ReclaimingJudaism.org. Not listed? Just ask and it will be done.

Enduring appreciation is due to the leadership of P'nai Yachadut–Reclaiming Judaism, the nonprofit that is the primary vehicle for my work in the world. The loving, steadfast support of executive committee members Dr. Sharon Uberg, Sarah Harwin, and Janice Rubin has made this remarkable forum for Jewish educational teaching, research, and development possible. My partner in the nonprofit's work, Rabbi Shohama Wiener is one of the world's quiet giants of Jewish life and learning; be sure to seek her out.

During the writing of this particular volume, I served as a consultant-in-residence on innovative Jewish programming at the 92nd Street Y in Manhattan. Through the guidance of Sol Adler, Helaine Geismar-Katz, Marty Maskowitz, Tony Giunta, Fretta Reitzes, Hanna Arie-Gaifman, and the team in the Bronfman Center for Jewish Life—Sharon Goldman, Leana Moritt, and Yaron Kapitulnik—new ways to express the joy of Jewishing for those unaccustomed to its beauty became possible and are incorporated into this work.

I close with abounding appreciation for all of my teachers, students, friends, and family.

—Reb Goldie

INDEX

Bar/Bat Mitzvah

The JGirl's Guide: The Young Jewish Woman's Handbook for Coming of Age
By Penina Adelman, Ali Feldman, and Shulamit Reinharz
This inspirational, interactive guidebook helps pre-teen Jewish girls address the many issues surrounding coming of age. 6 x 9, 240 pp, Quality PB, 978-1-58023-215-9 **$14.99**
Also Available: **The JGirl's Teacher's and Parent's Guide**
8½ x 11, 56 pp, PB, 978-1-58023-225-8 **$8.99**

Bar/Bat Mitzvah Basics: A Practical Family Guide to Coming of Age Together
Edited by Cantor Helen Leneman 6 x 9, 240 pp, Quality PB, 978-1-58023-151-0 **$18.95**

The Bar/Bat Mitzvah Memory Book, 2nd Edition: An Album for Treasuring the Spiritual Celebration *By Rabbi Jeffrey K. Salkin and Nina Salkin*
8 x 10, 48 pp, Deluxe HC, 2-color text, ribbon marker, 978-1-58023-263-0 **$19.99**

For Kids—Putting God on Your Guest List, 2nd Edition: How to Claim the Spiritual Meaning of Your Bar or Bat Mitzvah *By Rabbi Jeffrey K. Salkin*
6 x 9, 144 pp, Quality PB, 978-1-58023-308-8 **$15.99** *For ages 11–13*

Putting God on the Guest List, 3rd Edition: How to Reclaim the Spiritual Meaning of Your Child's Bar or Bat Mitzvah *By Rabbi Jeffrey K. Salkin*
6 x 9, 224 pp, Quality PB, 978-1-58023-222-7 **$16.99**; HC, 978-1-58023-260-9 **$24.99**
Also Available: **Putting God on the Guest List Teacher's Guide**
8½ x 11, 48 pp, PB, 978-1-58023-226-5 **$8.99**

Tough Questions Jews Ask: A Young Adult's Guide to Building a Jewish Life
By Rabbi Edward Feinstein 6 x 9, 160 pp, Quality PB, 978-1-58023-139-8 **$14.99** *For ages 12 & up*
Also Available: **Tough Questions Jews Ask Teacher's Guide**
8½ x 11, 72 pp, PB, 978-1-58023-187-9 **$8.95**

Bible Study/Midrash

Abraham's Bind & Other Bible Tales of Trickery, Folly, Mercy and Love *By Michael J. Caduto*
Re-imagines many biblical characters, retelling their stories.
6 x 9, 224 pp, HC, 978-1-59473-186-0 **$19.99** *(A book from SkyLight Paths, Jewish Lights' sister imprint)*

Ancient Secrets: Using the Stories of the Bible to Improve Our Everyday Lives
By Rabbi Levi Meier, PhD 5½ x 8½, 288 pp, Quality PB, 978-1-58023-064-3 **$16.95**

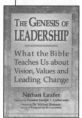

The Genesis of Leadership: What the Bible Teaches Us about Vision, Values and Leading Change *By Rabbi Nathan Laufer; Foreword by Senator Joseph I. Lieberman*
Unlike other books on leadership, this one is rooted in the stories of the Bible.
6 x 9, 288 pp, Quality PB, 978-1-58023-352-1 **$18.99**; HC, 978-1-58023-241-8 **$24.99**

Hineini in Our Lives: Learning How to Respond to Others through 14 Biblical Texts and Personal Stories *By Norman J. Cohen* 6 x 9, 240 pp, Quality PB, 978-1-58023-274-6 **$16.99**

Moses and the Journey to Leadership: Timeless Lessons of Effective Management from the Bible and Today's Leaders *By Dr. Norman J. Cohen*
6 x 9, 240 pp, Quality PB, 978-1-58023-351-4 **$18.99**; HC, 978-1-58023-227-2 **$21.99**

Self, Struggle & Change: Family Conflict Stories in Genesis and Their Healing Insights for Our Lives *By Norman J. Cohen* 6 x 9, 224 pp, Quality PB, 978-1-879045-66-8 **$18.99**

The Triumph of Eve & Other Subversive Bible Tales *By Matt Biers-Ariel*
5½ x 8½, 192 pp, Quality PB, 978-1-59473-176-1 **$14.99**; HC, 978-1-59473-040-5 **$19.99**
(A book from SkyLight Paths, Jewish Lights' sister imprint)

The Wisdom of Judaism: An Introduction to the Values of the Talmud
By Rabbi Dov Peretz Elkins
Explores the essence of Judaism. 6 x 9, 192 pp, Quality PB, 978-1-58023-327-9 **$16.99**
Also Available: **The Wisdom of Judaism Teacher's Guide**
8½ x 11, 18 pp, PB, 978-1-58023-350-7 **$8.99**

Or phone, fax, mail or e-mail to: **JEWISH LIGHTS** Publishing
Sunset Farm Offices, Route 4 • P.O. Box 237 • Woodstock, Vermont 05091
Tel: (802) 457-4000 • Fax: (802) 457-4004 • www.jewishlights.com
Credit card orders: (800) 962-4544 (8:30AM–5:30PM ET Monday–Friday)
Generous discounts on quantity orders. SATISFACTION GUARANTEED. Prices subject to change.

Children's Books by Sandy Eisenberg Sasso

Adam & Eve's First Sunset: God's New Day

Engaging new story explores fear and hope, faith and gratitude in ways that will delight kids and adults—inspiring us to bless each of God's days and nights.

9 x 12, 32 pp, Full-color illus., HC, 978-1-58023-177-0 **$17.95** *For ages 4 & up*

Also Available as a Board Book: **Adam and Eve's New Day**

5 x 5, 24 pp, Full-color illus., Board, 978-1-59473-205-8 **$7.99** *For ages 0–4*

(A book from SkyLight Paths, Jewish Lights' sister imprint)

But God Remembered

Stories of Women from Creation to the Promised Land

Four different stories of women—Lillith, Serach, Bityah, and the Daughters of Z—teach us important values through their faith and actions.

9 x 12, 32 pp, Full-color illus., Quality PB, 978-1-58023-372-9 **$8.99**; HC, 978-1-879045-43-9 **$16.95** *For ages 8 & up*

Cain & Abel: Finding the Fruits of Peace

Shows children that we have the power to deal with anger in positive ways. Provides questions for kids and adults to explore together.

9 x 12, 32 pp, Full-color illus., HC, 978-1-58023-123-7 **$16.95** *For ages 5 & up*

God in Between

If you wanted to find God, where would you look? This magical, mythical tale teaches that God can be found where we are: within all of us and the relationships between us. 9 x 12, 32 pp, Full-color illus., HC, 978-1-879045-86-6 **$16.95** *For ages 4 & up*

God's Paintbrush: Special 10th Anniversary Edition

Wonderfully interactive, invites children of all faiths and backgrounds to encounter God through moments in their own lives. Provides questions adult and child can explore together. 11 x 8½, 32 pp, Full-color illus., HC, 978-1-58023-195-4 **$17.95** *For ages 4 & up*

Also Available: **God's Paintbrush Teacher's Guide**

8½ x 11, 32 pp, PB, 978-1-879045-57-6 **$8.95**

God's Paintbrush Celebration Kit

A Spiritual Activity Kit for Teachers and Students of All Faiths, All Backgrounds

Additional activity sheets available:

8-Student Activity Sheet Pack (40 sheets/5 sessions), 978-1-58023-058-2 **$19.95**

Single-Student Activity Sheet Pack (5 sessions), 978-1-58023-059-9 **$3.95**

In God's Name

Like an ancient myth in its poetic text and vibrant illustrations, this award-winning modern fable about the search for God's name celebrates the diversity and, at the same time, the unity of all people.

9 x 12, 32 pp, Full-color illus., HC, 978-1-879045-26-2 **$16.99** *For ages 4 & up*

Also Available as a Board Book: **What Is God's Name?**

5 x 5, 24 pp, Board, Full-color illus., 978-1-893361-10-2 **$7.99** *For ages 0–4*

(A book from SkyLight Paths, Jewish Lights' sister imprint)

Also Available: **In God's Name video and study guide**

Computer animation, original music, and children's voices. 18 min. **$29.99**

Also Available in Spanish: **El nombre de Dios**

9 x 12, 32 pp, Full-color illus., HC, 978-1-893361-63-8 **$16.95**

(A book from SkyLight Paths, Jewish Lights' sister imprint)

Noah's Wife: The Story of Naamah

When God tells Noah to bring the animals of the world onto the ark, God also calls on Naamah, Noah's wife, to save each plant on Earth. Based on an ancient text.

9 x 12, 32 pp, Full-color illus., HC, 978-1-58023-134-3 **$16.95** *For ages 4 & up*

Also Available as a Board Book: **Naamah, Noah's Wife**

5 x 5, 24 pp, Full-color illus., Board, 978-1-893361-56-0 **$7.95** *For ages 0–4*

(A book from SkyLight Paths, Jewish Lights' sister imprint)

For Heaven's Sake: Finding God in Unexpected Places

9 x 12, 32 pp, Full-color illus., HC, 978-1-58023-054-4 **$16.95** *For ages 4 & up*

God Said Amen: Finding the Answers to Our Prayers

9 x 12, 32 pp, Full-color illus., HC, 978-1-58023-080-3 **$16.95** *For ages 4 & up*

Current Events/History

A Dream of Zion: American Jews Reflect on Why Israel Matters to Them
Edited by Rabbi Jeffrey K. Salkin Explores what Jewish people in America have to say about Israel. 6 x 9, 304 pp, HC, 978-1-58023-340-8 **$24.99**
Also Available: **A Dream of Zion Teacher's Guide** 8½ x 11, 32 pp, PB, 978-1-58023-356-9 **$8.99**

The Jewish Connection to Israel, the Promised Land: A Brief Introduction for Christians *By Rabbi Eugene Korn, PhD* 5½ x 8½, 192 pp, Quality PB, 978-1-58023-318-7 **$14.99**

The Story of the Jews: A 4,000-Year Adventure—A Graphic History Book
Written & illustrated by Stan Mack 6 x 9, 288 pp, illus., Quality PB, 978-1-58023-155-8 **$16.99**

Hannah Senesh: Her Life and Diary, the First Complete Edition
By Hannah Senesh; Foreword by Marge Piercy; Preface by Eitan Senesh; Afterword by Roberta Grossman
6 x 9, 368 pp, b/w photos, Quality PB, 978-1-58023-342-2 **$19.99**

The Ethiopian Jews of Israel: Personal Stories of Life in the Promised Land *By Len Lyons, PhD; Foreword by Alan Dershowitz; Photographs by Ilan Ossendryver* Recounts, through photographs and words, stories of Ethiopian Jews.
10½ x 10, 240 pp, 100 full-color photos, HC, 978-1-58023-323-1 **$34.99**

Foundations of Sephardic Spirituality: The Inner Life of Jews of the Ottoman Empire
By Rabbi Marc D. Angel, PhD 6 x 9, 224 pp, HC, 978-1-58023-243-2 **$24.99**

Judaism and Justice: The Jewish Passion to Repair the World
By Rabbi Sidney Schwarz 6 x 9, 352 pp, Quality PB, 978-1-58023-353-8 **$19.99**

Ecology/Environment

A Wild Faith: Jewish Ways into Wilderness, Wilderness Ways into Judaism
By Rabbi Mike Comins; Foreword by Nigel Savage
Offers ways to enliven and deepen your spiritual life through wilderness experience.
6 x 9, 240 pp, Quality PB, 978-1-58023-316-3 **$16.99**

Ecology & the Jewish Spirit: Where Nature & the Sacred Meet
Edited by Ellen Bernstein 6 x 9, 288 pp, Quality PB, 978-1-58023-082-7 **$18.99**

Torah of the Earth: Exploring 4,000 Years of Ecology in Jewish Thought
Vol. 1: Biblical Israel: One Land, One People; Rabbinic Judaism: One People, Many Lands
Vol. 2: Zionism: One Land, Two Peoples; Eco-Judaism: One Earth, Many Peoples
Edited by Arthur Waskow Vol. 1: 6 x 9, 272 pp, Quality PB, 978-1-58023-086-5 **$19.95**
Vol. 2: 6 x 9, 336 pp, Quality PB, 978-1-58023-087-2 **$19.95**

The Way Into Judaism and the Environment *By Jeremy Benstein, PhD*
6 x 9, 288 pp, Quality PB, 978-1-58023-368-2 **$18.99**; HC, 978-1-58023-268-5 **$24.99**

Grief/Healing

Healing and the Jewish Imagination: Spiritual and Practical Perspectives on Judaism and Health *Edited by Rabbi William Cutter, PhD*
Explores Judaism for comfort in times of illness and perspectives on suffering.
6 x 9, 240 pp, Quality PB, 978-1-58023-373-6 **$19.99**; HC, 978-1-58023-314-9 **$24.99**

Grief in Our Seasons: A Mourner's Kaddish Companion *By Rabbi Kerry M. Olitzky*
4½ x 6½, 448 pp, Quality PB, 978-1-879045-55-2 **$15.95**

Healing of Soul, Healing of Body: Spiritual Leaders Unfold the Strength & Solace in Psalms *Edited by Rabbi Simkha Y. Weintraub, CSW*
6 x 9, 128 pp, 2-color illus. text, Quality PB, 978-1-879045-31-6 **$14.99**

Mourning & Mitzvah, 2nd Edition: A Guided Journal for Walking the Mourner's Path through Grief to Healing *By Anne Brener, LCSW*
7½ x 9, 304 pp, Quality PB, 978-1-58023-113-8 **$19.99**

Tears of Sorrow, Seeds of Hope, 2nd Edition: A Jewish Spiritual Companion for Infertility and Pregnancy Loss *By Rabbi Nina Beth Cardin*
6 x 9, 208 pp, Quality PB, 978-1-58023-233-3 **$18.99**

A Time to Mourn, a Time to Comfort, 2nd Edition: A Guide to Jewish Bereavement *By Dr. Ron Wolfson*
7 x 9, 384 pp, Quality PB, 978-1-58023-253-1 **$19.99**

When a Grandparent Dies: A Kid's Own Remembering Workbook for Dealing with Shiva and the Year Beyond *By Nechama Liss-Levinson, PhD*
8 x 10, 48 pp, 2-color text, HC, 978-1-879045-44-6 **$15.95** *For ages 7–13*

Holidays/Holy Days

Rosh Hashanah Readings: Inspiration, Information and Contemplation
Yom Kippur Readings: Inspiration, Information and Contemplation
Edited by Rabbi Dov Peretz Elkins with Section Introductions from Arthur Green's These Are the Words
An extraordinary collection of readings, prayers and insights that enable the modern worshiper to enter into the spirit of the High Holy Days in a personal and powerful way, permitting the meaning of the Jewish New Year to enter the heart.
RHR: 6 x 9, 400 pp, HC, 978-1-58023-239-5 **$24.99**
YKR: 6 x 9, 368 pp, HC, 978-1-58023-271-5 **$24.99**

Jewish Holidays: A Brief Introduction for Christians
By Rabbi Kerry M. Olitzky and Rabbi Daniel Judson
5½ x 8½, 144 pp, Quality PB, 978-1-58023-302-6 **$16.99**

Reclaiming Judaism as a Spiritual Practice: Holy Days and Shabbat
By Rabbi Goldie Milgram
7 x 9, 272 pp, Quality PB, 978-1-58023-205-0 **$19.99**

7th Heaven: Celebrating Shabbat with Rebbe Nachman of Breslov
By Moshe Mykoff with the Breslov Research Institute
5⅛ x 8¼, 224 pp, Deluxe PB w/flaps, 978-1-58023-175-6 **$18.95**

Shabbat, 2nd Edition: The Family Guide to Preparing for and Celebrating the Sabbath
By Dr. Ron Wolfson 7 x 9, 320 pp, illus., Quality PB, 978-1-58023-164-0 **$19.99**

Hanukkah, 2nd Edition: The Family Guide to Spiritual Celebration
By Dr. Ron Wolfson. Edited by Joel Lurie Grishaver.
7 x 9, 240 pp, illus., Quality PB, 978-1-58023-122-0 **$18.95**

The Jewish Family Fun Book, 2nd Edition: Holiday Projects, Everyday Activities,
and Travel Ideas with Jewish Themes *By Danielle Dardashti and Roni Sarig. Illus. by Avi Katz.*
6 x 9, 304 pp, 70+ b/w illus. & diagrams, Quality PB, 978-1-58023-333-0 **$18.99**

The Jewish Lights Book of Fun Classroom Activities: Simple and Seasonal
Projects for Teachers and Students *By Danielle Dardashti and Roni Sarig*
6 x 9, 240 pp, Quality PB, 978-1-58023-206-7 **$19.99**

Passover

My People's Passover Haggadah
Traditional Texts, Modern Commentaries
Edited by Rabbi Lawrence A. Hoffman, PhD, and David Arnow, PhD
A diverse and exciting collection of commentaries on the traditional Passover Haggadah—in two volumes!
Vol. 1: 7 x 10, 304 pp, HC, 978-1-58023-354-5 **$24.99**
Vol. 2: 7 x 10, 320 pp, HC, 978-1-58023-346-0 **$24.99**

Leading the Passover Journey
The Seder's Meaning Revealed, the Haggadah's Story Retold
By Rabbi Nathan Laufer
Uncovers the hidden meaning of the Seder's rituals and customs.
6 x 9, 224 pp, HC, 978-1-58023-211-1 **$24.99**

The Women's Passover Companion: Women's Reflections on the Festival of Freedom
Edited by Rabbi Sharon Cohen Anisfeld, Tara Mohr, and Catherine Spector
6 x 9, 352 pp, Quality PB, 978-1-58023-231-9 **$19.99**

The Women's Seder Sourcebook: Rituals & Readings for Use at the Passover Seder
Edited by Rabbi Sharon Cohen Anisfeld, Tara Mohr, and Catherine Spector
6 x 9, 384 pp, Quality PB, 978-1-58023-232-6 **$19.99**

Creating Lively Passover Seders: A Sourcebook of Engaging Tales, Texts & Activities
By David Arnow, PhD 7 x 9, 416 pp, Quality PB, 978-1-58023-184-8 **$24.99**

Passover, 2nd Edition: The Family Guide to Spiritual Celebration
By Dr. Ron Wolfson with Joel Lurie Grishaver 7 x 9, 352 pp, Quality PB, 978-1-58023-174-9 **$19.95**

Inspiration

Happiness and the Human Spirit: The Spirituality of Becoming the Best You Can Be *By Abraham J. Twerski, MD*
Shows you that true happiness is attainable once you stop looking outside yourself for the source. 6 x 9, 176 pp, HC, 978-1-58023-343-9 **$19.99**

The Bridge to Forgiveness: Stories and Prayers for Finding God and Restoring Wholeness *By Rabbi Karyn D. Kedar*
Examines how forgiveness can be the bridge that connects us to wholeness and peace.
6 x 9, 176 pp, HC, 978-1-58023-324-8 **$19.99**

God's To-Do List: 103 Ways to Be an Angel and Do God's Work on Earth
By Dr. Ron Wolfson 6 x 9, 150 pp, Quality PB, 978-1-58023-301-9 **$16.99**

God in All Moments: Mystical & Practical Spiritual Wisdom from Hasidic Masters
Edited and translated by Or N. Rose with Ebn D. Leader
5½ x 8½, 192 pp, Quality PB, 978-1-58023-186-2 **$16.95**

Our Dance with God: Finding Prayer, Perspective and Meaning in the Stories of Our Lives *By Karyn D. Kedar* 6 x 9, 176 pp, Quality PB, 978-1-58023-202-9 **$16.99**
Also Available: **The Dance of the Dolphin** (HC edition of *Our Dance with God*)
6 x 9, 176 pp, HC, 978-1-58023-154-1 **$19.95**

The Empty Chair: Finding Hope and Joy—Timeless Wisdom from a Hasidic Master, Rebbe Nachman of Breslov *Adapted by Moshe Mykoff and the Breslov Research Institute*
4 x 6, 128 pp, 2-color text, Deluxe PB w/flaps, 978-1-879045-67-5 **$9.99**

The Gentle Weapon: Prayers for Everyday and Not-So-Everyday Moments—
Timeless Wisdom from the Teachings of the Hasidic Master, Rebbe Nachman of Breslov
Adapted by Moshe Mykoff and S. C. Mizrahi, together with the Breslov Research Institute
4 x 6, 144 pp, 2-color text, Deluxe PB w/flaps, 978-1-58023-022-3 **$9.99**

God Whispers: Stories of the Soul, Lessons of the Heart *By Karyn D. Kedar*
6 x 9, 176 pp, Quality PB, 978-1-58023-088-9 **$15.95**

Restful Reflections: Nighttime Inspiration to Calm the Soul, Based on Jewish Wisdom
By Rabbi Kerry M. Olitzky & Rabbi Lori Forman 4½ x 6½, 448 pp, Quality PB, 978-1-58023-091-9 **$15.95**

Sacred Intentions: Daily Inspiration to Strengthen the Spirit, Based on Jewish Wisdom
By Rabbi Kerry M. Olitzky and Rabbi Lori Forman 4½ x 6½, 448 pp, Quality PB, 978-1-58023-061-2 **$15.95**

Kabbalah/Mysticism

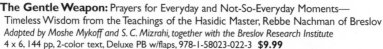

Awakening to Kabbalah: The Guiding Light of Spiritual Fulfillment
By Rav Michael Laitman, PhD 6 x 9, 192 pp, HC, 978-1-58023-264-7 **$21.99**

Seek My Face: A Jewish Mystical Theology *By Arthur Green*
6 x 9, 304 pp, Quality PB, 978-1-58023-130-5 **$19.95**

Zohar: Annotated & Explained *Translation and annotation by Daniel C. Matt; Foreword by Andrew Harvey* 5½ x 8½, 176 pp, Quality PB, 978-1-893361-51-5 **$15.99**
(A book from SkyLight Paths, Jewish Lights' sister imprint)

Ehyeh: A Kabbalah for Tomorrow
By Arthur Green 6 x 9, 224 pp, Quality PB, 978-1-58023-213-5 **$16.99**

The Flame of the Heart: Prayers of a Chasidic Mystic *By Reb Noson of Breslov. Translated by David Sears with the Breslov Research Institute* 5 x 7¼, 160 pp, Quality PB, 978-1-58023-246-3 **$15.99**

The Gift of Kabbalah: Discovering the Secrets of Heaven, Renewing Your Life on Earth
By Tamar Frankiel, PhD 6 x 9, 256 pp, Quality PB, 978-1-58023-141-1 **$16.95;**
HC, 978-1-58023-108-4 **$21.95**

Kabbalah: A Brief Introduction for Christians
By Tamar Frankiel, PhD 5½ x 8½, 208 pp, Quality PB, 978-1-58023-303-3 **$16.99**

The Lost Princess and Other Kabbalistic Tales of Rebbe Nachman of Breslov
The Seven Beggars and Other Kabbalistic Tales of Rebbe Nachman of Breslov
Translated by Rabbi Aryeh Kaplan; Preface by Rabbi Chaim Kramer
Lost Princess: 6 x 9, 400 pp, Quality PB, 978-1-58023-217-3 **$18.99**
Seven Beggars: 6 x 9, 192 pp, Quality PB, 978-1-58023-250-0 **$16.99**

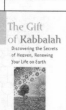

See also *The Way Into Jewish Mystical Tradition* in Spirituality / The Way Into... Series

Life Cycle
Marriage / Parenting / Family / Aging

The New Jewish Baby Album: Creating and Celebrating the Beginning of a Spiritual Life—A Jewish Lights Companion
By the Editors at Jewish Lights. Foreword by Anita Diamant. Preface by Rabbi Sandy Eisenberg Sasso.
A spiritual keepsake that will be treasured for generations. More than just a memory book, *shows you how—and why it's important*—to create a Jewish home and a Jewish life. 8 x 10, 64 pp, Deluxe Padded HC, Full-color illus., 978-1-58023-138-1 **$19.95**

The Jewish Pregnancy Book: A Resource for the Soul, Body & Mind during Pregnancy, Birth & the First Three Months
By Sandy Falk, MD, and Rabbi Daniel Judson, with Steven A. Rapp
Includes medical information, prayers and rituals for each stage of pregnancy, from a liberal Jewish perspective. 7 x 10, 208 pp, Quality PB, b/w photos, 978-1-58023-178-7 **$16.95**

Celebrating Your New Jewish Daughter: Creating Jewish Ways to Welcome Baby Girls into the Covenant—New and Traditional Ceremonies *By Debra Nussbaum Cohen; Foreword by Rabbi Sandy Eisenberg Sasso* 6 x 9, 272 pp, Quality PB, 978-1-58023-090-2 **$18.95**

The New Jewish Baby Book, 2nd Edition: Names, Ceremonies & Customs—A Guide for Today's Families *By Anita Diamant* 6 x 9, 336 pp, Quality PB, 978-1-58023-251-7 **$19.99**

Parenting as a Spiritual Journey: Deepening Ordinary and Extraordinary Events into Sacred Occasions *By Rabbi Nancy Fuchs-Kreimer*
6 x 9, 224 pp, Quality PB, 978-1-58023-016-2 **$16.95**

Parenting Jewish Teens: A Guide for the Perplexed
By Joanne Doades
Explores the questions and issues that shape the world in which today's Jewish teenagers live.
6 x 9, 200 pp, Quality PB, 978-1-58023-305-7 **$16.99**

Judaism for Two: A Spiritual Guide for Strengthening and Celebrating Your Loving Relationship *By Rabbi Nancy Fuchs-Kreimer and Rabbi Nancy H. Wiener; Foreword by Rabbi Elliot N. Dorff* Addresses the ways Jewish teachings can enhance and strengthen committed relationships. 6 x 9, 224 pp, Quality PB, 978-1-58023-254-8 **$16.99**

Embracing the Covenant: Converts to Judaism Talk About Why & How
By Rabbi Allan Berkowitz and Patti Moskovitz 6 x 9, 192 pp, Quality PB, 978-1-879045-50-7 **$16.95**

The Guide to Jewish Interfaith Family Life: An InterfaithFamily.com Handbook
Edited by Ronnie Friedland and Edmund Case 6 x 9, 384 pp, Quality PB, 978-1-58023-153-4 **$18.95**

Introducing My Faith and My Community
The Jewish Outreach Institute Guide for the Christian in a Jewish Interfaith Relationship
By Rabbi Kerry M. Olitzky 6 x 9, 176 pp, Quality PB, 978-1-58023-192-3 **$16.99**

Making a Successful Jewish Interfaith Marriage: The Jewish Outreach Institute Guide to Opportunities, Challenges and Resources *By Rabbi Kerry M. Olitzky with Joan Peterson Littman*
6 x 9, 176 pp, Quality PB, 978-1-58023-170-1 **$16.95**

The Creative Jewish Wedding Book: A Hands-On Guide to New & Old Traditions, Ceremonies & Celebrations *By Gabrielle Kaplan-Mayer*
9 x 9, 288 pp, b/w photos, Quality PB, 978-1-58023-194-7 **$19.99**

Divorce Is a Mitzvah: A Practical Guide to Finding Wholeness and Holiness When Your Marriage Dies *By Rabbi Perry Netter; Afterword by Rabbi Laura Geller.*
6 x 9, 224 pp, Quality PB, 978-1-58023-172-5 **$16.95**

A Heart of Wisdom: Making the Jewish Journey from Midlife through the Elder Years
Edited by Susan Berrin; Foreword by Harold Kushner
6 x 9, 384 pp, Quality PB, 978-1-58023-051-3 **$18.95**

So That Your Values Live On: Ethical Wills and How to Prepare Them
Edited by Jack Riemer and Nathaniel Stampfer
6 x 9, 272 pp, Quality PB, 978-1-879045-34-7 **$18.99**

Meditation

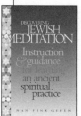

The Handbook of Jewish Meditation Practices
A Guide for Enriching the Sabbath and Other Days of Your Life
By Rabbi David A. Cooper Easy-to-learn meditation techniques.
6 x 9, 208 pp, Quality PB, 978-1-58023-102-2 **$16.95**

Discovering Jewish Meditation: Instruction & Guidance for Learning an Ancient
Spiritual Practice *By Nan Fink Gefen* 6 x 9, 208 pp, Quality PB, 978-1-58023-067-4 **$16.95**

A Heart of Stillness: A Complete Guide to Learning the Art of Meditation
By David A. Cooper 5½ x 8½, 272 pp, Quality PB, 978-1-893361-03-4 **$16.95**
(A book from SkyLight Paths, Jewish Lights' sister imprint)

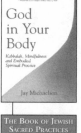

Meditation from the Heart of Judaism: Today's Teachers Share Their Practices,
Techniques, and Faith *Edited by Avram Davis*
6 x 9, 256 pp, Quality PB, 978-1-58023-049-0 **$16.95**

Silence, Simplicity & Solitude: A Complete Guide to Spiritual Retreat at Home
By David A. Cooper 5½ x 8½, 336 pp, Quality PB, 978-1-893361-04-1 **$16.95**
(A book from SkyLight Paths, Jewish Lights' sister imprint)

Ritual/Sacred Practice

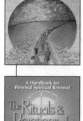

The Jewish Dream Book: The Key to Opening the Inner Meaning of
Your Dreams *By Vanessa L. Ochs with Elizabeth Ochs; Full-color illus. by Kristina Swarner*
Instructions for how modern people can perform ancient Jewish dream practices
and dream interpretations drawn from the Jewish wisdom tradition.
8 x 8, 128 pp, Full-color illus., Deluxe PB w/flaps, 978-1-58023-132-9 **$16.95**

God in Your Body: Kabbalah, Mindfulness and Embodied Spiritual Practice
By Jay Michaelson
The first comprehensive treatment of the body in Jewish spiritual practice and an
essential guide to the sacred.
6 x 9, 288 pp, Quality PB, 978-1-58023-304-0 **$18.99**

The Book of Jewish Sacred Practices: CLAL's Guide to Everyday & Holiday
Rituals & Blessings *Edited by Rabbi Irwin Kula and Vanessa L. Ochs, PhD*
6 x 9, 368 pp, Quality PB, 978-1-58023-152-7 **$18.95**

Jewish Ritual: A Brief Introduction for Christians
By Rabbi Kerry M. Olitzky and Rabbi Daniel Judson
5½ x 8½, 144 pp, Quality PB, 978-1-58023-210-4 **$14.99**

The Rituals & Practices of a Jewish Life: A Handbook for Personal Spiritual
Renewal *Edited by Rabbi Kerry M. Olitzky and Rabbi Daniel Judson*
6 x 9, 272 pp, illus., Quality PB, 978-1-58023-169-5 **$18.95**

The Sacred Art of Lovingkindness: Preparing to Practice
By Rabbi Rami Shapiro 5½ x 8½, 176 pp, Quality PB, 978-1-59473-151-8 **$16.99**
(A book from SkyLight Paths, Jewish Lights' sister imprint)

Science Fiction/Mystery & Detective Fiction

Mystery Midrash: An Anthology of Jewish Mystery & Detective Fiction
Edited by Lawrence W. Raphael; Preface by Joel Siegel
6 x 9, 304 pp, Quality PB, 978-1-58023-055-1 **$16.95**

Criminal Kabbalah: An Intriguing Anthology of Jewish Mystery & Detective Fiction
Edited by Lawrence W. Raphael; Foreword by Laurie R. King
6 x 9, 256 pp, Quality PB, 978-1-58023-109-1 **$16.95**

Wandering Stars: An Anthology of Jewish Fantasy & Science Fiction
Edited by Jack Dann; Introduction by Isaac Asimov
6 x 9, 272 pp, Quality PB, 978-1-58023-005-6 **$18.99**

More Wandering Stars: An Anthology of Outstanding Stories of Jewish Fantasy and
Science Fiction *Edited by Jack Dann; Introduction by Isaac Asimov*
6 x 9, 192 pp, Quality PB, 978-1-58023-063-6 **$16.95**

Spirituality

Journeys to a Jewish Life: Inspiring Stories from the Spiritual Journeys
of American Jews *By Paula Amann*
Examines the soul treks of Jews lost and found. 6 x 9, 208 pp, HC, 978-1-58023-317-0 **$19.99**

The Adventures of Rabbi Harvey: A Graphic Novel of Jewish
Wisdom and Wit in the Wild West *By Steve Sheinkin*
Jewish and American folktales combine in this witty and original graphic novel
collection. Creatively retold and set on the western frontier of the 1870s.
6 x 9, 144 pp, Full-color illus., Quality PB, 978-1-58023-310-1 **$16.99**

Rabbi Harvey Rides Again
A Graphic Novel of Jewish Folktales Let Loose in the Wild West *By Steve Sheinkin*
6 x 9, 144 pp, Quality PB Original, Full-color illus., 978-1-58023-347-7 **$16.99**

Ethics of the Sages: *Pirke Avot*—Annotated & Explained
Translation and Annotation by Rabbi Rami Shapiro 5½ x 8½, 192 pp, Quality PB, 978-1-59473-207-2
$16.99 *(A book from SkyLight Paths, Jewish Lights' sister imprint)*

A Book of Life: Embracing Judaism as a Spiritual Practice
By Michael Strassfeld 6 x 9, 528 pp, Quality PB, 978-1-58023-247-0 **$19.99**

Meaning and Mitzvah: Daily Practices for Reclaiming Judaism through Prayer, God,
Torah, Hebrew, Mitzvot and Peoplehood *By Rabbi Goldie Milgram*
7 x 9, 336 pp, Quality PB, 978-1-58023-256-2 **$19.99**

The Soul of the Story: Meetings with Remarkable People
By Rabbi David Zeller 6 x 9, 288 pp, HC, 978-1-58023-272-2 **$21.99**

Aleph-Bet Yoga: Embodying the Hebrew Letters for Physical and Spiritual Well-Being
By Steven A. Rapp. Foreword by Tamar Frankiel, PhD and Judy Greenfeld. Preface by Hart Lazer.
7 x 10, 128 pp, b/w photos, Quality PB, Layflat binding, 978-1-58023-162-6 **$16.95**

Does the Soul Survive? A Jewish Journey to Belief in Afterlife, Past Lives & Living
with Purpose *By Rabbi Elie Kaplan Spitz; Foreword by Brian L. Weiss, MD*
6 x 9, 288 pp, Quality PB, 978-1-58023-165-7 **$16.99**

First Steps to a New Jewish Spirit: Reb Zalman's Guide to Recapturing the
Intimacy & Ecstasy in Your Relationship with God *By Rabbi Zalman M. Schachter-Shalomi
with Donald Gropman* 6 x 9, 144 pp, Quality PB, 978-1-58023-182-4 **$16.95**

God in Our Relationships: Spirituality between People from the Teachings of Martin
Buber *By Rabbi Dennis S. Ross* 5½ x 8½, 160 pp, Quality PB, 978-1-58023-147-3 **$16.95**

Judaism, Physics and God: Searching for Sacred Metaphors in a Post-Einstein World
By Rabbi David W. Nelson 6 x 9, 368 pp, Quality PB, inc. reader's discussion guide, 978-1-58023-306-4 **$18.99**;
HC, 352 pp, 978-1-58023-252-4 **$24.99**

The Jewish Lights Spirituality Handbook: A Guide to Understanding,
Exploring & Living a Spiritual Life *Edited by Stuart M. Matlins*
What exactly is "Jewish" about spirituality? How do I make it a part of my life?
Fifty of today's foremost spiritual leaders share their ideas and experience with us.
6 x 9, 456 pp, Quality PB, 978-1-58023-093-3 **$19.99**

Bringing the Psalms to Life: How to Understand and Use the Book of Psalms
By Daniel F. Polish 6 x 9, 208 pp, Quality PB, 978-1-58023-157-2 **$16.95**;
HC, 978-1-58023-077-3 **$21.95**

God & the Big Bang: Discovering Harmony between Science & Spirituality
By Daniel C. Matt 6 x 9, 216 pp, Quality PB, 978-1-879045-89-7 **$16.99**

Minding the Temple of the Soul: Balancing Body, Mind, and Spirit through Traditional
Jewish Prayer, Movement, and Meditation *By Tamar Frankiel, PhD, and Judy Greenfeld*
7 x 10, 184 pp, illus., Quality PB, 978-1-879045-64-4 **$16.95**

One God Clapping: The Spiritual Path of a Zen Rabbi *By Alan Lew with Sherril Jaffe*
5½ x 8½, 336 pp, Quality PB, 978-1-58023-115-2 **$16.95**

There Is No Messiah ... and You're It: The Stunning Transformation of Judaism's
Most Provocative Idea *By Rabbi Robert N. Levine, DD*
6 x 9, 192 pp, Quality PB, 978-1-58023-255-5 **$16.99**

These Are the Words: A Vocabulary of Jewish Spiritual Life
By Arthur Green 6 x 9, 304 pp, Quality PB, 978-1-58023-107-7 **$18.95**

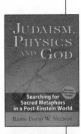

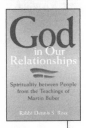

Spirituality/Lawrence Kushner

Filling Words with Light: Hasidic and Mystical Reflections on Jewish Prayer
By Lawrence Kushner and Nehemia Polen
5½ x 8½, 176 pp, Quality PB, 978-1-58023-238-8 **$16.99**; HC, 978-1-58023-216-6 **$21.99**

The Book of Letters: A Mystical Hebrew Alphabet
Popular HC Edition, 6 x 9, 80 pp, 2-color text, 978-1-879045-00-2 **$24.95**
Collector's Limited Edition, 9 x 12, 80 pp, gold foil embossed pages, w/limited edition silkscreened print, 978-1-879045-04-0 **$349.00**

The Book of Miracles: A Young Person's Guide to Jewish Spiritual Awareness
6 x 9, 96 pp, 2-color illus., HC, 978-1-879045-78-1 **$16.95** *For ages 9 and up*

The Book of Words: Talking Spiritual Life, Living Spiritual Talk
6 x 9, 160 pp, Quality PB, 978-1-58023-020-9 **$16.95**

Eyes Remade for Wonder: A Lawrence Kushner Reader *Introduction by Thomas Moore*
6 x 9, 240 pp, Quality PB, 978-1-58023-042-1 **$18.95**

God Was in This Place & I, i Did Not Know: Finding Self, Spirituality and Ultimate Meaning 6 x 9, 192 pp, Quality PB, 978-1-879045-33-0 **$16.95**

Honey from the Rock: An Introduction to Jewish Mysticism
6 x 9, 176 pp, Quality PB, 978-1-58023-073-5 **$16.95**

Invisible Lines of Connection: Sacred Stories of the Ordinary
5½ x 8½, 160 pp, Quality PB, 978-1-879045-98-9 **$15.95**

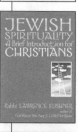

Jewish Spirituality—A Brief Introduction for Christians
5½ x 8½, 112 pp, Quality PB, 978-1-58023-150-3 **$12.95**

The River of Light: Jewish Mystical Awareness
6 x 9, 192 pp, Quality PB, 978-1-58023-096-4 **$16.95**

The Way Into Jewish Mystical Tradition
6 x 9, 224 pp, Quality PB, 978-1-58023-200-5 **$18.99**; HC, 978-1-58023-029-2 **$21.95**

Spirituality/Prayer

My People's Passover Haggadah: Traditional Texts, Modern Commentaries
Edited by Rabbi Lawrence A. Hoffman, PhD, and David Arnow, PhD Diverse commentaries on the traditional Passover Haggadah—in two volumes! Vol. 1: 7 x 10, 304 pp, HC 978-1-58023-354-5 **$24.99** Vol. 2: 7 x 10, 320 pp, HC, 978-1-58023-346-0 **$24.99**

Witnesses to the One: The Spiritual History of the *Sh'ma* By Rabbi Joseph B. Meszler; Foreword by Rabbi Elyse Goldstein 6 x 9, 176 pp, HC, 978-1-58023-309-5 **$19.99**

My People's Prayer Book Series

Traditional Prayers, Modern Commentaries *Edited by Rabbi Lawrence A. Hoffman*
Provides diverse and exciting commentary to the traditional liturgy, helping modern men and women find new wisdom in Jewish prayer, and bring liturgy into their lives. Each book includes Hebrew text, modern translation, and commentaries from all perspectives of the Jewish world.

Vol. 1—The *Sh'ma* and Its Blessings
7 x 10, 168 pp, HC, 978-1-879045-79-8 **$24.99**

Vol. 2—The *Amidah*
7 x 10, 240 pp, HC, 978-1-879045-80-4 **$24.95**

Vol. 3—*P'sukei D'zimrah* (Morning Psalms)
7 x 10, 240 pp, HC, 978-1-879045-81-1 **$24.95**

Vol. 4—*Seder K'riat Hatorah* (The Torah Service)
7 x 10, 264 pp, HC, 978-1-879045-82-8 **$23.95**

Vol. 5—*Birkhot Hashachar* (Morning Blessings)
7 x 10, 240 pp, HC, 978-1-879045-83-5 **$24.95**

Vol. 6—*Tachanun* and Concluding Prayers
7 x 10, 240 pp, HC, 978-1-879045-84-2 **$24.95**

Vol. 7—Shabbat at Home
7 x 10, 240 pp, HC, 978-1-879045-85-9 **$24.95**

Vol. 8—*Kabbalat Shabbat* (Welcoming Shabbat in the Synagogue)
7 x 10, 240 pp, HC, 978-1-58023-121-3 **$24.95**

Vol. 9—Welcoming the Night: *Minchah* and *Ma'ariv* (Afternoon and Evening Prayer) 7 x 10, 272 pp, HC, 978-1-58023-262-3 **$24.99**

Vol. 10—Shabbat Morning: *Shacharit* and *Musaf* (Morning and Additional Services) 7 x 10, 240 pp, HC, 978-1-58023-240-1 **$24.99**

Spirituality/Women's Interest

The Quotable Jewish Woman: Wisdom, Inspiration & Humor from the Mind & Heart
Edited and compiled by Elaine Bernstein Partnow
6 x 9, 496 pp, Quality PB, 978-1-58023-236-4 **$19.99**; HC, 978-1-58023-193-0 **$29.99**

The Divine Feminine in Biblical Wisdom Literature: Selections Annotated &
Explained *Translated and Annotated by Rabbi Rami Shapiro* 5½ x 8½, 240 pp, Quality PB,
978-1-59473-109-9 **$16.99** *(A book from SkyLight Paths, Jewish Lights' sister imprint)*

The Women's Haftarah Commentary: New Insights from Women Rabbis on the
54 Weekly Haftarah Portions, the 5 Megillot & Special Shabbatot
Edited by Rabbi Elyse Goldstein
6 x 9, 560 pp, Quality PB, 978-1-58023-371-2 **$19.99**; HC, 978-1-58023-133-6 **$39.99**

The Women's Torah Commentary: New Insights from Women Rabbis on the
54 Weekly Torah Portions *Edited by Rabbi Elyse Goldstein*
6 x 9, 496 pp, Quality PB, 978-1-58023-370-5 **$19.99**; HC, 978-1-58023-076-6 **$34.95**

The Year Mom Got Religion: One Woman's Midlife Journey into Judaism
By Lee Meyerhoff Hendler 6 x 9, 208 pp, Quality PB, 978-1-58023-070-4 **$15.95**

See Holidays for *The Women's Passover Companion: Women's Reflections on
the Festival of Freedom* and *The Women's Seder Sourcebook: Rituals &
Readings for Use at the Passover Seder.* Also see Bar/Bat Mitzvah for *The
JGirl's Guide: The Young Jewish Woman's Handbook for Coming of Age.*

Spirituality / Crafts

(from SkyLight Paths, Jewish Lights sister imprint)

The Knitting Way: A Guide to Spiritual Self-Discovery
By Linda Skolnick and Janice MacDaniels
Shows how to use the practice of knitting to strengthen our spiritual selves.
7 x 9, 240 pp, Quality PB, 978-1-59473-079-5 **$16.99**

The Quilting Path: A Guide to Spiritual Self-Discovery through Fabric,
Thread and Kabbalah *By Louise Silk*
Explores how to cultivate personal growth through quilt making.
7 x 9, 192 pp, Quality PB, 978-1-59473-206-5 **$16.99**

The Painting Path: Embodying Spiritual Discovery through Yoga, Brush
and Color *By Linda Novick; Foreword by Richard Segalman*
Explores the divine connection you can experience through art.
7 x 9, 208 pp, 8-page full-color insert, Quality PB, 978-1-59473-226-3 **$18.99**

The Scrapbooking Journey: A Hands-On Guide to Spiritual Discovery
By Cory Richardson-Lauve; Foreword by Stacy Julian
Reveals how this craft can become a practice used to deepen and shape your life.
7 x 9, 176 pp, 8-page full-color insert, b/w photos, Quality PB, 978-1-59473-216-4 **$18.99**

Travel

Israel—A Spiritual Travel Guide, 2nd Edition
A Companion for the Modern Jewish Pilgrim
By Rabbi Lawrence A. Hoffman 4¾ x 10, 256 pp, Quality PB, illus., 978-1-58023-261-6 **$18.99**

Also Available: **The Israel Mission Leader's Guide** 978-1-58023-085-8 **$4.95**

12-Step

100 Blessings Every Day: Daily Twelve Step Recovery Affirmations, Exercises for
Personal Growth & Renewal Reflecting Seasons of the Jewish Year
By Rabbi Kerry M. Olitzky; Foreword by Rabbi Neil Gillman
4½ x 6½, 432 pp, Quality PB, 978-1-879045-30-9 **$16.99**

Recovery from Codependence: A Jewish Twelve Steps Guide to Healing Your Soul
By Rabbi Kerry M. Olitzky 6 x 9, 160 pp, Quality PB, 978-1-879045-32-3 **$13.95**

Twelve Jewish Steps to Recovery: A Personal Guide to Turning from Alcoholism &
Other Addictions—Drugs, Food, Gambling, Sex ...
By Rabbi Kerry M. Olitzky and Stuart A. Copans, MD; Preface by Abraham J. Twerski, MD
6 x 9, 144 pp, Quality PB, 978-1-879045-09-5 **$15.99**

Theology/Philosophy

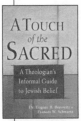

A Touch of the Sacred: A Theologian's Informal Guide to Jewish Belief
By Dr. Eugene B. Borowitz and Frances W. Schwartz Explores the musings from the
leading theologian of liberal Judaism. 6 x 9, 256 pp, HC, 978-1-58023-337-8 **$21.99**

Talking about God: Exploring the Meaning of Religious Life with
Kierkegaard, Buber, Tillich and Heschel *By Daniel F. Polish, PhD*
Examines the meaning of the human religious experience with the greatest theolo-
gians of modern times. 6 x 9, 160 pp, HC, 978-1-59473-230-0 **$21.99**
(A book from SkyLight Paths, Jewish Lights' sister imprint)

Jews & Judaism in the 21st Century: Human Responsibility, the
Presence of God, and the Future of the Covenant *Edited by Rabbi Edward Feinstein;
Foreword by Paula E. Hyman* Five celebrated leaders in Judaism examine contemporary
Jewish life. 6 x 9, 192 pp, Quality PB, 978-1-58023-374-3 **$19.99**; HC, 978-1-58023-315-6 **$24.99**

Christians and Jews in Dialogue: Learning in the Presence of the Other
By Mary C. Boys and Sara S. Lee; Foreword by Dr. Dorothy Bass
6 x 9, 240 pp, Quality PB, 978-1-59473-254-6 **$18.99**; HC, 978-1-59473-144-0 **$21.99**
(A book from SkyLight Paths, Jewish Lights' sister imprint)

The Death of Death: Resurrection and Immortality in Jewish Thought
By Neil Gillman 6 x 9, 336 pp, Quality PB, 978-1-58023-081-0 **$18.95**

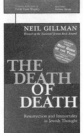

Ethics of the Sages: Pirke Avot—Annotated & Explained
Translation & Annotation by Rabbi Rami Shapiro
5½ x 8½, 208 pp, Quality PB, 978-1-59473-207-2 **$16.99** *(A book from SkyLight Paths, Jewish Lights' sister imprint)*

Hasidic Tales: Annotated & Explained *By Rabbi Rami Shapiro; Foreword by Andrew Harvey*
5½ x 8½, 240 pp, Quality PB, 978-1-893361-86-7 **$16.95**
(A book from SkyLight Paths, Jewish Lights' sister imprint)

A Heart of Many Rooms: Celebrating the Many Voices within Judaism
By David Hartman 6 x 9, 352 pp, Quality PB, 978-1-58023-156-5 **$19.95**

The Hebrew Prophets: Selections Annotated & Explained
Translation & Annotation by Rabbi Rami Shapiro; Foreword by Zalman M. Schachter-Shalomi
5½ x 8½, 224 pp, Quality PB, 978-1-59473-037-5 **$16.99** *(A book from SkyLight Paths, Jewish Lights' sister imprint)*

A Jewish Understanding of the New Testament
By Rabbi Samuel Sandmel; Preface by Rabbi David Sandmel
5½ x 8½, 368 pp, Quality PB, 978-1-59473-048-1 **$19.99** *(A book from SkyLight Paths, Jewish Lights' sister imprint)*

Keeping Faith with the Psalms: Deepen Your Relationship with God Using the Book
of Psalms *By Daniel F. Polish* 6 x 9, 320 pp, Quality PB, 978-1-58023-300-2 **$18.99**

A Living Covenant: The Innovative Spirit in Traditional Judaism
By David Hartman 6 x 9, 368 pp, Quality PB, 978-1-58023-011-7 **$20.00**

Love and Terror in the God Encounter: The Theological Legacy of Rabbi Joseph
B. Soloveitchik *By David Hartman* 6 x 9, 240 pp, Quality PB, 978-1-58023-176-3 **$19.95**

The Personhood of God: Biblical Theology, Human Faith and the Divine Image
By Dr. Yochanan Muffs; Foreword by Dr. David Hartman 6 x 9, 240 pp, HC, 978-1-58023-265-4 **$24.99**

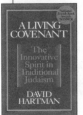

Traces of God: Seeing God in Torah, History and Everyday Life *By Neil Gillman*
6 x 9, 240 pp, Quality PB, 978-1-58023-369-9 **$16.99**; HC, 978-1-58023-249-4 **$21.99**

We Jews and Jesus: Exploring Theological Differences for Mutual Understanding
By Rabbi Samuel Sandmel; Preface by Rabbi David Sandmel
6 x 9, 176 pp, Quality PB, 978-1-59473-208-9 **$16.99** *(A book from SkyLight Paths, Jewish Lights' sister imprint)*

Your Word Is Fire: The Hasidic Masters on Contemplative Prayer
Edited and translated by Arthur Green and Barry W. Holtz
6 x 9, 160 pp, Quality PB, 978-1-879045-25-5 **$15.95**

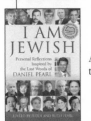

I Am Jewish
Personal Reflections Inspired by the Last Words of Daniel Pearl
Almost 150 Jews—both famous and not—from all walks of life, from all around
the world, write about many aspects of their Judaism.
Edited by Judea and Ruth Pearl
6 x 9, 304 pp, Deluxe PB w/flaps, 978-1-58023-259-3 **$18.99**
**Download a free copy of the *I Am Jewish Teacher's Guide* at our website:
www.jewishlights.com**

Theology/Philosophy/The Way Into... Series

The Way Into... series offers an accessible and highly usable "guided tour" of the Jewish faith, people, history and beliefs—in total, an introduction to Judaism that will enable you to understand and interact with the sacred texts of the Jewish tradition. Each volume is written by a leading contemporary scholar and teacher, and explores one key aspect of Judaism. *The Way Into...* series enables all readers to achieve a real sense of Jewish cultural literacy through guided study.

The Way Into Encountering God in Judaism
By Rabbi Neil Gillman, PhD
For everyone who wants to understand how Jews have encountered God throughout history and today.
6 x 9, 240 pp, Quality PB, 978-1-58023-199-2 **$18.99**; HC, 978-1-58023-025-4 **$21.95**
Also Available: **The Jewish Approach to God:** A Brief Introduction for Christians
By Rabbi Neil Gillman, PhD
5¼ x 8½, 192 pp, Quality PB, 978-1-58023-190-9 **$16.95**

The Way Into Jewish Mystical Tradition
By Rabbi Lawrence Kushner
Allows readers to interact directly with the sacred mystical text of the Jewish tradition. An accessible introduction to the concepts of Jewish mysticism, their religious and spiritual significance and how they relate to life today.
6 x 9, 224 pp, Quality PB, 978-1-58023-200-5 **$18.99**; HC, 978-1-58023-029-2 **$21.95**

The Way Into Jewish Prayer
By Rabbi Lawrence A. Hoffman, PhD
Opens the door to 3,000 years of Jewish prayer, making available all anyone needs to feel at home in the Jewish way of communicating with God.
6 x 9, 208 pp, Quality PB, 978-1-58023-201-2 **$18.99**

Also Available: **The Way Into Jewish Prayer Teacher's Guide**
By Rabbi Jennifer Ossakow Goldsmith
8½ x 11, 42 pp, Quality PB, 978-1-58023-345-3 **$8.99**
Visit our website to download a free copy.

The Way Into Judaism and the Environment
By Jeremy Benstein, PhD
Explores the ways in which Judaism contributes to contemporary social-environmental issues, the extent to which Judaism is part of the problem and how it can be part of the solution.
6 x 9, 288 pp, Quality PB, 978-1-58023-368-2 **$18.99**; HC, 978-1-58023-268-5 **$24.99**

The Way Into *Tikkun Olam* (Repairing the World)
By Rabbi Elliot N. Dorff, PhD
An accessible introduction to the Jewish concept of the individual's responsibility to care for others and repair the world.
6 x 9, 304 pp, Quality PB, 978-1-58023-328-6 **$18.99**; 320 pp, HC, 978-1-58023-269-2 **$24.99**

The Way Into Torah
By Rabbi Norman J. Cohen, PhD
Helps guide in the exploration of the origins and development of Torah, explains why it should be studied and how to do it.
6 x 9, 176 pp, Quality PB, 978-1-58023-198-5 **$16.99**

The Way Into the Varieties of Jewishness
By Sylvia Barack Fishman, PhD
Explores the religious and historical understanding of what it has meant to be Jewish from ancient times to the present controversy over "Who is a Jew?"
6 x 9, 288 pp, Quality PB, 978-1-58023-367-5 **$18.99**; HC, 978-1-58023-030-8 **$24.99**

About Jewish Lights

People of all faiths and backgrounds yearn for books that attract, engage, educate, and spiritually inspire.

Our principal goal is to stimulate thought and help all people learn about who the Jewish People are, where they come from, and what the future can be made to hold. While people of our diverse Jewish heritage are the primary audience, our books speak to people in the Christian world as well and will broaden their understanding of Judaism and the roots of their own faith.

We bring to you authors who are at the forefront of spiritual thought and experience. While each has something different to say, they all say it in a voice that you can hear.

Our books are designed to welcome you and then to engage, stimulate, and inspire. We judge our success not only by whether or not our books are beautiful and commercially successful, but by whether or not they make a difference in your life.

For your information and convenience, at the back of this book we have provided a list of other Jewish Lights books you might find interesting and useful. They cover all the categories of your life:

Bar/Bat Mitzvah
Bible Study / Midrash
Children's Books
Congregation Resources
Current Events / History
Ecology/ Environment
Fiction: Mystery, Science Fiction
Grief / Healing
Holidays / Holy Days
Inspiration
Kabbalah / Mysticism / Enneagram

Life Cycle
Meditation
Parenting
Prayer
Ritual / Sacred Practice
Spirituality
Theology / Philosophy
Travel
12-Step
Women's Interest

Stuart M. Matlins

Stuart M. Matlins, Publisher